BLACK KETTLE

BLACK KETTLE

THE CHEYENNE CHIEF WHO SOUGHT PEACE BUT FOUND WAR

THOM HATCH

John Wiley & Sons, Inc.

Published by John Wiley & Sons, Inc., Hoboken, New Jersey
Published simultaneously in Canada

Illustration credits: pages 84 (both), 86 (both), and 87 (both) courtesy of the Denver Public Library; pages 85 (both) and 187 (top) courtesy of the Colorado Historical Society; pages 185 and 186 courtesy of Special Collections, Tutt Library, Colorado College, Colorado Springs, Colo.; pages 188 (both) and 189 (top) courtesy of Steve Black; page 187 (bottom) from author's collection; and page 189 (bottom) courtesy of Lynn Cahill.

Maps copyright © 2004 by Kenneth West. All rights reserved

For general information about our other products and services, please contact our Customer Care Department within the United States at (800) 762-2974, outside the United States at (317) 572-3993 or fax (317) 572-4002.

Wiley also publishes its books in a variety of electronic formats. Some content that appears in print may not be available in electronic books. For more information about Wiley products, visit our web site at www.wiley.com.

Library of Congress Cataloging-in-Publication Data:

Hatch, Thom, date.
   Black Kettle : the Cheyenne chief who sought peace but found war /
Thom Hatch.
      p.   cm.
Includes bibliographical references and index.
ISBN 0-471-44592-4 (cloth)
   1. Black Kettle, Cheyenne clief, d. 1868. 2. Cheyenne Indians—
Kings and rulers—Biography. 3. Cheyenne Indians—Wars, 1864.
4. Sand Creek Massacre, Colo., 1864. I. Title.

E99.C53 B58   2004
973.8'1'092—dc22

                                        2003021830

10 9 8 7 6 5 4 3 2 1

To my lovely and talented wife, Lynn, and precious daughter, Cimarron, who make every moment special

CONTENTS

Illustrations

MAPS

INTRODUCTION

ONE OF THE MOST COMPELLING AND TRAGIC STORIES OF THE nineteenth-century American West is the plight of the Native American tribes that found themselves in the pathway of white expansion. Individual tribes reacted to this threat in various ways, primarily by waging war. Great Native American leaders, such as Sitting Bull, Crazy Horse, and Geronimo, challenged the might of the U.S. Army, believing that they could drive away their enemy and once again be free to roam their traditional territory. Each of these noble endeavors ended in failure and resulted in the sacrifice of countless lives.

There was one chief, however, who understood that the white man would ultimately dominate the homeland of his tribe. In an effort to prevent the extinction of his people, he worked relentlessly to establish peace between the two races without bloodshed. This perceptive and courageous man, destined to become the most significant chief of the Cheyennes, was named Black Kettle.

The book in your hands, surprisingly, is the first biography ever written about this intriguing man. While other chiefs have captured the imagination of historians by their defiance and violent temperaments, Black Kettle has been overlooked due to the misconception that his story does not portray the thrilling exploits that have become the hallmark of frontier sagas. Nothing could be further from the truth.

Few nineteenth-century Native American chiefs or warriors hadas important a role on history's stage or participated in more notable events than this Cheyenne chief did. And his own actions throughout the years were anything but passive. Time and again, Black Kettle put his life on the line with personal acts of heroism that could be called nothing less than intrepid. Whether brazenly riding into the thick of the fighting to prevent a slaughter of soldiers or brushing aside warnings against his life from members of his own tribe who disdained peace, he demonstrated a bravery and a determination matched by few chiefs or warriors in history.

As a young warrior, Black Kettle proved his courage and leadership skills in battles against enemy tribes, as traditional rivals established and protected their territories on the Great Plains. When elevated to chief, he became a visionary figure as an advocate for peace and was the principal spokesman and negotiator for his tribe in treaty councils with the U.S. government. His peaceful intentions, however, could not prevent Black Kettle and his tribe from being victimized in two of the most widely known and controversial episodes of the Plains Indian Wars.

The betrayal of Black Kettle by authorities in Colorado Territory resulted in the 1864 Sand Creek Massacre and the slaughter of innocent Cheyenne men, women, and children. In November 1868, Lieutenant Colonel George Armstrong Custer attacked Black Kettle's village on the Washita River, which cost the chief his life and outraged the nation.

But this is not merely the story of the tragedies that defined the life of Black Kettle; it is also the story of the Cheyennes, for the two are inseparable. Events in Black Kettle's life chronicle the rise to prominence of the Cheyennes as a people and their fall in the conquest of the southern plains at the hands of the white man. Throughout this book, every aspect of Black Kettle's existence reflects his selfless commitment to his tribe and to the welfare of his people. The vow that he took when he became a chief, that every decision would be made for the good of the entire tribe, was never compromised or broken.

This journey through Black Kettle's life and the early days of the Cheyennes features in-depth information about social, political, cultural, and historical events of the time, including treaties, race relations, battles and massacres, and tribal histories and customs, and presents a cast of fascinating characters, both famous and lesser known, all of which are vital to understanding this era of Western expansion.

Above all, with his story finally told, perhaps Black Kettle, the peacemaker, will now be recognized for his remarkable personal traits and will gain the status and the respect formerly given to his peers who viewed war as the only answer.

1

EARLY LIFE

THE NORTH AMERICAN GREAT PLAINS ENDURE AS A BREATHTAKING, postcard-perfect scene of boundless prairie covered with a blanket of undulating grasses that extends without interruption to the horizon.

Meandering waterways hidden within verdant recesses and guarded by majestic cottonwoods create life-giving oases. The sky—by day the brilliance of a blue jay's tail feathers and an inky-black dome of pulsating star masses at night—can be overwhelming in its dominance. Spectacular showers of gold and red and pink explode each evening when the sun yields to the earth's rotation. These thousands of square miles, rich with esthetically appealing natural assets, provide a home to an abundance of wildlife.

The character of this land, however, can transform in the blink of an eye from one of benevolent beauty to that of a cruel adversary. Within its disposition exists the propensity to terrify and destroy.

Sudden, blinding dust storms or devastating tornadoes can carve paths of destruction across the vulnerable earth. Torrential cloudbursts can swamp the land in a matter of minutes and unleash hailstones the size of a man's fist. Storms that dump an avalanche of snow are often accompanied by bitter, barbed-wire blasts of frigid air that lower the chill factor below human endurance. Dryness and heat can combine to roast the earth to the brink of mummification and wilt the most hardy crop. And the wind—the wind is in motion to some degree most of time, inciting near madness in a person as it interminably roars across the barren flatland.

People who choose to take up residence in this forbidding land are obliged to adapt to its temperament and harsh climate. This is not the sort of place on which mankind can impose its will and hope to survive.[1]

Yet there was an ancient race of man known as Native Americans that migrated to this land of vivid contrast and extreme weather and became its first inhabitants. Although existence at times presented extreme hardships and challenges, these people roamed this majestic realm in relative freedom and from its unspoiled wellspring invented ways to develop a unique lifestyle of self-sufficiency. One Native American tribe that learned to thrive on the Great Plains was called the *Cheyennes*.

In the winter months, the various bands of Cheyennes sought refuge for their camps in tree-sheltered valleys and rarely ventured any distance from those places. They survived on food that had been preserved and stored during the hunting and harvesting seasons and trusted that it would sustain them until the spring thaw.

These people never stayed for any length of time at one particular campsite during the summer season. Their prime motivation for frequently moving was the need to follow the buffalo and other game herds. Also, they moved from place to place as each offered up its harvest of edible roots and vegetables or wild fruits and berries. Another reason for this nomadic lifestyle was that the resources in one area could not support a village and a sizable pony herd for very long.

Commonly, each Cheyenne band traveled over a traditional route or trail, arriving at approximately the same hunting, harvesting, and gathering times and places from year to year. This seasonal route was occasionally altered, due to the presence of stronger enemies or if game herds shifted from their usual habitat, but otherwise the bands' movements were predictable.

No matter the location of the Cheyenne camp, the bleached-white, buffalo-hide lodges, or tepees, could be found arranged in a circle, broken only by an opening that faced the rising sun, with water and timber close by. Daily camp life was also structured, and each person abided by long-standing rituals of proper etiquette.

Accordingly, the day that Black Kettle was born would have been like any other in the Cheyenne camp.

At first light the women began their daily chores by visiting the nearby stream and filling containers with fresh water—they believed that yesterday's water was dead, and the Cheyennes would drink only living water. The water-bearers wore dresses, or smocks, that fell to midway between the knee and the ankle, with capelike sleeves that hung loosely around the elbows. These everyday work clothes, designed with freedom of movement in mind, had been handmade from the skins of deer, elk, or antelope and were quite plain. On ceremonial occasions, however, the women adorned themselves in skin garments decorated with colorful beads, bells, porcupine quills, and perhaps teeth from an elk.[2]

When the first golden rays of the sun spread across the land, the men and the boys, with toddlers in tow, straggled to the stream and, regardless of the weather, washed away all sickness and were made hardy and healthy with a morning bath. Upon completion of this ritual, the male members of the tribe returned to their lodges and without fail pulled on their breechcloths—those scanty pieces of animal skin that covered their loins and hips. Custom dictated that a man would lose his manhood if he did not wear his precious breechcloth. Boys, as soon as they could walk, wrapped around their tiny waists the string to which the breechcloth would someday be attached.[3]

The camp was bustling with activity by the time the sun peeked above the horizon. Women, assisted by daughters and other female members of the extended family, attended to the morning meal, their cooking pots hanging over smoking fires, the pleasant aromas teasing the men, who chatted nearby while anxiously waiting to be fed. Boys rode out to drive the pony herd toward fresh grazing grass and selected certain mounts—usually the war horses—to be tied in front of lodges, in the event that they might be needed at a moment's notice.

While families settled in to eat breakfast, the Crier strolled through the camp, beginning at the opening of the circle, and announced the news of the day. In a loud voice, repeating his words as he moved along, he relayed orders from the chiefs, perhaps about how long the camp would remain in that place, to notify everyone that a certain soldier band planned a dance for that evening, or to mention items that had been lost or found. Most anticipated were the latest tidings of a personal nature—possibly about a child having been born during the night or the previous day. In this manner, the camp had been informed about the birth of Black Kettle.[4]

With breakfast completed, a number of the men readied their horses and weapons and rode out to hunt. Cheyenne men were exclusively big game hunters, favoring buffalo, antelope, deer, elk, and wild sheep, in that order. Wolves and foxes were hunted only for their fur, and other smaller animals were usually ignored by the men. Small game, however, was hunted by the boys as a learning exercise.

Men who chose to remain in camp that day gathered around lodges or under shade trees to smoke and gossip, while repairing a bow, fashioning a pipe, making arrows, or working on some other necessary implement. The older men entertained the workers by recounting tales of tribal history, contacts with neighboring tribes or the white man, and other notable events, both real and mysterious, which were discussed and debated for hours.[5]

Several curious boys could be found sitting at a respectful distance, listening to the grown-ups talk. Most of the boys, however, assembled in small groups to engage in various spirited activities. Swimming was a favorite, as were running foot races, wrestling, practicing with bow and arrows, riding ponies, throwing sticks at targets, and other games that symbolized their status as warriors-in-training.[6]

The unmarried young men did not normally participate in the morning discussions with their elders or play with the boys, choosing instead to devote considerable time to improving their personal appearance. Each morning they painstakingly plucked every visible strand of hair from their faces and eyebrows and patiently combed and braided their long hair. They finally dressed in their finest clothing, perhaps wearing their "war shirts," which fell to the knees and may have been ornamented with beads or quills or, more commonly among the Cheyennes, with colorful designs and dark-green fringes. Afterward, they paraded around the camp for everyone—particularly the young ladies of courting age—to see and admire.[7]

Cheyennes were not hasty about getting married, and the formal courtship process could extend for as long as four or five years. When a female child reached puberty, she was initiated into womanhood by a ceremony, usually performed by her grandmother, and no longer talked to her older brothers or associated with the boys in her age group. At that time she began receiving instructions from her mother regarding proper conduct with respect to relationships. Premarital sex was strictly forbidden among the Cheyennes, and a young lady who brazenly flirted with a potential suitor was considered immoral. George Grinnell states:

> The women of the Cheyennes are famous among all western tribes for their chastity. In old times it was most unusual for a girl to be seduced, and she who had yielded was disgraced forever. The matter at once became known, and she was taunted with it wherever she went. It was never forgotten. No young man would marry her.[8]

A young man courted the girl of his choice with such romantic acts as playing his flute for her, which was thought to be a means of casting a love spell over a reluctant maiden; whistling at her from a distance; and eventually lingering near her lodge for a chance to speak with her when she returned from her chores.

When a match had been made, an elderly relative of the young man would discuss the marriage arrangement with the girl's father, which might include gifts of horses and other valuable items. If the young woman's family approved of the union, family members would send presents to the young man and, if well-to-do, would perhaps also give the daughter horses to serve as her dowry. The young lovers would be married several days later, in what was often an elaborate ceremony with gifts and food. The groom occasionally carried the bride on a blanket to his father's lodge, which was where the couple would reside until the two constructed their own home.[9]

The primary responsibility of a Cheyenne man was to provide food and other material needs for his family. The men were also obliged to protect their wives and children, as well as the collective interests of the tribe, from any outside threat. The noted anthropology professor Dr. E. Adamson Hoebel here describes the typical Cheyenne man:

> Reserved and dignified, the mature adult Cheyenne male moves with a quiet sense of self-assurance. He speaks fluently, but never carelessly. He is careful of the sensibilities of others and is kindly and generous. He is slow to anger and strives to suppress his feelings, if aggravated. Towards his enemies he feels no merciful compunctions, and the more aggressive he is, the better. He is neither flighty nor dour. Usually quiet, he has a lightly displayed sense of humor. His thinking is rationalistic to a high degree and yet colored with mysticism. His ego is strong and not easily threatened. He is serene and composed, secure in his social position, capable of warm social relations.

Cheyenne women exhibited many of the same characteristics as the men but were more artistically creative. The woman was by all means accomplished in domestic relations and was expected to care for the children and perform every household duty. Contrary to the customs of some Plains tribes, the relationship between the Cheyenne husband and the wife was an equal partnership—the women were not considered chattels—and most marriages endured for life. Women were the rulers of the camp and, although not permitted to participate in tribal councils, made their wishes known through their husbands, who obediently acted on any request, whether with respect to the tribe or to the family.[10]

While the men pursued their morning endeavors, the women, assisted by the older girls, resumed their daily housekeeping routine. With babies on cradle-boards and toddlers close by, they might prepare or sew skins for clothing or a new lodge, pound berries for use in pemmican, or decorate robes—usually in the company of friends. Women who had decorated at least thirty robes without assistance were highly respected and were initiated into a quilling society, which permitted them to learn certain ceremonies and work on ceremonial robes, lodges, and other special items.[11]

At some point during the morning, small parties of women and girls ventured off into the hills to gather firewood, berries, or roots. Their basic tool was the dibble, or digging stick, which was given to them by the Great Medicine Spirit. This was a time of laughter and merriment for the women, who viewed the work not as a tiresome chore but as an outing, an opportunity to discuss camp news, gossip, and engage in practical jokes.

Occasionally, men or boys charged out of camp on horseback to "attack" the women and the girls who were returning with their bundles of roots or berries. The men attempted to "count coup," touch their "enemy," while their intended victims pelted them. Any man struck by a thrown missile was eliminated from the game, and only a man who had distinguished himself in warfare was permitted to actually capture any roots or berries for himself.[12]

By midday, as the sun beat down on the camp, most people sought refuge inside their lodges to escape the heat. Later in the afternoon, men who had gone out hunting rode back into camp. They dismounted in front of their lodges, handed over their kill to the women for washing and preparing, and then relaxed, perhaps gathering here and there to boast about their hunting skills, pass along information, or speculate about the location and the availability of game.[13]

The camp came alive once more when the sun began its descent. Daily tasks were set aside in favor of leisurely and festive amusements. Preparation for the evening meal commenced, fires were ablaze, and children could be seen scurrying around the circle of lodges with invitations to guests for dinner. The boys drove the horses in to a safe, fresh grazing area, while turning out other mounts for the night.

Eventually, the sound of music and drumming could be heard, and people of all ages wandered around the camp to share a feast, attend a social dance, play games, court that special young woman, gamble, or simply enjoy the companionship of their fellow tribe members. Story-telling was a big part of the evening, as certain men known for their talent to entertain with tales drew audiences to their lodges. This bustle of activity was punctuated by frequent shouts and laughter, combined with the incidental whinny of a horse, the bark of a dog, or the howl of a distant coyote. Some people might choose to seek solitude, perhaps by chanting a prayer to the spirits or playing a flute on a nearby hill. For several hours, illuminated by the comforting glow of huge bonfires, the camp celebrated the simple pleasures of a satisfying lifestyle.

One by one, the fires burned down, the music faded away, and visitors drifted back to their own lodges. The camp gradually became silent, and another harmonious day for the Cheyennes came to an end. The people slept with the knowledge that scouts, known as "wolves," were patrolling the vicinity of the village and would alert them to any potential danger, such as an approaching enemy.[14]

This was the traditional daily routine that greeted the entrance of Black Kettle into the world. The exact day and the year that the old Crier carried the announcement of Black Kettle's birth throughout the Cheyenne camp, however, is unknown.

Reference works, such as encyclopedias and biographical dictionaries, cite Black Kettle's date of birth as somewhere between the years 1803 and 1807, yet fail to note any sources from which this information was derived. Most researchers have chosen one of those dates—mainly, 1803—to incorporate into the text of books when relating later events in the life of Black Kettle. This date may or may not be accurate.[15]

Edward Wynkoop, an Indian agent who was intimately acquainted with Black Kettle, said in an 1868 address to the United States Indian Commission: "I would state that Black Kettle was 56 years of age at the time of his death." If that was true, Black Kettle, who died in 1868, would have been born in the year 1812.[16]

Another interesting—and perhaps a more credible—source about Black Kettle's later life is the reminiscences of George Bent, an educated half-Cheyenne, half-white man who married the chief's niece. Bent stated in his memoirs that Black Kettle was sixty-seven years old when he died, which would mean that he had been born in 1801.[17]

Another matter of mystery has been Black Kettle's family heritage. The first official record of a Cheyenne chief by the name of "Black Kettle" came in 1860 at Fort Wise, when Commissioner A. B. Greenwood entertained a number of Cheyenne chiefs in treaty negotiations.

By that time, Black Kettle was certainly middle-aged or older and, inasmuch as the Cheyennes did not maintain written documentation of births, deaths, or marriages, rather relying on oral tradition, there can be no way in which to research his family tree, other than by the later memories and the hearsay of those who were acquainted with him.

George Bent noted that Black Kettle was the son of Swift Hawk Lying Down, who was never a chief. Bent also listed two brothers, Gentle Horse and Wolf, and one sister, Wind Woman.[18]

The woman said to have been Black Kettle's sister, Wind Woman, told George Bird Grinnell in 1913 that the name of their father, who died young, was Hawk—perhaps a shortened version of Swift Hawk Lying Down.[19]

Grinnell also had been informed by Wolf Chief, a Cheyenne who supplied much relevant information over the years, that Black Kettle's father was Hawk Stretched Out and his mother, Sparrow Hawk Woman or Little Brown-Back Hawk Woman. Black Kettle was said to be the oldest child, followed by Gentle Horse, Wind Woman, and Stone Teeth.[20]

Major General William S. Harney mentioned at the Medicine Lodge Treaty council in 1867 that he had first encountered Black Kettle in 1825 at the mouth of the Teton River. Harney told reporters that Black Kettle was the son of High Back Wolf, who was a chief.[21]

This claim by Harney was supported by the Indian agent Edward Wynkoop to the United States Indian Commission when he said, "He [Black Kettle] was the son of High Back Wolf, once a principal chief of the Cheyenne nation, and the particular friend of Gen. Harney, who many years ago took considerable interest in the boy Black Kettle. Upon the death of High Back Wolf, his son Black Kettle succeeded him."[22]

Chief High Back Wolf, however, was a prominent figure and the subject of much documentation throughout Cheyenne history of the mid-1850s. No mention has been made in various reliable sources that would indicate that Black Kettle was in any manner related to this chief. In addition, Black Kettle himself became a chief while High Back Wolf was still alive. The Harney-Wynkoop account likely suffers from either poor translation or perhaps a well-meaning but baseless attempt by one or both of the men to elevate Black Kettle to tribal "royalty" status by birth. It is also doubtful that a young, obscure warrior such as Black Kettle would have been brought to the attention of General Harney as early as 1825.[23]

The location where Black Kettle was born in the early 1800s is also a matter of speculation, but the approximate vicinity can be determined by tracing the movements of his tribe.

The origin of these native people with Algonquin roots cannot be accurately documented, but it is believed that they once lived north of the Great Lakes in southern Canada. By 1673, according to a map attributed to the French-Canadian explorer Louis Joliet, the Cheyennes were occupying permanent villages along the upper Mississippi River—on the present-day Wisconsin side, across the border from present-day Minnesota. Within ten years, the tribe had relocated to the western reaches of the Minnesota River valley, where tribe members farmed, hunted, gathered wild rice, and fashioned pottery.[24]

During this period of time, the tribe that called itself *Tsistsistas*, meaning "beautiful people" or "the People," received another name. The Sioux, a neighboring tribe, called these beautiful people *Shai ena*, which means "red talkers" or "people of a different speech." Over time, other tribes and the white man would corrupt the words from the Siouan language, and as a result the Tsistsistas became commonly known as the *Cheyennes*.[25]

By the late 1600s, constant warfare with the more aggressive Minnesota tribes—the Sioux and the Ojibway (also known as the Chippewa)—convinced the People, the Cheyennes, to move westward into present-day North Dakota, where they established a principal village of about seventy lodges on the Sheyenne River, twelve miles southeast of present-day Lisbon. Evidence reveals that the Cheyennes remained concerned about their powerful adversaries and fortified their villages in the event of an attack. They lived in earthen lodges that measured forty feet in diameter and continued to practice their age-old agrarian lifestyle—with one exception.[26]

The Cheyennes, perhaps informed by friendly neighbors, became aware of great herds of buffalo that roamed on the plains to the west. The newcomers quickly learned that this shaggy beast was a dependable source for nearly every item required for basic survival needs and could also provide luxuries that offered a higher standard of living.

During the early nineteenth century, Great Plains buffalo herds were estimated to total upward of 75 to 100 million, an impressive figure when one considers that each animal weighed around a ton, with most bulls tipping the scale at a ton and a half. Nowhere else in the annals of food resources can such an infinite provider of sustenance be documented.

There has been a continuing debate about whether the by-products derived from the buffalo were vital to the health and the welfare of the average Plains Indian. Granted, there was an abundance of other wild game, and these animals were assuredly part of the menu and the wardrobe. But the native tribes could sustain a thriving self-sufficiency by ingeniously utilizing every portion of the buffalo but the bellow.

The most obvious, and important, benefit was food. The buffalo was truly a four-legged commissary. The muscle was high in protein, and other parts supplied more than the daily requirements of vitamins and minerals. What was not readily consumed could be preserved for the long winter months. One manner of preservation was by simply drying the meat under the sun; another was by pounding berries and other fruit into the dried meat to create pemmican—a treat that provided every element necessary for a balanced diet.

Within the village proper, the first items to catch the eye were the lodges, which were constructed mainly from tanned buffalo hides. Inside the lodges were warm coats and sleeping robes, also fashioned from those hairy hides, and summer blankets made soft by scraping off the hair and tanning both sides. Dressed hides were also sewn into shirts, leggings, moccasins, carrying bags, and women's dresses, as well as into drums and shields.

Green skins provided serviceable kettles for drinking and cooking. Horns were used for ladles, spoons, cups, and other containers. Bones could be carved into arrowheads, spear tips, or needles. Hooves were boiled down to make glue for many applications. Buffalo hair was braided into ropes and pony reins. Bull boats to traverse rivers were made water-tight with stretched hides. Sinew became bowstrings. Skin became battle shields. Axes and hoes were made from shoulder blades, sledge runners from ribs, and paint from blood. Hair was used to stuff pillows. Fly swatters and whisk brooms were made from the tails. The black beard became an ornament to adorn clothing. Primitive toys, including baby rattles, were constructed from various parts. And the list goes on and on.[27]

In the early days, however, the Cheyennes were without horses and conducted winter buffalo hunts on foot, with participation by every able-bodied person in the tribe—men, women, and children—as well as dogs. The hunting party first sought an ideal location, then surrounded an isolated herd of buffalo and with the assistance of the dogs drove the herd into deep drifts. While the animals struggled to escape the hindering snow, the men dashed up close and shot as many as possible with arrows. The buffalo were butchered, and the meat dragged home in bundles attached by thongs to the dogs' necks. In other instances, the tribe was known to drive a herd over a cliff, then the hunters would take what they could carry and leave the remainder behind to feed the wolves and other scavengers that followed the hunt.[28]

Sometime after 1750, during their stay in these permanent settlements on the Sheyenne River, the People were introduced for the first time to the horse, an event that changed their way of life forever. The sturdy descendants of horses that had been brought to the continent by the Spanish in the early 1500s were plentiful and easily captured and tamed. The animals required little attention, for they were accustomed to providing for themselves and possessed excellent endurance. Best of all, mounted Cheyennes could now more effectively hunt buffalo, whenever and wherever they desired, and could transport larger quantities back to camp. In addition, it was much easier to move the village with beasts of burden to carry the load.

Although the tribe continued to raise corn and other vegetables, this newfound mobility marked the beginning of a transformation. From that point on, the Cheyennes would depend less on agriculture for subsistence, in favor of the buffalo.[29]

Between 1770 and 1790, the Cheyennes, perhaps due to an attack on their village by the Chippewa, migrated westward to establish residence on the Missouri River near the present-day boundary of North and South Dakota. One village of earthen lodges located on Porcupine Creek was reportedly larger than any had been on the Sheyenne River. During this time, the People became friendly with the Arikaras, the Hidatsas, and the Mandans, and intermarried with these neighboring tribes.[30]

One particular group of nomadic people, known as the Sutaios, or singularly Suhtai, also called the "Buffalo People," had been an enemy of the Cheyennes for many years. Following one great battle, however, the two tribes held a parley. At that time, it was discovered that they spoke a similar language—Sutaio was a more guttural dialect that sounded "funny" to the Cheyennes. In addition, both of them had Algonquin roots and believed that they had common ancestors. This realization encouraged the two tribes to make a lasting peace. One faction of the Sutaios then headed north and was never heard from again. Another group remained with the Cheyennes and was gradually incorporated into the tribe. This faction, however, may have remained distinct and might not have camped within the Cheyenne village until the mid-1860s.[31]

This was an important event, because according to his sister, Wind Woman—as well as to George Bent—Black Kettle was born into the Sutaio faction of the tribe. His father and mother, although their names cannot be confirmed, were assuredly both full-blooded Suhtai. Perhaps this fact alone dispels any notion that Black Kettle was the son of High Back Wolf, who from all indications was a Cheyenne and likely would have been born before the Sutaios joined the People.[32]

In addition to being the tribe into which Black Kettle was born, the Sutaio people brought with them rich traditions that were shared with the Cheyennes and that influenced the lifestyle of the tribe forever. The People were introduced to such ceremonies as the Sacred Buffalo Hat, the Sun Dance, the Sweat Lodge, and other rituals pertaining to the buffalo, which would become an important part of their cultural identity and religion.[33]

It was during the latter half of the eighteenth century, perhaps partly due to the influence of the Sutaios, that the Cheyennes completed their transition from planters to archetypical nomadic Plains buffalo hunters. Villages and crops were abandoned, and individual bands could be found wandering over a vast territory that extended from west of the Black Hills to the Missouri River on the east, and south as far as the Arkansas River. Another factor for this gradual withdrawal to the south was likely the emergence of the Lakota Sioux, known as the Inviters, a tribe that had recently arrived on the Great Plains from Minnesota and was aggressively establishing its own territory.[34]

Although the People had encountered French trappers and traders traveling through their territory over the years, the first historical documentation of contact with whites came in October 1804, when Meriwether Lewis and William Clark, as representatives of President Thomas Jefferson, were visiting the Arikaras and happened upon two nearby Cheyenne villages. Then, in August 1806, Lewis reported entering a Cheyenne camp that consisted of 120 lodges. Later, the chief of another village initially refused Clark's offer of an American medal, stating, "He knew that the white people were all medecine [sic] and that he was afraid of the medal or any thing that white people gave them." The chief, who was finally persuaded to accept the medal, also admitted that he had no grievance with the white man and that his only enemy was the Sioux.

Lewis and Clark drew a map showing that the Cheyennes at this point in history were the dominant tribe living in the vicinity of the Black Hills, having earlier driven out the Kiowas. This mountainous wilderness area, which presents a striking contrast to the monotonous flatland of the plains, is located along the Dakota-Wyoming border and runs roughly one hundred miles from north to south and sixty miles east to west. The various Cheyenne bands did not necessarily reside within the Black Hills but roamed separately over a vast area that formed a rough semicircle to the east, the west, and the south. It would have been here, certainly within sight of the Black Hills, that Black Kettle was born.[35]

Knowledge of the exact date and the place of Black Kettle's birth, or the family into which he was born, is not necessary to understand his childhood experiences.

The Cheyennes cherished their children—to the extent that youngsters were never punished but rather were gently scolded and shown proper behavior by example and patient guidance. The birth of a male child in particular was cause for celebration. From birth until perhaps the age of five or six, Black Kettle (Mo-ta-vato, Moketavato, or Moka-ta-va-tah, in Cheyenne) was called by a pet name, some term of endearment, then received a more permanent name—as well as a nickname by which he was commonly called. Children were usually named by a relative and almost always after a paternal family member.[36]

Black Kettle was wrapped snugly in blankets and carried around in his mother's arms until he developed enough strength to be safely laced onto a baby-board, or cradle-board. He spent most of his infanthood strapped to this convenient device, which, when leaned against the side of the lodge or hung from a lodge pole, permitted him to watch his mother as she went about her daily chores. When the camp moved, the cradle-board was attached to his mother's back or onto a saddle or a travois pole.[37]

Black Kettle's umbilical cord, when it had dried and fallen off, was beaded into the shape of a turtle and placed with him inside his cradle-board to ward off evil spirits. A fake beaded umbilical cord was put on the outside of the cradle-board, which was intended to fool evil spirits. This same procedure was employed for the umbilical cords of girls, except that a lizard was fashioned, rather than a turtle.[38]

Black Kettle was doted upon by his mother. She spent countless hours playing with him and from the earliest age also taught him his first behavioral lesson, that of self-control. Crying babies were quickly quieted or taken out of the lodge, away from camp, so as not to disturb anyone. This was particularly important at night, to avoid alerting enemies to the camp's location. This education in showing self-effacement while in the presence of adults or elders remained with Black Kettle throughout his youth.[39]

Black Kettle had his ears pierced when he was between three and six months old, most likely during a Sun Dance or another important ceremony. This ritual, which was performed by a noted warrior who was rewarded by the father for his service, symbolized a lightning strike that was said to make the child invulnerable when someday he went into battle.[40]

Black Kettle's formative years were relatively carefree but were filled with purpose. He engaged in playful endeavors, much as today's children do—digging in the dirt, casually throwing rocks or sticks at targets, wrestling, fishing, swimming, sledding down snowy hills, all the while watching and emulating older boys and men. In the case of a Cheyenne child, these activities extended to serious, competitive practice with bows and arrows, stalking birds and wild game, and contests that taught him how to attack an enemy, as well as how to repulse an attack. Boys learned to ride ponies almost from the moment they could walk and by the age of seven or eight were accomplished riders who were trusted to help manage the tribe's pony herd.

At about the age of twelve, Black Kettle's training became more formal. His father, uncles, and grandfathers instructed him in the ways of a man, emphasizing the attributes of bravery in battle and the skills of hunting. The relationship between the generations was that of pupil and student—and the student had already learned to be deferential.

The child was told about his status within the tribe, how he must always obey commands without question, and about the need for humility and for living in harmony with fellow Cheyennes. The punishment for violating rules or engaging in improper conduct would not be physical but instead would be ridicule from other warriors, a most humiliating penalty. Professor Adamson Hoebel states that Cheyenne children were constantly urged by their elders:

Be brave, be honest, be virtuous, be industrious, be generous, do not quarrel! If you do not do these things, people will talk about you in the camp;

they will not respect you; you will be shamed. If you listen to this advice you will grow up to be a good man, and you will amount to something.[41]

Black Kettle was taught from the earliest age that religion embraced every aspect of his daily life, from hunting and warfare to personal relationships. He learned about Maheo, the All Father, the Great Spirit or God, who created the earth—which was called Our Grandmother—and every living thing above and below. Maheo also created Maheyuno, the four Sacred Persons, who guarded the four corners of the universe; Esseneta'he, who lived in the southeast, where the sun rises, and who originated light and life itself; Onxsovon, of the northwest, who symbolized the beauty and the perfection of the setting sun; Sovota, who dwelled in the southwest and provided warmth and rain to nourish Grandmother Earth; and Notamota, who lived in the northeast and brought stormy weather, blizzards, disease, and death. Each Sacred Person was represented in ornamentation by a different color—Esseneta'he by white; Onxsovon by golden yellow, the color of the sunset; Sovota by red; and Notamota by black.[42]

Black Kettle came to understand that he possessed a spirit or a soul, known as the Ma'tasooma, which would depart his body at the moment of his death and soar across the Milky Way Galaxy to Maheo, where he would be reunited with those who had already passed away. Se'han was a place much like the white man's heaven, where he would ride the fastest ponies through great herds of buffalo and want for absolutely nothing. There was no alternative, for hell did not exist in the hereafter but could be found here on earth by experiencing ridicule or even banishment from the tribe if a warrior brought shame upon himself and did not display the honorable character traits that were expected of him throughout his life. Suicide would banish the spirit into darkness, to wander forever off the path of the Milky Way.[43]

Black Kettle also learned that Maheo had created Maiyun, the Sacred Powers, which served the Sacred Persons. Heammawihio, or Wise One Above, and Ahtunowihio, whose domain was below the earth, could appear as some bird or animal that lived on the earth. These beneficial powers, which provided such necessities as food, shelter, and clothing, were expressed through various sacred ceremonies and the possession of venerated objects.[44]

The most important Cheyenne ceremony was the Sacred Arrow Renewal, a four-day observance that took place roughly at the time of the summer solstice, but not necessarily on a regular basis. It was held most often when warriors were killed in battle or was invoked as a manner in which to end some hardship that had befallen the People. The arrows were also renewed if one Cheyenne happened to kill another Cheyenne. In this instance, blood would appear on the Sacred Arrow points, which required renewal.

This rite centered around four Sacred Arrows—two painted for hunting and two for battle. These arrows were a supernatural gift given by Maheo to Sweet Medicine, a Cheyenne ancestral hero, when he journeyed to a cave near Bear Butte, an extinct volcano on the northern fringe of the Black Hills. The two hunting arrows, when pointed at animals, would render them helpless and thereby easily killed. The two war arrows were carried into battle by a trusted warrior, who rode ahead of the others and pointed the arrows at an enemy prior to the attack. This act would blind and confuse the enemy and ensure success in the ensuing battle.

The Sacred Arrows, therefore, were the People's greatest protection against starvation and defeat by an enemy and were kept in a bundle with other sacred objects that symbolized the collective existence of the Cheyenne tribe.

Arrow Renewal was a time of feasting, singing, curing the sick, renewing old acquaintances, and perhaps repairing or making new battle shields—punctuated by solemn rituals. The ceremony to renew the power of the arrows also served to renew the Cheyennes as a nation, for the arrows were the embodiment of the tribal soul.[45]

The other important fetish, a sacred symbol of great power, was the Buffalo or Medicine Hat. This hat, made from fur taken from a buffalo's head, with the horns still attached, and decorated with blue beads, had been the property of the Sutaio tribe. An honored member of that tribe was always designated as the keeper of the hat. The Sacred Hat Lodge in which it was kept was considered a sanctuary, a place where people spoke in hushed tones and children were forbidden to approach.

The Medicine Hat held great power over the health and the welfare of the tribe, assuring that food, shelter, and clothing would be plentiful, especially with respect to successful buffalo hunting, the staple of Cheyenne subsistence. It was displayed during Sacred Arrow Renewal ceremonies or when needed to ward off diseases—for its primary purpose was to foster health and healing—and was worn into battle by a trusted warrior only when the entire tribe went to war.[46]

Perhaps the most fascinating ceremony to Black Kettle and the other youngsters was the Sun Dance, known to the People as the Medicine Lodge, or "new-life-lodge." This ritual, which was common to most Plains tribes, was held for eight days once a year, usually when the tribe gathered for the summer buffalo hunt. The Sun Dance was performed as a supernatural way to seek power from the spirits for the purpose of reviving and renewing Grandmother Earth's resources and restoring harmony among all of her inhabitants. This ceremony of rebirth was a ceremonial time for the tribe, accompanied by dances, feasts, and the exchanging of gifts.

The most memorable and spectacular part of the ritual, however, was performed by warriors who suspended themselves from poles by two ropes fastened into gashes in their chests. This form of voluntary self-torture, according to George Bird Grinnell, was "a sacrifice of self to bring good fortune or to avert misfortune in the future." The sacrificer remained attached to the ropes, dancing while fastened to the pole, possibly throughout the night, until his skin was torn loose and he fell to the ground. If he managed to hang through the entire night, the medicine man would cut the flesh to end his ordeal.[47]

The Massaum ceremony, which was also shown to Sweet Medicine on his sacred journey, was an amusing hunting ritual performed by men who dressed and acted like various animals. These actors were then "hunted" by members of the Bowstring Society, who, much to the delight of the onlookers, humorously stalked their prey.

Black Kettle had watched as his father and the other men showed respect and asked for protection and blessings from the Sacred Persons, as well as from Maheo, by smoking the sacred pipe, fasting, and praying and through various personal sacrifices and ceremonial sweats. The sacred pipe, when smoked, was the link between man and nature and the supreme deity. The Cheyennes addressed their sacred spirits, Maiyun and Maheyuno—as well as Maheo—asking that their prayers be heard. They began the ritual by pointing their pipes first to the sky, then to Grandmother Earth, and to the four directions—east, south, west, and north.

Also, Cheyenne shamans were always available, when needed, to perform healing rituals that required the use of animal parts and medicinal plants and minerals.[48]

An important rite of passage came when Black Kettle was permitted to accompany the men on his first controlled buffalo hunt. He had been schooled in every aspect of the hunt, the habits of the buffalo, how to ride and shoot, and how to obey orders from the leader, which would increase his chances of success. If he happened to kill a calf, it would be cause for great celebration, perhaps even a feast, and his father would boast about the son's prospects of becoming a capable warrior.

Within a year or two after his first buffalo hunt, Black Kettle's final step in becoming a man was much more dangerous—his first war party. Beforehand, he was reminded of the importance of fighting with bravery and of not necessarily killing an enemy but trying to count coup. This practice of touching an enemy with a lance known as a coup stick or with his bare hand was considered the bravest feat a warrior could achieve. He could also hope to capture a weapon or a shield or perhaps even take a scalp, items that could be displayed later at a victory ceremony. In most cases, however, the young man would be given the duty of holding the horses for the older warriors.[49]

Young Black Kettle was keenly aware that the benefits of becoming a successful warrior, whether from hunting or from raiding an enemy, meant prestige for himself and his family, material wealth, and a voice at tribal councils. He was now prepared to demonstrate that he had learned his lessons well and was anxious to show the prowess, the determination, and the courage required to become a respected Cheyenne warrior.

2

WARRIOR

THE CORNERSTONE OF CHEYENNE SOCIAL STRUCTURE—THE ULTIMATE
constitutional authority of the tribe—rested in the hands of forty-four
peace chiefs, each representing a particular band. Four of the forty-
four were old chiefs; the other forty were selected by the ten bands—
four from each. These distinguished men, all of whom had been respected warriors, were chosen for possessing such admirable personal
traits as wisdom, generosity, selflessness, and fairness. This Council of
Forty-four conducted the day-to-day business of the tribe, ruling on
internal disputes and common issues, making decisions regarding alli-
ances with other tribes, and, when necessary, declaring war. Therefore,
the control of the tribe was not in the hands of aggressive war leaders
but was governed by men who rarely rode off into battle but served as
evenhanded protectors of the People.[1]

Every Cheyenne warrior dreamed of one day attaining a position
on the Council of Forty-four, but first he had to prove himself worthy.
The first step toward this goal was for every able-bodied youngster to
join a military, or soldier, society. These societies functioned like a fra-
ternity and were the military arm and the police force of the tribe.
There were five soldier bands from which a young man could choose—
Bowstring Soldiers, Dog Soldiers (or the Dog Men), Elkhorn Scrapers,
Kit Foxes, and Red Shields. The headmen of these societies made decisions about tribal matters, which were presented to the Council Chiefs
for discussion and finally a vote.[2]

Black Kettle, at about the age of fourteen or so, joined the Bowstrings, perhaps because his father was a member. He likely remained
with this soldier band throughout his teen years, wearing animal skins
cut like a poncho in the tradition of that society.[3]

When he approached manhood, however, he engaged in a self-mutilation ritual similar to that performed in the Sun Dance, in an effort to seek a vision and summon a guardian spirit who would protect him in future battles. Following that experience, Black Kettle changed allegiances and became a member of the Elkhorn Scrapers (Himoweyuhkis), which was also known as the Hoof Rattles or Crooked Lances. Each Elk member had in his possession a rattling instrument carved from a piece of elk horn, painted yellow above and blue below, with a snake's head on one end and the tail on the other. This relic represented the blue racer snake, which was said to have come from the sun. The Elkhorn Scrapers were noted dancers, who, before such formal occasions, purified their rattles four times with the smoke of burning sweet grass.[4]

At some point after Black Kettle's vision quest and entrance into the Elkhorn Scrapers, a young lady caught his eye. Her name was Little Sage Woman, and all that is known about her is that she was said to be "fine looking." Black Kettle and Little Sage subsequently married, and, in the tradition of the Cheyenne, he went to live with her family.[5]

In the early 1830s, bands of the People, including Black Kettle and Little Sage, had gradually drifted south and east from the Black Hills to settle within an area that encompassed the eastern plains of Colorado Territory and into Kansas, mainly along the verdant banks of the Arkansas River (which they called Flint Arrowpoint). This group would become known as the "Southern" Cheyennes.

Other Cheyenne bands remained for the most part north along the headwaters of the Platte in the old country and eventually aligned with their aggressive former enemies, the Lakota Sioux. The Southern and Northern factions of the tribe often camped and traveled together but over time adopted their own particular contrasting lifestyles.

By that time, a steady stream of whites was passing through the region—trappers, mountain men, and other adventurers, such as Jim Bridger, Kit Carson, and Thomas Fitzpatrick. Bent's Fort, a trading post located about six miles from present-day La Junta, Colorado, on the Arkansas River was established in about 1834 by William Bent. This post, the first in Colorado (with William Bent being the first American settler in the territory that would become the state of Colorado), sold general merchandise to both whites and the neighboring tribes, which included the Cheyennes.[6]

Other than a few isolated incidents, relations between the whites and the Cheyennes could be called accommodating, even friendly, during this time of moderate expansion.

The vast western domain, however, was a battleground for warfare between the various tribes. The Southern Cheyennes fought constantly with the Kiowas, the Comanches, the Utes, the Crows, the Shawnees, and the Pawnees.

The first military intervention by the United States came in 1835 when Colonel Henry Dodge led an expedition to Bent's Fort for the purpose of negotiating an end to the intertribal wars. Dodge met with representatives of the Cheyenne, the Arapaho, the Gros Ventres, the Arikara, the Pawnee, and the Blackfoot tribes. These peace emissaries were welcomed by the Cheyennes, and, in the end, Dodge departed believing that he had established at least a temporary truce. He was incorrect in his assumption—the Cheyennes and the Pawnees skirmished time and again during the ensuing years.[7]

It was the Kiowas, known as the Greasy Wood People, however, who became the primary enemy of the Southern Cheyennes in the summer of 1837. A party of forty-two Bowstring warriors had set out on foot to raid Kiowa horse herds in the Washita River Valley. These Cheyennes were noticed along the way by a Kiowa hunter, who spread the alarm. Kiowa and Comanche warriors eventually surrounded the Bowstrings and killed and scalped them all.[8]

This act of treachery by the Kiowas outraged the Cheyenne nation, and the cry for vengeance echoed throughout the camps. The stage had been set for a climactic battle to gain revenge, but any action would have to be postponed for the time being, due to the advent of winter. The People chose to camp beside the Arkansas River, just below Bent's Fort, to wait out the winter of 1837–1838.

This village was quite large, and that presented many problems, the most significant of which was supplying enough wild game to adequately feed everyone. Black Kettle and his fellow hunters diligently searched for buffalo. Just one small herd would have provided enough meat and hides to sustain their needs throughout the cold months. But to the dismay and the frustration of these expert hunters, not even a lone buffalo was observed during the entire winter.

When the weather became extreme, with heavy snow and bitterly cold winds, the suffering became worse. To add to the misery, all of the horses belonging to one band were stolen by enemy raiders. Other horses starved to death, due to lack of forage. Many people were also in danger of starvation. Finally, in order to survive, small groups left the village to venture off on their own.

Mercifully, spring arrived and brought with it the buffalo. When the bellies of the hungry were filled, the thoughts of the People turned to the loss of their loved ones at the hands of the Kiowas, the Greasy Wood People. Family members desired to collect the bones of their loved ones for proper burial, while the various warrior societies vowed to punish the Kiowas for killing the forty-two Bowstring Soldiers. The chiefs held a council and decided that the wishes of the People would be honored. It would be war.

Every band was summoned from its winter camp, and together the entire village, which numbered about 3,500 people, moved south by way of William Bent's Fort, where they obtained supplies—including a number of Hudson's Bay guns, with flint, powder, and balls. The Cheyennes, armed with their new weapons, then traveled down the Arkansas in search of the Kiowas. They eventually halted about six or seven miles above Chouteau's Island, not far from an encampment of Southern Arapahoes, the Cloud People.[9]

At some point in the early nineteenth century, the Arapahoes, another Algonquin tribe, had allied themselves with the Cheyennes. The two tribes camped and hunted together and occasionally intermarried. Around 1835, the Arapahoes had divided into two groups— the Northern Arapahoes settled just east of the Rocky Mountains along the headwaters of the Platte River in Wyoming; and the Southern Arapahoes moved to an area along the Arkansas River of Colorado to associate with the People who became the Southern Cheyennes.[10]

The two tribes enjoyed a huge feast that night before the great impending battle against the Kiowas, with the Arapahoes vowing to fight side by side to the death with the Cheyennes. The Kiowas would be supported by their traditional tribal ally, the Comanches, known as the Rattlesnake People.

In the morning, the Cheyennes and the Arapahoes moved south and within several days had halted on Crooked Creek, a small tributary of the Cimarron River. On the evening of their arrival, the chiefs chose a group of scouts, known as wolves, each one a fast runner, to seek out the camp of the Greasy Wood People, which was presumed to be somewhere in the vicinity of the mouth of Wolf Creek. Wolf Road was named to lead this second scouting party, whose members would include the brothers Gentle Horse and Black Kettle.[11]

These wolves moved swiftly on foot toward the head of Wolf Creek but initially traveled too far west and passed the location of the Kiowa village without noticing it. One day, however, they were scouting down a ravine between Wolf and Beaver Creeks when a hunting party of Kiowa and Comanche warriors appeared into view. The Cheyenne wolves dipped into the water, concealed themselves in the rushes, and watched as these enemy hunters chased a small herd of buffalo. At one point, a young warrior on a bay mule rode within a few yards of the Cheyenne hiding place, but his eyes were trained on a running buffalo, which he shot and killed.

Black Kettle and the others patiently waited while the hunters butchered their kill, packed the meat, and rode away. It was now evident that although they had not determined the precise location, the enemy camp was without question nearby. The Cheyenne wolves cautiously made their way down the ravine and ran as fast as they could for home.

The return of the scouts to the village, which had by then moved to a place down Beaver Creek, was greeted with much excitement. Each scout in turn entered the circle of lodges, howling like a wolf, an indication that the enemy camp had been discovered. One by one, the wolves stood in front of the chiefs to report what they had observed.

The chiefs immediately sent the old Crier around the village to announce that they would move out that night, with intentions of attacking the hated Kiowas and the Comanches at dawn on the following morning.

Fragrances of sweet grass, sage, and cedar wafted throughout the area as the men blessed and purified their war shirts and shields, painted their faces, arranged their war medicines, readied their weapons, sang their war songs, and painted and decorated their war ponies. The women built platforms on which to store their possessions for safekeeping, for the lodges would be left standing.[12]

The Crier once again made his rounds, telling the warriors to assemble with their societies for the ceremonial march around the village, a traditional prelude to marching off to war.

The parade was a glorious mingling of motion, music, and color. War Bonnets swayed in time to the dancing movements of the war horses, while sunshine flashed from the beaten-silver hair plates trailing from the scalp locks of many a younger warrior. The men's war clothing glowed with the soft, rich shades of the sacred colors—red, yellow, black, blue, and green. These colors symbolized the Four Directions, the Sky, the Earth—the places from which sacred power came pouring in upon the people, blessing them and giving them new life. . . . It was a sight which never failed to make the People's hearts sing.[13]

The two combined tribes, Cheyennes and Arapahoes—men, women, children, horses, and even the dogs—marched southeast that night. Guards from the various warrior societies, including Black Kettle and the Elkhorn Scrapers, were positioned in the advance and on the flanks to make certain that anxious young warriors did not bolt ahead and compromise the element of surprise. The Dog Soldiers performed that same duty in the rear, which was their traditional place as watchdogs of the People. During the journey, in which the column paused four times to rest, warriors from each society took turns singing war songs that served to instill confidence and proclaim that they would be rewarded with victory in this impending battle.

Black Kettle and his fellow Elkhorn Scrapers sang their society song, the words of which professed that the Elks would always assist each other, no matter how tough the battle:

My Friends:
I am ready to help them out
Whenever they need help![14]

At dawn, however, the column found itself at the Canadian River, far below its intended destination. The guides had lost their bearings in the darkness, and now, to correct this miscalculation, they turned westward, arriving at Wolf Creek well after the sun had risen above the horizon. This blunder opened the door for an opportunist to seize upon.

Porcupine Bear, who months earlier had lost his position as chief of the Dog Soldiers and was exiled from camp with his family when he killed another man while drunk, was aware that the People were planning to attack the Kiowas. He and his small outlaw band had been riding independently just west of the main column toward Wolf Creek. His line of travel brought him directly opposite the camp of the enemy, and, before long, he happened to spot a group of about thirty Kiowas heading out to hunt buffalo.

Porcupine Bear secreted his seven Cheyenne outlaw warriors down a ravine and, with his back to the hunters as if watching something on the distant prairie, exposed himself on the crest of a hill and rode back and forth to indicate that he had located a buffalo herd. The men and women hunters, believing that this was a fellow Kiowa hunter, headed in his direction at the gallop.

When the Kiowas approached within speaking distance, Porcupine Bear sprang his trap. He grabbed his lance and, with the other outlaws close behind, wheeled around and charged into the group of unsuspecting buffalo hunters.

The surprised Kiowas had no chance to prepare their weapons and were caught defenseless. Porcupine Bear and his outlaws swept through the ranks of their fleeing enemy, lancing and shooting them down at will. All thirty men and women were killed by the seven outlaws, and their horses were captured.

Thus began the monumental Battle of Wolf Creek, with an outlaw band counting first coup—an honor that would not be officially recognized. In fact, this attack had been made before the ceremony of the Sacred Arrows had taken place, which nullified the supernatural power of the arrows against the enemy. This was the reason given later for the loss of so many people in the battle that followed.[15]

The Cheyenne and Arapaho women, children, and older men were secured at a safe place in the hills while the warriors—about a thousand of them, set to face an equal number of the enemy—rode down into the valley.

It was perhaps ten o'clock, well into the morning, when warriors of the main column first came upon scattered groups of their prey. A Kiowa man and woman ventured into sight and were immediately attacked and killed. Twelve women who had been digging roots were killed, then two men were cut down.

The column continued down a tributary of Wolf Creek until the Kiowa camp came into sight. The Elk Horn Scrapers, the warrior society to which Black Kettle belonged, were given the honor of charging first and thundered toward the lower end of the village. The waterway that these warriors had to negotiate, however, was deep and muddy, with slick banks that caused their horses to struggle and impeded progress. But the determined warriors fought their way forward, battling with their Kiowa and Comanche enemies, pulling back when facing superior numbers—once luring a group of Kiowas into a trap by wheeling around from a false retreat and then charging.

The other warrior societies struck the camp in several different places as separate detachments. The area surrounding Wolf Creek was a scene of mass chaos as the Cheyenne and the Arapaho warriors tore into the unsuspecting Kiowa-Comanche village. Running people, men and women, were cut down, while others were toppled from their horses.

The morning was ablaze with gunfire and the eerie sound of arrows zipping through the air. Great plumes of smoke from spent black powder cartridges combined with clouds of dust stirred up by the horses to obscure vision and make it difficult to discern friend from foe. Cries of agony and encouragement, war whoops, screams of terrified women and children, and the shrill whinnies of the frightened and wounded mounts created a macabre quality that would be forever imbedded in the minds of the participants.

Most of the fierce battle was waged hand to hand in close quarters, which tested the skill and the bravery of the most accomplished warrior. Some Kiowas fought from behind breastworks, but those isolated pockets of resistance were quickly routed. Duels on horseback between individuals and small groups were commonplace. The Cheyennes charged and beat back countercharges, with no quarter given by either side and casualties steadily mounting. It was evident throughout the afternoon, however, that the Cheyennes and the Arapahoes were successfully avenging the deaths of the forty-two Bowstring Soldiers who had been killed the previous year.

The Cheyenne wounded were taken as they fell during the day to a place down the valley where the women could care for them. At one point in the fighting, the women moved closer to the village to watch and were noticed by the Kiowas, who were not able to distinguish their identity and believed that they were another detachment of braves ready to attack. This greatly disheartened the Kiowa observers and caused many to flee into the surrounding timber to escape this presumed new assault by fresh warriors.

The sun had dipped low in the western sky before the fighting slackened and the Cheyenne warriors gradually returned to camp. The Battle of Wolf Creek had concluded, and the Greasy Wood People and the Rattlesnake People had been severely chastised—fifty to sixty of them had been killed, countless others wounded, and the remainder of the tribe had fled in disarray from the scene of the carnage.[16]

Nothing has been recorded about the specific actions of Black Kettle on that day, but there can be no doubt that he was in the thick of the fighting, from the initial charge throughout the entire engagement. Many of the dead Bowstring Soldiers likely had been friends with whom he had shared his youth when he was a member of that soldier society. Black Kettle would have fought with a personal vengeance in his heart and remained on the field until the final opportunity to shed the blood of his enemy has passed.

This battle on Wolf Creek, however, was a bittersweet victory for the Southern Cheyennes. True, they had avenged their murdered brethren, but there was much weeping that night as the names of the dead were revealed. Chiefs White Thunder (also known as Gray Thunder, in some texts) and Gray Hair, as well as twelve warriors, had been killed.

It was unthinkable to the People that White Thunder, the Keeper of the Sacred Arrows, the holiest man among them, had fallen. Although the arrows had been saved, the death of this revered man compelled many strong warriors to accompany the women in wailing to mourn the tragic loss.[17]

The death of White Thunder also affected the Bent family. The previous year, William had married Owl Woman, Chief White Thunder's daughter—the couple would have four children, including George, whose memoirs would prove so valuable.[18]

The Cheyennes and the Kiowas engaged in several minor skirmishes, as well as the customary horse-stealing forays, throughout the following year, but, perhaps surprisingly, the summer of 1840 brought with it the promise of peace between the rival tribes.

An emissary from the Prairie Apaches, known as the People Using the Rasp Fiddle, who were allies of the Kiowas and the Comanches, professed that those tribes were interested in making a lasting peace with the Cheyennes and the Arapahoes.

The People and the Cloud People were agreeable to that proposal. Runners were dispatched to carry the news that the Cheyennes were willing to make peace and had promised that they would not send out war parties while talks progressed.[19]

Within days, the entire Southern Cheyenne camp packed up and moved toward Bent's Fort, in order to trade for gifts that they would present as tokens of friendship to the Kiowas and the Comanches. From there, the Cheyennes, now accompanied by the Arapahoes, traveled to the mouth of Two Butte Creek and camped to await the arrival of their former enemies.

Two days later, chiefs of the Kiowa, the Comanche, and the Apache tribes, led by the Kiowa Little Mountain, presented themselves at the camp. The chiefs of the Cheyennes and the Arapahoes welcomed them and led their former enemies to the center of the camp circle, where they sat facing each other in a long line. Eagle Feather lit his pipe and moved along the row of Cheyenne chiefs, offering the pipe to each man in turn. After each chief had taken one puff from the pipe, peace was declared.[20]

The visitors had brought with them, wrapped in a colorful Navajo blanket, the scalps of the forty-two Bowstring warriors whom they had killed three years earlier. High Back Wolf, however, displayed great wisdom when he refused to accept them, saying, "Friend, these things if shown and talked about will only make bad feeling. The peace is made now; take the heads [scalps] away with you and use them as you think best; do not let us see them or hear of them."[21]

The Cheyenne people came forward and presented gifts, then the tribes sat down together for a great feast. The Kiowa and the Comanche chiefs invited their new friends to meet them just below Bent's Fort in the near future, where they would trade additional presents—such coveted items as horses, blankets, beads, brass kettles, and guns—and they would all enjoy another feast.[22]

And so an end to hostilities between the People and the Cloud People with their former enemies the Greasy Wood People, the Rattlesnake People, and the People Using the Rasp Fiddle came to pass—and this peace treaty would never be broken.

This was the first time that Black Kettle witnessed a peace treaty. With the smoking of the pipe—the equivalent of a solemn handshake or the touching of the pen in the white man's world—two bitter, traditional enemies had set aside all differences between them and vowed to become friends and allies from that day forth.

For years, these tribes had slaughtered one another, stolen each other's horses on raiding parties, and lived every day with the realization that their enemy could swoop down upon them at any moment and take their lives. Now, they could share gifts and sit together in friendship at a feast, with the comforting knowledge that no member of either tribe, after having watched their chiefs take this sacred vow, would ever consider breaking their word.

And High Back Wolf, with his refusal to receive the scalps of the Cheyenne warriors killed by the Kiowas, had demonstrated to Black Kettle that all the killing and the misery, all the grieving and the tears wept by the women, could be summarily forgiven and the perpetrators of the deeds instantly pardoned.

Perhaps this event made enough of an impression upon Black Kettle that it served as a lesson in shaping his future role as a man who believed that peace with any enemy—even the white man—was attainable if both parties were honorable and sincere with their promise to become friends.

One year after peace between the tribes had been made, the first emigrant wagon train rumbled west along the South Platte River, headed for Oregon. For years the People had been in contact with white fur trappers and traders, with whom relations had been cordial. But as this trickle of covered wagons became a flood that gushed across the Plains, the tribes were confronted with a different type of white man, one who displayed hostility and had no regard for natural resources.

These emigrants thought little of cutting and wasting precious timber—and the isolated stands of cottonwood trees along streams within the barren prairie were the only places where the tribes could find adequate shelter in winter. The travelers also allowed their herds of livestock to graze in one spot until nothing remained but dirt. And they slaughtered buffalo by the score and simply left the carcasses to rot.

The curious braves who approached these wagon trains to trade for tobacco and other goods were usually treated with arrogance or outright fear. No effort was made by either side to establish an understanding and an acceptance of cultural differences.

Throughout the 1840s, however, incidences of conflict between the travelers and the Plains tribes were relatively minor in nature. The chiefs, for the most part, managed to control the impulsive young warriors from interfering with the white intrusion, and offenses were generally limited to running off stock, although the temptation to count coup did result in an occasional killing. The frustrations and the aggressions of the People during this time of white expansion were mainly vented with skirmishes against traditional enemies, such as the Pawnees, the Crows, the Utes, the Delawares, and the Shawnees.

The U.S. Army, in an effort to maintain order on the principal trails west, also became more of a presence. By 1849, two forts, Laramie and Kearny, had been garrisoned for the purpose of patrolling the emigrant trails.[23]

That same year, the discovery of gold in California initiated another influx of wagon trains passing through the Plains. This particular invasion would have a tragic result for many of the Plains tribes. The emigrant trains not only brought more whites through the territory but also spread the deadly cholera disease.

The symptoms of this infection were acute diarrhea and vomiting, a loss of fluid and salts, muscle cramps, severe thirst, chills, wrinkled skin, and often circulatory collapse. Coma and death could occur within a few hours of contracting cholera.

And the Cheyennes and their neighbors, through whose homelands the infected wagon trains passed, contracted the disease in alarming numbers.

George Bent described this terrible scourge, which had originated in the ports of New Orleans and New York and was carried to the Plains by the gold rushers:

> "Cramps" the Indians called it, and they died of it by the hundreds. On the Platte whole camps could be seen deserted with the tepees full of dead bodies, men, women, children. The Sioux and Cheyennes, who were nearest to the road, were the hardest hit. . . . Our tribe suffered very heavy loss; half the tribe died, some old people say. . . . The people were soon in a panic. The big camps broke up into little bands and family groups, and each party fled from the rest.[24]

Miraculously, Black Kettle and Little Sage Woman were spared as this cholera epidemic decimated the Cheyennes and other Plains tribes. In late winter, after the disease had run its course, the couple traveled to a place on the Arkansas River near Bent's Fort, where the rest of the People who had survived began straggling in, to assemble once again as a tribe. It was a time of great sorrow as the dead were mourned—and the living were given another reason to resent the presence of the white man in their land.

Thomas Fitzpatrick, the mountain man and guide known as "Broken Hand," had been appointed as Indian agent for the Upper Platte and the Arkansas rivers in 1846. Two summers after the cramping sickness, he managed to convince the U.S. Congress that a treaty was necessary to maintain peace among the Plains tribes, and appropriations were subsequently approved.

In September 1851, more than ten thousand members of the various Plains tribes—including the Southern Cheyennes and the Southern Arapahoes—gathered at Horse Creek, about thirty-five miles east of Fort Laramie, to discuss peace with the U.S. government. Tensions

Southern Cheyenne–Arapaho Territory, Horse Creek Treaty of 1851

were as taut as a bowstring as enemies camped within sight of each other, and, despite such notables as Jim Bridger and Father Pierre Jean De Smet being in attendance to soothe relations, a few incidents of violence did occur. But on September 17, after a week of negotiations, the Treaty of Horse Creek, or Fort Laramie, was signed.

This treaty provided the Southern Cheyenne and Arapaho tribes with goods and provisions in the amount of $50,000 per year for fifty years (later reduced by Congress to ten years) as compensation for the destruction of buffalo ranges. The Cheyennes would control the vast territory between the trails to Oregon and Santa Fe, which included most of the Colorado plains, southeastern Wyoming, and parts of Kansas and Nebraska, that had been their homeland. The treaty also officially confirmed that the Southern bands were separate from their Northern counterparts, the Northern Cheyennes, although in reality various bands of the tribe, whether Northern or Southern in designation, frequently camped together. And the Cheyennes as a tribe remained as one for ceremonies, such as the Sacred Arrow renewal and the Sun Dance.

In return, the chiefs promised to refrain from waging war against the whites and to permit the government to build roads and military posts within their territory.

Black Kettle would certainly have been impressed by the wealth of the white man in the form of presents that were distributed whenever one of the Council Chiefs "touched the pen." The chiefs, much less the tribal members, however, likely did not understand or perhaps even take the treaty that seriously. They were confident of their security within the boundaries of their traditional territory and had maintained good relations with the white man. The promise of gifts alone would have been enough motivation to sway their decision to sign. Nonetheless, for the most part, both sides abided by the treaty, and relations would remain peaceful for many years.[25]

Peace might have been made with the Kiowas and the Comanches and now with the white man, but the Cheyennes did not lack enemies—the Pawnees, the Wolf People, in particular. Ten years earlier, the Pawnees had captured the Cheyenne Sacred Arrows during a battle along the Platte River. The bundle had been tugged off the lance of Medicine Man Bull when he attempted to strike an enemy warrior. The Cheyennes had fought desperately to recover the arrows but failed. Although they had made four new medicine arrows and two of the originals were subsequently recovered, this had been one of the greatest tragedies to ever befall the People.

The Pawnees made peace overtures at Horse Creek but were rebuffed by the Cheyennes. Memories of those who had been lost in battle—as well as of the capture of the Sacred Arrows—were too strong in the hearts of many chiefs to consider peace at that time with the Wolf People.[26]

Within a year of the Horse Creek Treaty, in the summer of 1852, 230 members representing all 5 soldier societies, along with allied Arapaho, Sioux, Apache, and Kiowa warriors, engaged in a battle with a Pawnee buffalo hunting party. In the ensuing fierce struggle, the Cheyennes finally drove the Wolf People away but paid dearly. Eight men of the People had been killed, including Chief Alights on the

Cloud, who was considered the most important man of the Cheyenne tribe at the Horse Creek councils. He was widely admired for his handsome appearance, bravery, and kindness, and his death evoked much sorrow that night in the camp of the People.[27]

Several months following this battle, Little Robe, a prominent Dog Soldier chief whose son had also been killed that day, carried the pipe to all the scattered camps of the People. He was on a personal mission to convince all the bands that they must unite and wipe the Wolf People off the face of the earth. Now was the time, he told them, to avenge the blood of their loved ones, and the people responded positively to that cry for justice.

This effort by Little Robe finally brought him to the main village, which was located at the mouth of Beaver Creek on the South Platte, where once again he pled his case. The Council Chiefs retired to the confines of their huge lodge to discuss this grave matter.

Eventually, the Crier was dispatched to announce to everyone the decision of the chiefs. He rode around the circle of lodges and declared that the Sacred Arrows and the Sacred Medicine Hat would be moved without delay against the Pawnees. War had been declared.

Scouts were immediately sent out to learn the location of the Pawnee camp, and within days these wolves returned to report that the enemy had been found. The People, with much excitement and anticipation, tore down their lodges and packed all of their possessions. In one great column, the Cheyennes moved steadily south until arriving at the Arikara Fork of the Republican River, where they made final preparations for war with the Wolf People. The village was the scene of great bustle as the People prepared for war. Young men readied their weapons and purified shields, while singing songs and painting themselves and their mounts.[28]

The next day, the village moved downstream on a collision course with the camp of the Pawnee. All was now in place—the Cheyennes would attack in the morning.

That day, while the women and the children waited out of sight, the men engaged in their final ceremonies before going into battle.

Long Chin, the chief of the Dog Soldiers, was selected to wear the Sacred Buffalo Hat. The hat was reverently raised from its bed of white sage and placed on his head. As he began to tie the hat in place, however, one of the leather strings snapped. This was a terrible omen, for even the slightest damage to the Sacred Hat could spell disaster for the People. Long Chin, in an effort to make the best of a bad situation, vowed to give a woman, to be passed on the prairie, as a sacrifice to right this wrong. He knotted the broken string and finished tying the hat in place.

When it was time to choose a special man to be honored by carrying the Sacred Arrows into battle, the Keeper approached Black Kettle, the brave and respected warrior from the Elkhorn Scraper Society. The four arrows were securely lashed onto the end of Black Kettle's war lance, and he proudly rode to the head of the line of Southern Cheyenne warriors, where he was joined by Long Chin.

Black Kettle with the Sacred Arrows and Long Chin wearing the Sacred Buffalo Hat would lead the charge into the Pawnee camp.[29]

While these ceremonies had been taking place, however, Big Head and seven others had secretly slipped away from the main party, with intentions of counting the first coup on the Pawnees. To ride ahead of the two Great Covenants—the Sacred Arrows and the Sacred Hat— was a violation of Cheyenne law and could diminish the power or even eliminate the medicine promised to the People.

Black Kettle and Long Chin, unaware of Big Head's transgression, led the charge toward the enemy camp. Behind them, the men pushed their ponies to great speeds in their haste to engage the Wolf People. But when the honored warriors reached the presumed location of the Pawnee camp, there was no one to be found—nothing except the ashes of burned-out fires.

Black Kettle and the lead warriors searched the surrounding area, riding upstream and then turning back to look for any sign of the Wolf People. Before long, a small group of warriors appeared and advanced toward them. Believing these men to be Pawnee, Black Kettle and the others charged with weapons at the ready. But it was Big Head, waving a scalp and calling out that "the camp is right over the hill. Go slowly, for there are many of them."

The Cheyennes had lost that all-important element of surprise. The Pawnees, compliments of Big Head and his party, had been afforded enough advance warning that they were able to move their women, children, and ponies downstream, where they would be protected by the high banks. The men had then assumed defensive positions behind natural breastworks along the banks. Although greatly outnumbered by the Cheyennes and their allies, the Wolf People had averted the disaster that would certainly have been their fate had not the glory-seeking Big Head prematurely given away the presence of the People. The Cheyenne warriors raced through the Pawnee camp and charged the streambank positions. The Pawnee men, however, did not come out into the open to fight but rather held the People at bay with a withering fire. Throughout the afternoon, Black Kettle and the other warriors attempted time and again to penetrate the Pawnee defenses but on each occasion were thwarted by the effective defense along the streambank.

The Cheyennes did manage to fight their way into the Wolf People's camp, where they destroyed the lodges and confiscated the hide covers and any other property that they desired.

They were completing the systematic dismantling of the Pawnee camp when a party of strangers was observed advancing toward them. Several Kiowas recognized these people as Potawatomis, an Eastern tribe that had been moved West. These strangers had adopted many customs of the white man, such as wearing civilized clothing, and were known to always be well-armed.

The Kiowas headed toward the Potawatomis with intentions of initiating a parley. The Potawatomi warriors, however, were in no mood to talk. Instead, these newcomers commenced firing at the Cheyennes. It was evident to the People that a runner had been sent by the Pawnees to request assistance from the Potawatomis. They would now have to defeat or chase off the Potawatomis before resuming efforts to dislodge the Pawnees from their hiding places.

The unexpected, blistering barrage that greeted them from Potawatomi rifles, however, compelled the Cheyennes to retreat. Then, overcoming their initial shock, the warriors wheeled their horses around and charged toward this enemy. The Potawatomis lived up to their reputation as expert marksmen. One after another Cheyenne warrior was shot from his saddle. The Cheyennes prudently pulled back to regroup and formulate another plan of attack.

The Potawatomi warriors boldly advanced to the places where dead Cheyennes lay on the ground. The People watched with horror as this new enemy dismounted, cut open the chests of fallen Cheyennes, then removed the hearts and stuffed these into their bullet pouches. It had been rumored that this tribe made strong medicine from enemy hearts, which was then rubbed on bullets to improve warriors' aim when in battle.

This rumor had come true right before their eyes, which struck fear into the hearts and the souls of the People. The power of their own medicine had been broken by Big Head's rash act, and it was apparent that the Potawatomi medicine was strong. Black Kettle and the other Cheyenne warriors were completely unnerved and fled en mass from the Pawnee camp.

Later, when the dead were counted, the People had lost eighteen men; the Kiowas and the Prairie Apaches had both suffered two killed; and one Arapaho had lost his life. There would be much weeping in the camps during that summer of 1853.[30]

That same summer, Southern Cheyenne warriors led by War Bonnet conducted the tribe's first raid into Mexico. For years, the Kiowas had told them about the quality of horseflesh that was there just waiting to be taken. Although the journey would be difficult, with water holes few and far between, the reward was worth perhaps losing a man or two to thirst. The great horse herds—as well as Mexican women and children captives—that the Kiowas displayed were enough proof to inspire War Bonnet to act.

War Bonnet's raid, however, ended in tragedy when Mexican soldiers happened upon his party and killed several of them, while the remainder limped home, empty-handed. Subsequent raiding parties were more successful and yielded a fair bounty of horses, mules, and a few captives.[31]

In 1854, the People met at Fort St. Vrain at the request of John W. Whitfield, the Indian agent who had replaced Thomas Fitzpatrick. Whitfield asked that the chiefs order their bands to quit raiding into Mexico and turn over to him any people whom they had captured. Following some discussion, the chiefs agreed to end their forays against the Hairy Nostriled White Men, as the Cheyennes called them, with the promise that the Mexicans would also cease hostilities. The Cheyennes subsequently released to Whitfield a white boy and two Mexicans who had been taken prisoner.[32]

The People then moved from Fort St. Vrain down to Sand Hill Timbers, on the Arkansas River. From this camp, two members of the Scabby Band decided to hunt buffalo and ventured down the Cimarron River. Days passed, and these men did not return. Several parties rode out to search for their brethren and finally discovered their bodies buried in a camp that had been recently vacated by Mexican buffalo hunters.[33]

Soon afterward, the Council of Forty-four convened to discuss tribal business. The chiefs of the Scabby Band raised the issue regarding their two warriors who had been killed by the Hairy Nostriled White Men. These murders had occurred after the chiefs had promised Agent Whitfield that the tribe would not raid into Mexico. That pledge, however, had been made with the provision that the Mexicans would also cease any violence against the Cheyennes. Now, with the killing of the two warriors by Mexicans, the leaders of the Scabby Band argued that the chiefs were no longer bound by their pledge, and a war party should be organized without delay to settle accounts.

The subject of reprisal against the Mexicans was a matter of lengthy debate, at times contentious, among the chiefs. In the end, they were unable to arrive at a consensus opinion about whether or not to retaliate. The council adjourned without resolving the issue.

The idea of avenging these two murders remained a prominent topic of discussion within the tribe, with the young warriors encouraging the chiefs to act. Not every chief had abandoned the thought of organizing a war party to punish the Mexicans for their treachery, but there was enough dissent to set aside an immediate decision.

To Black Kettle, however, the murders were an affront that could not be ignored. He was a seasoned warrior, a prominent member of the Elkhorn Scrapers who carried the war pipe—a man of respect whom the younger men were eager to follow into battle. While others hesitated, Black Kettle stepped forward and seized the initiative. Regardless of promises made by the chiefs, he was determined to take action to right this blatant atrocity by the Mexicans. He announced that he would lead a war party into Mexico and see to it that the Mexicans paid dearly for killing the two innocent Cheyennes.

Feathered Shin, Frog, and Wolf Chief—each carrying a war pipe—along with fifteen capable warriors, volunteered to join Black Kettle on this quest. Two women would accompany the war party—Frog's wife, Red Eye Woman; and Little Sage Woman, the wife of Black Kettle. The women would be of great service to the men by performing necessary domestic chores and taking charge of the plunder that the men intended to appropriate.

Black Kettle led his small party south through desolate, rugged terrain under a scorching sun on a strenuous trek that tested the resoluteness of the Cheyennes and the endurance of their mounts. But with relentless determination, he kept them steadily moving through long stretches with no water, pushing deeper into enemy territory, riding for many difficult days through Texas until finally arriving in southern Mexico.

This adventure by Black Kettle was quite remarkable. In addition to enduring natural elements, his war party would have had to pass through the territories of countless tribes and nomadic bands that would not have looked kindly upon an intrusion by the Cheyennes. And, unlike previous raids by the Cheyennes, there was now more of a military presence on both sides of the border. Danger, without question, lurked over every bluff, down every ravine, and if the Cheyennes were to be spotted on the open prairie, they would not have a safe avenue of escape.

Upon arriving at their destination, deep into Mexico, the Cheyenne avengers swept through the countryside, raiding isolated rancheros and terrorizing the inhabitants as repayment for the killing of their two brethren. Employing hit-and-run tactics, Black Kettle's war party struck quickly, stealing stock and other property, then hastening away before any resistance or pursuit could be organized. When Black Kettle had determined that their actions had exacted sufficient punishment to the Hairy Nostriled White Men, the jubilant war party headed north, leading a great number of stolen horses that were heavily laden with plunder.

The return trip proved to be another arduous journey, and it was with great relief when they finally made it into fertile country near the foot of the mountains between the South Canadian and the Cimarron rivers. Black Kettle and the other pipe bearers were riding in the advance, when up ahead they noticed a man on foot, leading a horse, patiently following a trail as if he had lost something and was looking for it.

Red Moon and Timber were summoned and ordered to discern the identity of this stranger. The two young Cheyenne warriors galloped away and were closing on the man when he noticed them. He leaped onto his horse and raced off, with Red Moon and Timber in hot pursuit. Black Kettle and the others followed with the horse herd and watched as this stranger and the two warriors disappeared over the crest of a bluff.

Within moments, Red Moon and Timber reappeared and raced back toward the war party, all the while making signs indicating that everyone should flee. The destination of the stranger had been a large camp occupied by Utes—known to the Cheyennes as the Black People—and a handful of Mountain Apaches, where he was presently spreading the alarm about the Cheyenne intruders.

Instead of abandoning the horse herd, which would have made flight more expedient, Black Kettle and his men attempted to control the animals as they wheeled around to escape this sudden threat. Several young men lagged behind and waited with intentions of holding off the enemy long enough for the others to get away.

The sight of an overwhelming number of Ute and Mountain Apache warriors thundering over the top of the bluff, however, compelled the advance guard to retreat, and the enemy quickly overtook the main party. The fighting was fierce as Black Kettle rallied his men against this superior force.

Little Sage Woman was in the thick of the battle when her saddle cinch snapped, and she was thrown from her horse to the ground. Black Kettle managed to catch his wife's pony and lead it to her, but she was unable to mount the wild-eyed, shying animal.

By now, the Cheyennes were completely surrounded by the Black People, and the only manner in which to save themselves was to fight their way out of the closing circle of fury in order to flee.

Black Kettle and several others continued their attempts to rescue Little Sage, who had now become the primary target of the enemy, but they were pushed farther and farther away from her by the furious onslaught. Feathered Shin was killed, and Black Kettle and Red Moon were both wounded as they fought to free the woman. The beleaguered Cheyennes could only watch in horror and rage as Little Sage was grabbed and swept onto a horse by a Ute warrior, who rode off with her in the direction of the camp.

The attention of the Utes now turned to Red Eye Woman, who also had been unable to escape the closing ring of warriors. The Cheyennes were determined to save her and fought desperately. Frog, her husband, refused to leave her side and lost his life battling to protect her. In spite of their efforts, the Cheyennes were beaten back, and Red Eye Woman was taken in the same manner as Little Sage.

At this time, the Ute and the Mountain Apache warriors broke contact and contentedly returned to their camp. They had killed three of their enemy, captured two women, and rounded up the Cheyenne horse herd with its load of valuable plunder. The prospect of inspecting their newly acquired horseflesh and the opportunity to rummage through the packs far outweighed the desire to annihilate their enemy. There would be a great celebration that night in the camp of the Black People.

Black Kettle no doubt was tormented over the loss of Little Sage Woman, and in his angry heart he must have wanted to rush into the enemy camp to save her. Perhaps he was physically restrained or convinced by the level-headed advice of the others from committing such a rash act. It is also possible that the wound Black Kettle sustained had incapacitated him—the extent of his injury has not been noted anywhere. More than likely, however, he came to the understanding that any attempt to rescue the two women would be tantamount to suicide.

With only the horses they were riding, Black Kettle and the heartsick survivors of this tragic encounter reluctantly headed for home.

The war party had expected to arrive triumphantly in their camp to the joyous sound of victory songs in their ears, honoring them for avenging the two warriors killed by the Mexicans—not to mention excitement over the property that they had taken in southern Mexico. Instead, Black Kettle and his beaten, weary war party were greeted by the wails and the tears of women who mourned the loss of their loved ones.

It would not have been prudent to mount a rescue party and return to the location of the fight with the hope of freeing Little Sage and Red Eye. The Utes would have certainly moved their camp by then, and the trail would have eventually gone cold. There was nothing to do but grieve for the dead and the missing.

Later, Mexican traders were persuaded to help locate the two women captives and arrange a trade. Time passed without any word, and Little Sage Woman and Red Eye Woman were never heard of again. The two women possibly spent the remainder of their lives as slaves for the hated Black People or some other tribe. Or, in an ironic twist of fate, the Utes could have traded them to *comancheros*, that shady group of traffickers, who may have then sold them to a wealthy Mexican family, where they would have become servants or field workers at a large ranchero.

The grief-stricken Black Kettle perhaps privately admonished himself for taking his wife along on such a perilous mission. As a man with the heart of a warrior, however, he would not have regretted that he had served his people well, once again proving his bravery and leadership skills by avenging the murders of his fellow tribesmen.[34]

After an appropriate and respectful period of mourning, Black Kettle took another wife. Her name was Medicine Woman Later, and she was a member of the Wotap band (plural, Wotapio), who were recognized for their excellent eye for horseflesh and the fine, roomy lodges that they built. Black Kettle, in the tradition of the Cheyenne, moved in with his wife's family.

In the winter of 1854, Bear Feather, the chief of the Wotapio, went to be with the spirits. When it came time to choose a successor to Chief Bear Feather, the Wotap band—perhaps surprisingly—turned to their new brother, the man who had married Medicine Woman Later. Black Kettle, the warrior born of Suhtai parents, was named a chief of the Southern Cheyennes and a member of the prestigious Council of Forty-four.[35]

This man who had distinguished himself in countless battles and had suffered great personal loss would now be called upon to assume a prominent role in a changing era. Chief Black Kettle would be challenged to summon every ounce of experience and wisdom gained from his days as a warrior to lead his people as they contended with the most powerful force that the tribe had yet encountered—the white man.

3

THE MIGHT
OF THE U.S. ARMY

By the early 1850s, tensions between the white man and the various Cheyenne bands—as well as other Plains tribes—had progressively heightened. The heartland that had provided such a prosperous existence for the Native Americans was suffering from disease, hunger, despair, and uncertainty—the result of the increasing white civilian invasion and the threatening presence of armed troops. Incidences of violence had escalated to the point that militant factions from both sides were on the brink of declaring war.

Oddly enough, it was a relatively minor event that ignited the powder keg into one monumental explosion. This incident and its aftermath forever changed the tactics employed by the U.S. Army against the Plains tribes and initiated an era of armed hostilities that did not abate for decades.

On August 17, 1854, an ox from a wagon train of Mormon emigrants happened to stray close to a Lakota Sioux camp east of Fort Laramie. This animal, portrayed as lame and worn out or crippled and left by the wayside, was killed within sight of its owner by an arrow fired from the bow of a Sioux brave named High Forehead. The precise reason for this act has failed to stand the test of time, and versions abound. Most likely, High Forehead killed the animal out of mischief rather than hunger. Relations had degenerated to the point that both races derived pleasure from provoking one another.

Regardless of High Forehead's motives, the indignant Mormons reported the incident to the fort and demanded satisfaction. Brave Bear, the Sioux chief, was summoned and informed of the affair by Lieutenant Hugh B. Fleming, the post commander who was two years removed from West Point.

Brave Bear considered the affair inconsequential but readily offered to make restitution. Fleming, however, ignored that gesture. Instead, Fleming ordered that High Forehead be brought to the fort for disposition. The chief refused, stating that not only did he lack such authority over High Forehead but Fleming's demand was in direct violation of the 1851 Horse Creek Treaty, which provided for each tribe to punish its own guilty parties in crimes against whites. Fleming then vowed to send troops the following morning to arrest the culprit.

Word of this threat reached the Lakota camp, and High Forehead was plainly terrified. The white man's practice of arrest and incarceration was alien to the Plains tribes, and the brave feared that he would be murdered if removed from his people. That night, the warriors in the various nearby camps sang songs as they painted themselves and readied their medicines in preparation for war.

One officer at the post, a recent West Point graduate named Second Lieutenant John L. Grattan, was chomping at the bit to prove his prowess in battle. He had yet to hear a shot fired in anger but nonetheless was known to boast that his primitive enemy would be no match for the might of the U.S. Army. Grattan, unfortunately, was cut from a mold of army officers all too common in the frontier West, those who preferred confrontation rather than compromise. He convinced Lieutenant Fleming to permit him to command the detail assigned to arrest High Forehead, the killer of incapacitated Mormon oxen. Fleming might have set aside any action for the time being, but Grattan was so insistent that the post commander finally acquiesced.

Grattan, as promised, set out in the morning from the fort with a detachment of twenty-nine troopers, an interpreter, a small mountain howitzer, and a twelve-pound fieldpiece.

Meanwhile, some twelve hundred Lakota Sioux warriors had assembled around the bluffs surrounding the camp to await Grattan's arrival.

Grattan, who some reports say had bolstered his courage with drink, passed through this gauntlet of warriors to enter the camp. He summoned Chief Brave Bear and made it clear that he intended to arrest High Forehead. The chief consulted the guilty party, who stated that he would die, perhaps even commit suicide, before he would submit. Negotiations continued for another half hour, with Brave Bear repeating his offer of compensation for the dead ox.

Grattan refused to bargain and insisted that High Forehead deliver himself. Finally, the lieutenant lost patience and ordered his men to ready their weapons, perhaps as a "saber-rattling" tactic to display his determination.

It is not clear which side shot first—most say that Grattan gave the order—but within moments the air was thick with bullets and arrows as the soldiers and the Sioux opened fire on each other. The first to fall was Brave Bear, struck with at least three bullets—perhaps initially shot in the back by Grattan. Artillery rained on the camp, but the guns had been aimed too high and blasted harmlessly through the tops of the lodges.

The outnumbered soldiers panicked, broke ranks, and ran. The Lakota chased them down and killed them all. Grattan was found with twenty-four arrows piercing his body and his skull crushed beyond recognition. He could be identified only by his pocket watch.

The riled-up warriors then turned their attention toward raiding a nearby trading post and gathering support for an assault on Fort Laramie. Eventually, however, the level-headed chiefs convinced their brethren that the prudent course of action would be to immediately withdraw from that place. The triumphant Lakota Sioux packed up their lodges and departed to participate in their annual buffalo hunt.[1]

The Eastern press reported with great embellishment the massacre of this gallant young officer and his troops. An inflamed public called for revenge against the red devils responsible for this unprovoked, outrageous deed.

The War Department ignored testimony from officers at Fort Laramie who professed that Grattan was responsible for the incident and also pointed out that the attempted arrest was a violation of the treaty. The War Department decided that military action was in order.

The man selected to punish the Lakota for their treachery was Brigadier General William S. Harney, a fifty-four-year-old hero of the Mexican War. Harney, who was in Paris at the time, would soon begin assembling his troops at Fort Leavenworth, Kansas, for the march west.

In August 1855, a new Indian agent was appointed for the Upper Platte. Thomas S. Twiss, a West Point graduate recently discharged from the army, arrived at Fort Laramie and lost little time getting down to business. Twiss dispatched runners to the Lakota camps to advise the chiefs that all friendly Indians were to report to the fort, where they would be protected and provided with rations. Otherwise, they would be considered hostile and could expect the army to pay them an inimical visit.

This edict was taken seriously by most of the Lakota bands, who reconsidered any idea that they might have had about engaging in war with the white man. By early September, hundreds of lodges had peacefully assembled in a village on the Laramie Fork, thirty-five miles from the fort.[2]

One Sioux band of about 40 lodges—250 people—led by Chief Little Thunder, however, remained camped on Bluewater River, a tributary of the Platte, 6 miles northwest of Ash Hollow and 100 miles east of Fort Laramie. Runners warned Little Thunder about the danger of defying the order, but the chief argued that his people had been out buffalo hunting and required sufficient time to dry the meat. Little Thunder and his people had always been considered friendly, and therefore he dismissed any notion that he would be attacked. In this instance, he judged wrong.

On September 3, General Harney, with six hundred troops and artillery, approached Little Thunder's camp. This unexpected visit was quite a shock to those present, and the chiefs rode out to intercept the general and request a parley.

Harney was willing to listen but had already deployed his cavalry in a secreted location above the camp and continued to march his infantry toward his objective.

When the chiefs failed to halt Harney's advance, they galloped away to spread the alarm, with the army opening fire as they gave chase.

The panicked Lakota within the village fled from the foot soldiers—only to run directly into the cavalry. And, in what could only be called a massacre, revenge for Lieutenant John Grattan and his men was exacted.

When the firing had ceased, eighty-six Sioux had been killed, with five wounded and another seventy women and children taken prisoner. The village and its valuable contents had been destroyed and the pony herd captured. Those who managed to escape were mostly on foot, running for their lives with nothing but the shirts on their backs.[3]

Although Harney's report does not mention the fact, it was highly probable that those counted as killed were not exclusively warriors but actually included an unknown number of women and children. General Winfield S. Scott later "objected seriously to the killing of women and children that had occurred at Ash Hollow."[4]

The destruction of Little Thunder's camp had been a catastrophe of proportions previously unheard of in the annals of Plains warfare.

Never before had another tribe, much less the white man, killed so many of them or captured their wives and children in such great numbers, or had a village been so thoroughly ravaged.

The gauntlet had been thrown down in challenge by the U.S. Army. Total war, a ruthless tactic that subjected the civilian populace, not just the warriors, to a reign of terror, had been declared. The army, as evidenced by General Harney's actions, had concluded that invading the enemy's homeland and mercilessly destroying property and taking women and children prisoners, if not killing them, would break the will of the red man to fight, and resistance to peace entreaties favorable to the white man would diminish. And the commanders, acting under the orders of the War Department, rarely bothered to distinguish the innocent from the guilty—while those who had committed misdeeds ran for the hills to hide, the soldiers could always easily locate some friendly camp to punish.

The Lakota Sioux, the most powerful tribe on the Plains, had been humbled by the soldiers at Ash Hollow. Word of this tragedy spread among the various nomadic bands and tribes like a Plains wildfire. Every tribe, without exception, was clearly frightened by the ruthlessness displayed by the army. The message had been delivered that any tribes that refused to submit to the wishes of the United States of America would be in danger of losing their property, loved ones, and territory rights by force.

While Harney marched against the Sioux, a surveying party made its way through the central Plains to map out a proposed wagon road that would cut through the heart of buffalo ranges from the Kansas, the Solomon, and the Smoky Hill rivers to Bent's Fort on the Arkansas. This new Smoky Hill Trail would soon bring an even greater wave of emigrants across traditional Cheyenne territory. And the army was determined to protect the travelers from any threat by hostile tribes.[5]

At a March 1856 council with General Harney at Fort Pierre, the chastised Sioux leaders readily agreed to hand over the murderers of Lieutenant Grattan and his men. Seven men were surrendered, and they and their women were subsequently imprisoned at Fort Leavenworth, Kansas.[6]

At the same time, Harney spoke to representatives of several Northern Cheyenne bands. Roads had been surveyed through Cheyenne territory, and the flow of emigrants, perhaps as many as 20,000 in the previous year, had led to a number of minor depredations by aggressive young warriors. Harney, in no uncertain terms, told the Cheyenne chiefs—without distinguishing between Northern and Southern factions—that they must restrain their warriors from engaging in raiding parties against the Pawnee and the Sioux, which were a danger to people passing through; that they could hunt only in territory designated by the Fort Laramie Treaty (i.e., the Horse Creek Treaty); and that they must withdraw from the vicinity of the Platte Road to assure the safety of travelers. If they disobeyed, Harney warned, he would "sweep them from the face of the earth." The chiefs grudgingly agreed to do their best to make the young men comply.[7]

The general, however, detected defiance in the attitude of the Cheyenne chiefs and recommended to Washington that an expedition be mounted against that tribe at some future date. Major William Hoffman, the commanding officer at the fort, relayed Harney's opinion by writing: "The Cheyennes are an unruly race and I have little confidence in their promises of good conduct unless they are kept in dread of immediate punishment for their misdemeanors."[8]

In April, the month of the spring moon, an incident occurred near the Upper Platte River Bridge that added fodder to General Harney's belief that the Cheyennes indeed were a hostile and uncompromising tribe. This bridge, about 125 miles from Fort Laramie, near present-day Casper, Wyoming, was a primary crossing for emigrant wagon trains and was guarded by a small detachment of soldiers.

A party of Northern Cheyenne warriors, including Two Tails and Fire Wolf, was in the area to trade and found four horses running loose on the open prairie. The men rounded up these horses and returned to their camp. Before long, word was sent to the Cheyenne camp that the rightful owner of the horses wanted his property returned and would pay a reward.

Two Tails, Wolf Fire, and two others, leading three horses, went to the fort. The fourth animal, they told the commanding officer, had not been found in the same location as the other three and the description given by the alleged owner did not fit that particular horse.

The officer became enraged and ordered that the Cheyennes be arrested and placed in leg irons until the horse in question was returned. The warriors resisted and attempted to fight off the soldiers. One warrior, Bull Shield, was shot and killed, and two others, including Wolf Fire, were locked in chains. Two Tails was wounded but managed to escape and ran to spread the word of this incident to his camp.

The Cheyenne men, women, and children were terrified that a repeat of the Ash Hollow Massacre was imminent and fled in panic toward the Black Hills, leaving behind their lodges and family possessions. Those fears were not without merit. Within moments, the troops arrived and looted and burned down the abandoned camp.

Wolf Fire's relatives, outraged that he had been imprisoned, came upon a trapper named Ganier that night and killed him. Two Tails, who would gain fame under the name Little Wolf during the 1878 Dull Knife outbreak, and the entire band then headed south to seek refuge with Black Kettle and the main group of Southern Cheyennes that was camped on the Arkansas River.

A minor misunderstanding about the ownership of a horse had been once again settled with confrontation, rather than compromise, and had led to violence and engendered further distrust and bitterness between the two races.[9]

The summer solstice, however, allowed the Cheyennes to temporarily set aside their problems with the white man to participate in the sacred ceremonies of this season of renewal. Black Kettle and the other chiefs of the Council of Forty-four summoned all the bands from their winter seclusion to gather together in one huge village. In this time when the days were longest, the People socialized, renewed acquaintances, and celebrated the rituals of the Sun Dance. Perhaps this year's renewal of life was even more important than usual to the tribe, given recent indications that their traditions were being threatened by a ruthless adversary who refused to accept or respect their culture and customs. When the festivities had been completed, the entire village moved to a site closer to the buffalo herds to take part in the annual communal hunt.[10]

Black Kettle and his fellow chiefs, with what must have been considerable effort, managed to control the young men of their tribe throughout those warm summer months. The various bands remained within an area between the Platte and the Arkansas rivers, hunting and occasionally visiting Bent's Fort, and, other than a couple of isolated incidents, they ignored the intrusion of the emigrant wagon trains and army patrols that passed through their territory. The Cheyennes were confident that they were at peace with the white man.[11]

That same sentiment, however, did not extend to the Pawnees, the Wolf People. Although General Harney had warned the Cheyennes to cease raiding against the Pawnees—that warriors painted for battle roaming the prairie would not be tolerated—age-old traditions were difficult to break.

In late August, the time when the cherries are ripe, a war party of about eighty Cheyennes headed north with the intention of attacking a Pawnee camp that was located near the Platte Road, not far from Fort Kearny.

On a cold and rainy day, the party halted and built war lodges within sight of the road in order to keep dry. The men took out their pipes to smoke but realized that everyone was out of tobacco. Shortly, a wagon could be seen coming along the road, headed for Fort Kearny. Two young men were sent out to meet the wagon and try to beg or trade for a piece of tobacco.

The driver of this mail wagon was clearly unnerved by the approach of the braves and motioned for them to leave him alone. One of the men persisted, until finally the frightened driver pulled out a pistol and shot at the young Cheyenne, barely missing him. The driver then whipped his mules in an effort to reach the safety of the fort. The angry warriors fired several arrows at the fleeing driver, one of which struck him in the arm.

The older warriors were incensed that the young man had wounded the driver and whipped him with their quirts. The members of the war party then settled into their lodges to wait out the chilly day.[12]

The wounded driver raced his mules into Fort Kearny and re-ported to Captain Henry Wharton, the commanding officer. He told the captain that he had been attacked by Cheyenne warriors and dis-played as evidence his wounded arm—as well as arrows that were imbedded in the wagon. Wharton immediately ordered that Captain George H. Stewart saddle up a detail of forty-one men from the 1st Cavalry and punish the perpetrators.

Meanwhile, the Cheyenne warriors, careful to avoid any travelers on the road, had moved on to Grand Island, where they camped at the edge of a dense stand of trees.

By late morning on the following day, Stewart and his troopers had located their unsuspecting prey. The soldiers appeared at the camp so suddenly that the Cheyennes were completely taken by surprise. The warriors dropped their bows and made signs that they would not fight. The soldiers, however, ignored these peace entreaties and fired a barrage at the defenseless warriors. With bullets filling the air all around them, the Cheyennes had no other choice but to run away on foot, leaving behind everything they owned.

Stewart reported that ten Indians were killed, another eight or ten severely wounded, and his men had confiscated twenty-two horses, two mules, and various items, including battle shields, buffalo robes, saddles, bridles, lances, and personal effects. The Cheyennes, however, disputed the number of those killed, claiming that six had been left behind on the battlefield.[13]

When the news of this atrocity reached the main camp, which was now located on the Republican River, Black Kettle and the other Council Chiefs immediately sent the old Crier on his rounds with a message meant to pacify the anger that pervaded among the People.

This overreaction by the soldiers, afflicting punishment that was way out of proportion for the wounding of the driver, however, served to inflame the entire Cheyenne nation and perhaps acted as a last straw in any effort to maintain peaceful relations with the white man.

Many hot-blooded warriors, mainly from the Northern bands, snuck away from camp in small groups to seek vengeance for their murdered brothers. Four Mormons from a wagon train were killed that night. Several days later, a woman was killed, her four-year-old boy was captured, and all their livestock was driven off. On September 2, a carriage carrying three men who were transporting public funds and important papers to Salt Lake City from Fort Kearny was ambushed and the men killed. The following night, four people were killed and a woman taken captive.[14]

Agent Thomas Twiss, in an attempt to calm tensions, held two parleys with Northern chiefs at Fort Laramie and listened to their side of the story. The chiefs explained how difficult it was to control young men who had witnessed their friends shot down in cold blood. In a third council, which was attended by Black Kettle and the rest of the Council of Forty-four, Twiss professed that he was convinced that the army was more to blame than the Cheyennes were for the recent bloodshed. He did, however, make the council promise to abide by General Harney's original demands. An exchange of prisoners was arranged, but by the time the Cheyennes returned home, the captives had been allowed to escape. Both sides were now apparently satisfied that relations, at least for the time being, were peaceful.[15]

The People, both Northern and Southern, assembled to camp on the Solomon to wait out the winter of 1856. One day some of the older men were taking a sweat bath, when Bear Man told them that he had seen a vision that showed the Pawnee, the Wolf People, headed toward their camp. Four days later, it was discovered that a large number of horses had been stolen during the night. Further investigation turned up a Pawnee arrow, evidence of the identity of the culprits. Bear Man's vision had come true.

Chief Black Kettle's Wotapio band had not been victimized by the Pawnee raid, but, nonetheless, he volunteered to lead the war party that would ride out in an attempt to recover the stolen ponies.

Black Kettle and his small group departed camp in the morning and followed the trail of the Pawnee toward the forks of the Solomon River. He moved his men steadily along the trail from morning until late afternoon, when at last they located fresh signs of the Wolf People near a small stream that flowed into the forks of the Solomon. Black Kettle called for a halt in a place surrounded by grazing buffalo, camp was made, and they settled in to rest and plan their next move.

Most of the warriors had been riding ordinary mounts and were leading their trusted war horses. Others, however, had lost their best ponies in the raid and did not have an adequate horse to mount when engaging the Pawnees.

Black Kettle assessed this situation and came to the conclusion that warriors who were riding the slower horses could be a hindrance during an attack. Therefore, he said, "We are getting close to the Wolf People. All of you who have good horses must saddle them now. Leave your poor horses here. Those of you who have only slow horses, stay here and watch those horses."

Two older men, Thin Face, who was Black Kettle's brother-in-law, and Lump Nose, had lost their best horses in the Pawnee raid and were reduced to riding common stock. Both wanted to recapture their stolen mounts and voiced displeasure about being left behind. Black Kettle, in an effort to ward off any resentment, appointed them leaders of those who would stay behind and requested that they go out and kill a few buffalo cows for a feast while the war party was gone. In addition, he asked them to maintain a fire throughout the night so that the war party could find them after their raid. Black Kettle's wise decision appeased the two men—if a warrior could not participate in a raid of the enemy, then hunting was about the next best thing.

The chief assembled the warriors who possessed trusted war horses and once again struck the trail of the Pawnees. They cautiously followed this fresh sign for some time along the banks of the Solomon River, when Black Kettle abruptly called a halt. He told his men to arrange their horses in a line, then to dismount and stand in one long row.

Black Kettle walked out in front of this line of expectant warriors and removed an arrow from his quiver—one that was known to hold sacred powers. In dramatic, ceremonial fashion, he raised this sacred arrow before him and aimed it toward the crest of a nearby bluff. Then, drawing the arrow backward, he turned to his men and said, "Do you see the point of that hill over there? Right under it the Wolf People are resting and eating."

No one questioned the words of this seasoned warrior chief, whose medicine was powerful. With great anticipation, the warriors mounted and galloped off in the direction of the hill that Black Kettle had indicated. Upon arrival, however, they found a camp by a creek with fires burning and buffalo meat roasting—but no sign of the Pawnees.

Black Kettle was unfazed and led them down the narrow waterway for a short distance until finally the enemy came into sight. Ahead, they observed seven Pawnees, who were frantically attempting to round up the stolen Cheyenne horses and flee.

The Southern Cheyenne avengers closed with these thieves and quickly killed and scalped five of them who tried to escape into the dense timber. Two others, however, managed to mount the fast horses that belonged to Thin Face and Lump Nose. The Cheyennes were aware that none of their horses could match the speed of those two superior mounts, and they could only watch as the Pawnee raiders faded away into the pale dusk of impending night.

The loss of the two swift horses was of little consequence, however. By dark, nearly every other mount that had been stolen was rounded up by the jubilant, whooping Cheyenne warriors.

Black Kettle and his recaptured horse herd headed back toward the temporary camp, riding through the night, and finally stopping beside a creek when the sun broke the horizon. While resting, the men dressed the scalps of the dead Pawnee raiders. They gleefully planned, as was the custom of war parties, to shake these scalps in the faces of the others when they arrived at camp.

"We must not show these scalps to the other men until we get near them," Black Kettle told his warriors. Instead, they would play a joke on their friends by hiding the scalps until the last possible moment, then pulling them out as a surprise.

Thin Face, Lump Nose, and the others were waiting with antici-pation when Black Kettle's war party and horse herd approached the camp. The warriors who had recaptured the horses were anxious to remove the Pawnee scalps and proudly shake them in their faces of their brethren. Before they could do that, however, Thin Face stepped forward, produced a scalp, and happily waved it at them. The joke was now on Black Kettle and his surprised warriors.

While the war party had been gone, Thin Face and the others had noticed a Pawnee who was herding eight head of horses—unbroken mares that had been missing from the herd that Black Kettle recap-tured. The Pawnee had fought desperately but was killed by Lump Nose, and the mares had been recovered.

The Southern Cheyenne war party, sharing stories as they enjoyed roasted buffalo meat around the fire, celebrated their dual success of regaining the stolen horses and punishing the culprits—without losing a man.

Later, Black Kettle and his triumphant war party, with the horse herd in tow, headed for home. The chief proudly rode at the head of his warriors on the victory charge into the village and shook the five Pawnee scalps in the air as he passed through cheering people around the circle of lodges.[16]

This minor victory over a Pawnee horse raiding party did not obscure the fact that severe problems remained with respect to the U.S. Army.

The primary topic of discussion throughout the winter within the tribe—as well as among Black Kettle and the Council of Forty-four—was the devastating consequences brought into their lives by the white men who had invaded their homeland. Hundreds of Cheyennes had died of disease. Buffalo and other wild game were being slaughtered in unheard-of numbers. Hunger and misery ravaged every band. And now, their young men were being murdered at will by the soldiers.

Angry, mourning relatives of those who had died in the attack of Captain Stewart's troops pleaded with the chiefs and the warrior soci-eties to avenge these tragic deaths by declaring war.[17]

Adding to those already mourning were the friends and the rela-tives of Wolf Fire, the alleged horse thief, who had been taken prisoner the previous spring. Word reached the camp that Wolf Fire had died from the effects of his imprisonment while bound with chains in the white man's jail cell. Furthermore, the post commander had refused permission for his relatives to recover and properly bury his body.[18]

Inevitably, the chiefs agreed, it would be necessary at some point in the future to shed the blood of the white man in order to preserve what was rightfully their own. If not, it was feared that the People would be driven from their traditional territory to face an uncertain fate in a place not of their choosing.

This opinion was further bolstered by the warriors Ice (also known as White Bull) and Dark, who had received a mysterious power that they claimed would cause the rifles of the soldiers to malfunction and render their bullets useless. The two warriors were invited by the chiefs to perform their ceremonies inside the Council lodge. Black Kettle and the other chiefs were impressed by Ice and Dark but reserved judgment about sanctioning war. They would wait to make a decision for peace or for war when the intentions of the soldiers became known.

Many of the young men, however, had great faith in the power that had consumed Ice and Dark and commenced preparations to retaliate against the white man once the weather turned warm.[19]

In the spring, William Bent, the father of George, who had married into the Cheyenne tribe, informed a party of the People who were visiting Bent's Fort that he had heard that the soldiers were planning a campaign against them. The chiefs responded by saying that if that were true, they would "kill all they want, and get plenty of white women for prisoners."[20]

When June, the season that the horses got fat, arrived, the Southern Cheyennes separated into small bands and moved toward summer buffalo hunting ranges, while the Northerners headed north. Within days, the Northern People returned to report that they had observed columns of soldiers but were hesitant to engage them in battle. That disturbing news—combined with William Bent's warning and assurances from Ice and Dark that their power was strong—was enough to compel some of the warriors to ride off in search of soldiers to kill. Most other bands, however, resumed hunting buffalo, and the main body of the tribe eventually came together to camp on the banks of the Solomon River.[21]

The soldiers who had been spotted by the Northerners were members of an army expedition, which totaled about 400 men—6 troops of cavalry and 3 of infantry, supported by 4 mountain howitzers—that had marched west from Fort Leavenworth on May 18 under the command of Colonel Edwin V. Sumner.

The War Department and General Harney had determined that the raids by the Cheyennes along the Platte Road that took the lives of innocent travelers late the previous year, in addition to other assorted atrocities, must be avenged. Colonel Sumner had been ordered to severely punish the tribe for its treachery, in the hope that this would teach the Cheyennes a lesson. Agent Thomas Twiss argued that the Cheyenne chiefs had made great efforts to restrain their young men and should be given the benefit of the doubt; perhaps another council would be in order. But the army was unyielding—the red man understood only force, and Sumner was prepared to show them plenty of that.

By mid-July, Colonel Sumner's column had bivouacked on the South Platte. Delaware and Pawnee scouts, mortal enemies of the People, were dispatched to comb the area and locate the main Cheyenne camp.[22]

Meanwhile, Black Kettle and his people had been contently hunting buffalo, unaware as yet that they were being stalked by Colonel Sumner, but they remained alert to this potential danger. Scouts had kept constant watch over the soldiers, briefing the chiefs almost daily with respect to every movement.

By the end of July, the moon when the buffalo bulls are rutting, the circle of lodges could be found on Solomon's Fork of the Kansas River. Then it finally became clear to the chiefs that the increased activity by the army in the heart of Cheyenne territory was not without purpose. According to the scouts, the soldiers displayed every sign of deliberate aggression. There could be no mistaking it now; the army had a military objective, and the People were the obvious intended target. War with the white man was at hand.

The Council of Forty-four discussed strategy at length, while the exhilarated warriors prepared their horses and weapons and arranged their medicines. Black Kettle and the other chiefs arrived at the conclusion that since a battle was imminent, this confrontation should, if possible, be fought away from the village to assure the safety of their women and children. There was a valley fifteen miles north, a familiar camping place, that would serve their purpose.[23]

On July 29, Colonel Sumner was informed by his scouts about the present location of the Cheyenne camp. He worried that his elusive prey would escape before he could get close to them and ordered his cavalry to mount up and ride off toward this camp without delay. The infantry and the artillery followed at a slower pace, lagging behind by as much as three miles.[24]

Cheyenne scouts noticed this flurry of activity and rushed back to camp, howling like wolves to let everyone know that the soldiers were coming. The Council Chiefs assembled and initially proposed that they move the camp and avoid any conflict. Predictably, this idea did not sit well with the warriors—the young men were spoiling for a fight and nothing the chiefs could say would stop them now.

Ice and Dark supported the warriors' position and produced a powerful white powder that they claimed would assure that every bullet fired by the Cheyennes would hit its intended target. This was an important element, inasmuch as the weapons owned by the warriors were greatly inferior and in lesser numbers than the modern carbines and pistols carried by the army. Most of the rifles were old short-range smooth-bores that had been obtained over the years from traders and were not very accurate or dependable. Ice and Dark loaded these rifles, one by one, with the magical white powder—which one warrior later discovered to be ordinary gunpowder. The two warriors then performed the sacred ceremony that would make the bullets of the soldiers fall harmlessly from the muzzles of their rifle barrels.[25]

By mid-morning, when the ceremonies had concluded, more than three hundred battle-ready, painted Cheyenne warriors rode away from the village. They eventually descended into the valley on the south fork of the Solomon, heading toward the location that had been designated by the chiefs for the fight. The long column finally halted at a favorite camp-site, near a stand of cottonwood along the sparsely foliated banks of Solomon's Fork of the Smoky Hill River in northwest Kansas, not far from a small, sparkling lake. They would wait in that place for the appearance of the soldiers.

This would be the first time that Black Kettle and most of the tribe had ever faced white soldiers in battle. The impending engagement, however, was not viewed with the remotest fear of defeat but rather with the knowledge and the faith that everything possible had been accomplished to assure victory. These soldiers were no different from any other enemy, and, with the powerful medicine that Ice and Dark had provided to protect the Cheyennes, the odds were certainly in their favor. In addition, this fight would be waged at a place of their choosing, away from the village, which, in a display of confidence, had been left standing. The soldiers would not catch them by surprise, resting in their lodges, with vulnerable women and children about, as had been the case with the Sioux at Ash Hollow.

It was early afternoon, about one o'clock, when the Cheyenne wolves came galloping into sight over a distant bluff. The scouts slowed their pace, then wheeled their ponies around in a circle, the traditional sign that buffalo—or, in this case, soldiers—had been spotted.

Every warrior leaped onto his favorite war horse, made one last check of his weapons, and trotted off to assume a position with his soldier society as the Cheyennes formed one long battle line across the prairie, facing their oncoming enemy. Rays of the sun reflected off shields, lances, and rifles; colorful feathers and fringe rustled in the breeze; the nervous ponies snorted and stomped about; and the anxious men, squinting into the distance for any sign of their enemy, sang songs boasting of the bravery and the achievements of their particular society. With the Sacred Arrows and the Sacred Medicine Hat at the front, the Cheyennes were prepared to do battle with the U.S. Army.

Although the chiefs rarely rode into battle, it was likely that Black Kettle had taken a position near the Elkhorn Scrapers, his former society, and offered words of encouragement to instill confidence in every fast-beating heart.

The column of cavalrymen steadily approached, riding around a large rock formation until entering the valley of the south fork of the Solomon River. Colonel Sumner called for them to halt, and every eye focused on the east end of this two- to three-mile wide valley and viewed for the first time the long line of 300 mounted, painted Cheyenne warriors. The spectacle of the colorful assemblage that spread boldly across the terrain to their front certainly would have made quite an impression in the mind of every blue-clad trooper. Colonel Sumner formed his men into one long battle line that faced the line of Cheyennes.

As if on cue, the two disciplined adversaries advanced straight toward each other, closing gaps in ranks, none wavering, first at a walk, then a trot, the warriors singing their songs and death chants, perhaps punctuating their words with loud whoops. The sight and the sounds of the Cheyenne warriors must have unnerved many troopers, most of whom were untested in battle, but none of them hesitated as the two groups of combatants drew nearer and nearer, quickly narrowing the distance between them.[26]

This battle, however, would prove to be less than noteworthy for the Cheyennes.

Within moments, Colonel Sumner gave the order for two cavalry companies to split from the main body and attack the flanks of the Cheyennes, while the remainder of the troops maintained their advance.

The Cheyennes watched this movement with the confidence that they could easily overwhelm the soldiers once it was proven that Ice and Dark had rendered the army carbines and pistols useless.

When the cavalrymen came within carbine range, Sumner gave the command to draw sabers and charge. Yelling wildly, the blades of their sabers flashing in the sun, the horsemen galloped toward the massed Cheyenne warriors.

The sight of these long knives in the hands of the onrushing soldiers evoked astonishment and struck fear into the hearts of many warriors. They abruptly halted their advance to watch the charge with growing trepidation as the society chiefs rode along the line, shouting words of encouragement.

Sumner's troopers thundered across the prairie, their long knives pointed menacingly at the line of hesitant Cheyenne fighting men.

The medicine of Ice and Dark did not include power over such weapons as these long knives, and this turn of events had without question broken the medicine. The warriors became flustered over this realization, and an uneasy murmuring gradually escalated into words of doubt.

Sumner's cavalrymen had now closed the gap between them to about one hundred yards.[27]

The warriors, at the urging of the society chiefs, fired a hasty, ineffective volley of arrows at the soldiers. Then, without a shot being fired by the cavalrymen, the panicked warriors wheeled their ponies around and fled, scattering in small groups in their haste to escape the impending onslaught.

The cavalrymen chased the various bands of fleeing Cheyennes for some five to seven miles, overtaking a number of them along the way. Isolated engagements, or running battles, between the desperate warriors and the soldiers, often fought hand to hand, were waged in the area south of Solomon's Fork. Most of the Cheyennes, however, were mounted on their fastest ponies, which enabled them to easily ride out of danger. By about three o'clock, Sumner feared that his men and their exhausted horses were becoming too widely scattered around the countryside, and he had the recall sounded. The battle of Solomon's Fork had ended in a total rout of the Cheyennes by the horse soldiers.[28]

Sumner claimed that his men killed nine warriors; the Cheyennes placed that number at four. The army lost two troopers killed and another eight wounded—as well as one officer wounded. Lieutenant James E. B. (Jeb) Stuart, the future Confederate Civil War hero, had been shot point blank in the chest. Stuart, in a most admirable display of courage, would days later lead a small group of wounded soldiers over 120 miles of rugged terrain to reach Fort Kearny after Sumner had moved on without them.

A worse blow to the People, however, occurred two days later when Sumner located their abandoned village, where about 170 lodges remained standing. The women had hurriedly departed to join the men on their flight south toward the Arkansas River and had taken with them only the possessions that they could carry on their backs.

Sumner's troops burned the lodges (which averaged about fifteen hides each to construct) and the heavy lodge poles, in addition to destroying or confiscating at least 20,000 pounds of buffalo meat and countless hides, blankets, articles of clothing, lodge furnishings, robes, cooking utensils, and many other necessary items—enough of a loss to impoverish the entire tribe.[29]

Sumner then marched his troops up the Arkansas in pursuit of his prey. He halted briefly at Bent's Fort, where he confiscated the issue of Cheyenne annuities and distributed them among his command and to friendly Arapahoes and other tribes, which had not participated in the battle with their allies. Sumner had intended to resume hunting down the outlaw Cheyenne bands and further chastise them, but, by the first part of September, he received orders to join an expedition to Utah, where the Mormons were rebelling against the U.S. government. The 1857 Cheyenne Expedition had come to an end.

Black Kettle and the rest of the beleaguered Cheyennes, in the meantime, had fled south of the Arkansas River to take refuge in Kiowa and Comanche country. They remained in that area until the fall, when the various Southern bands returned to their traditional territory in the vicinity north of the Arkansas, and the Northern bands journeyed to their homeland north of the Platte.[30]

War had been waged on the army with disastrous results. Black Kettle and many of the Council Chiefs now understood that peaceful relations with the white man must be established, or the Cheyennes as a tribe were in danger of facing annihilation.

4

GOLD IN COLORADO TERRITORY

In the days following the debacle at solomon's fork, black Kettle and the other chiefs sequestered themselves inside their sacred Council Lodge for countless hours to discuss the troubling turn of events. A few of the military society chiefs, the Dog Soldiers in particular, may have encouraged them to make a declaration of war, but that idea would have been readily dismissed without debate. Rather, the conversation centered around what could be done to prevent another confrontation with the blue-clad, saber-wielding horse soldiers.

The proposal that at last was adopted by the Council called for an initiative to open doors of communication with the white man in order to present the Southerners' side of the story and emphasize their desire for peace. Council Chief High Back Wolf, along with Chiefs White Antelope, Tall Bear, and Starving Bear, would visit Bent's Fort and plead their case to William Bent, a man who could be trusted to have their best interests at heart. Bent had always acted as an unofficial liaison and would relay their intentions to the proper authorities.[1]

William Bent had been born in St. Louis in 1809 and entered the fur trade with family members while in his late teens. In 1834, with business partners Ceran St. Vrain and his brother Charles, he established Bent's Fort on the north side of the Arkansas River, about fifteen miles above the mouth of the Purgatorie River. While his partners traveled around the West, William settled at the fort and opened trade with fur trappers and nearby Indian tribes. In about 1837 he married Owl Woman, the daughter of the Cheyenne chief White Thunder. Four children were born to the couple in Owl Woman's lodge near the fort—Mary (1838), Robert (1840), George (1843), and Julia

(1847). Owl Woman, however, died giving birth to Julia. Sometime later, William married Owl Woman's younger sister, Yellow Woman, who gave birth to one son, Charles.

In 1853, William sent four of his children—Mary, Robert, George, and Charles—east to reside with his sister, Dorkas Bent Carr, in Westport, Missouri, near Kansas City, where they attended school under the guardianship of his business associate Albert Boone, Daniel's grandson. That same year, the Bents moved their trading post downstream to a new location on the north bank of the Arkansas River, several miles west of present-day La Junta, Colorado. At the point in time that the Southern Cheyenne chiefs had decided to visit William in October 1857, William's sons George and Charles were enrolled at Webster College, rooming with the son of Ceran St. Vrain.[2]

When the four Council Chiefs rode into Bent's New Fort that late October day to speak to William, they came as representatives of the South Platte and the Arkansas River Cheyenne bands and made it clear that they were not speaking for the Northern factions.

The chiefs patiently presented a detailed review of events since the Horse Creek Treaty had been signed some six years earlier and claimed that they had not broken the provisions of that agreement. The only tribes that they had engaged in war during that period were the Pawnees, the Wolf People, and the Utes, the Black People, neither of which had smoked the pipe with the People at Horse Creek.

Furthermore, it had been the soldiers who violated the treaty by seizing the alleged horse thieves at Fort Kearny and, by overreacting to minor transgressions, instigated other episodes that resulted in the punishment and the death of innocent Cheyenne warriors. Captain Stewart's attack was also unwarranted, they argued, inasmuch as the Kiowas, not the Cheyennes, had been guilty of the spring 1856 incidents. And, to their credit, in spite of these wrongs committed against them by the white man, the People had not sought revenge, although the opportunity had presented itself on many occasions.

The chiefs explained that the raids and the skirmishing that had taken place the previous summer could be blamed on the actions of the Northern Cheyenne bands, and only a very small number of the more aggressive young men from their South Platte and Arkansas bands had participated.

The four Council Chiefs returned to their village, satisfied that they had spoken from the heart and that their explanation and intentions, when passed on to the white man, would, it was hoped, exonerate them and restore peaceful relations.[3]

William Bent was convinced that the Southern bands were, for the most part, blameless and had been punished for the crimes of others—namely, the Northerners. He wrote to the superintendent, Colonel John Haverty, and, in addition to forwarding the letter from the Cheyenne chiefs, asserted in his own message that the Northern bands were the ones that had "commenced the fracus and ortof [ought to have] shared a part of the thrashing." Perhaps the opinion of the white man who probably understood the Cheyennes better than any other would have some bearing in shaping the future attitude and the actions of the government.[4]

Those who subscribe to the Harney-Wynkoop premise that Black Kettle was the son of High Back Wolf explain this appearance at Bent's New Fort by High Back Wolf—after he was alleged to have been dead—as pointing to a case of mistaken identity: that it was actually Black Kettle and not his "father" who attended the meeting. William Bent and the regulars at the fort, however, would never have mistaken the aged, familiar High Back Wolf for Black Kettle, with whom they were probably also acquainted.[5]

Needless to say, the winter of 1857–58 was a most difficult time for the Southern Cheyennes—and not simply due to severe weather conditions or lack of food. The tribe lived—perhaps *existed* would be a better word—under a gloomy shroud of desperation, derived from the realization that their age-old lifestyle was under attack from elements that, perhaps for the first time in history, were beyond their control.

No longer could they look forward to the prospect that when the weather turned warm, they could roam free across boundless stretches of prairie in search of buffalo or enemy pony herds to raid. The affair with Colonel Sumner's troops had served as a warning that the chiefs must sternly caution their warriors that any minor conflict, especially with emigrants, could bring retaliation. Black Kettle and his fellow chiefs also came to the conclusion that a peace treaty, perhaps at any cost, must be negotiated with the white man. Otherwise, there would be much weeping in Cheyenne camps.

The position that had been taken by the chiefs, however, served to plant seeds of discontent within the tribe. The People had grown strong through the centuries by forming an enduring internal cohesiveness—one mind and one purpose. Now, many warriors, as well as certain military society chiefs, privately questioned the wisdom of the ruling Council.[6]

It would be reasonable to conclude that by this time, Black Kettle was one of the more outspoken proponents for peace with the white man. He was not that far removed from his days as a warrior, and the passion for battle assuredly must have burned within him. But he had witnessed the reaction of the warriors when they faced the charge of Colonel Sumner's long-knives—an action that he and the other chiefs had approved, perhaps rashly—and the memory of the Ash Hollow massacre was also fresh in his mind. The chief could only speculate with dread about what might have happened—what loss of life and how many women and children would have been taken captive—had Sumner caught them by surprise in their village.

The Cheyennes were few when compared to the great numbers of whites that were arriving each year. Before long, if not at present, these white men who invaded the territory would greatly outnumber the Cheyennes. If war was to be waged, the weapons and the manpower of the Cheyennes would be no match for the might of the U.S. Army.

And it was no secret that the buffalo were being slaughtered and their migration routes altered by the influx of travelers, ranches, farms, and settlements. One day in the not-too-distant future this animal would be gone. The question was posed, time and again—how could the Cheyennes live without this shaggy beast, which had always provided for all their needs?

And worse yet, this tragedy had been foretold. The disappearance of the buffalo had been prophesied many years earlier by Sweet Medicine. This great man had experienced a vision and told them about a strange animal that would someday graze where buffalo had roamed. The People could now recognize the description of the strange animal that Sweet Medicine had seen as resembling the white man's oxen and cattle herds.[7]

Through the dismal winter months, Black Kettle, a man of great perception and intelligence, awakened to the fact that he must accept the challenge to assume a leadership role and strive to bring about an honorable peace with the white man. Although he certainly was aware that his position on this issue might become unpopular, he vowed to remain committed to this cause, no matter what the consequences. The fierceness with which he had fought as a warrior now would be redirected toward peace, for the good of his tribe.

There was one bright spot for the People in the spring of 1858, when Robert C. Miller, the newest Indian agent for the Upper Arkansas, reported to his superiors that in his opinion, the Southern bands had been sufficiently punished for any perceived or real depredations. Miller recommended that the tribe be paid its annuities that summer— if only to discourage it from raiding along the vulnerable Santa Fe road.[8]

Before any official action could be taken by the U.S. government to address the concerns of Black Kettle and the Southern Cheyennes, however, another event with the potential to impact the lifestyle of the People was taking place in Colorado Territory.

Also that spring, a man named William Green Russell, a native of Georgia, along with a party of about seventy Cherokee Indians and white men, ventured from Kansas to the foothills of the Colorado mountains. These men were chasing rumors that a California-bound party of Cherokees had noticed signs of gold at some point along the South Platte River. The prospectors made their way along the Platte and found a small amount of color in several places, but not in paying quantities.

The Russell party was working the mouth of Cherry Creek in mid-July when another group of fortune hunters from Lawrence, Kansas, led by John Easter, joined the dig. Together, they were able to fill several tiny goose quills with gold dust, which was not even enough for a man to live on for a week in a town.

But the word that prospectors were panning for gold had a way of creating a fever in men desperate to gain riches by means other than mundane, conventional endeavors. And those goose quills filled with color, no matter how sparse in content, became the subject of exaggerated tales of abundant wealth that was available for the digging in Colorado Territory—on land promised to the Southern Cheyennes and the Arapahoes in the Treaty of Horse Creek of 1851.[9]

On July 19, while the fortune hunters continued their quest for gold, Indian Agent Robert Miller visited the camp on the Pawnee Fork of the Arkansas River, where all the Upper Arkansas tribes—the Cheyennes, the Southern Arapahoes, the Kiowas, the Comanches, and the Prairie Apaches—had assembled in anticipation of receiving their annuity goods.

When the time came for the Southern Cheyenne chiefs to address their new agent, each in turn related his wishes that a new treaty be negotiated. The battle with Colonel Sumner had been quite convincing, they told the agent, and the People now understood the folly of fighting the white man, for soon he would dominate the entire territory.

Then an idea that Chief Yellow Wolf had proposed in 1847, which at that time was ignored, was revived and presented to Miller. Without question, this proclamation surprised, yet pleased, the agent.

The People told him that they were aware that the buffalo would soon vanish—it had been prophesied—and in order to survive they must adopt a new lifestyle. In a startling declaration that must have sounded outlandish to even their ears, the chiefs professed a willingness to learn the white man's way of tilling the soil and requested that plows and other farming implements be provided, as well as farmers to teach them.[10]

Chief Black Kettle stood before Miller, his long-stemmed pipe resting across his left forearm, his fringed and intricately beaded pipe bag—the symbol of his position on the Council of Forty-four—hanging beneath. He echoed the sentiments of the Southern Cheyenne chiefs when he said they

> had eyes and were not blind. They no longer listened to their young men who continually clamored for war. They hoped their Great Father, the white chief in Washington, would listen to them, and give them a home where they might be protected for and protected against the encroachments of their white brothers until at least, like them, they had been taught to cultivate the soil and other arts of civilized life."[11]

Agent William Miller departed the meeting with renewed confidence that peace was at hand. He certainly had not expected to hear the revelation that these nomadic hunters were willing to lay down their weapons and stand behind a plow. This information would be well received by his superiors in Washington, and Miller hoped that a treaty would be forthcoming.

Miller was not aware, however, that the handful of Southern Cheyenne chiefs present did not speak on behalf of the entire tribe.

Noticeably absent from this conference on the Pawnee Fork were the chiefs of the Northern bands, the headmen of the soldier societies, and most of the young men. Word of this proposal, which called for them to transform from hunters to farmers, was met with fierce opposition. Custom dictated, they argued, that a warrior prove his manhood by hunting buffalo, fighting with enemies, and raiding pony herds—and by doing so, he would accumulate wealth for his family and for the tribe as a whole. Farming, although admittedly an ancestral livelihood of the Cheyennes, was not an agreeable practice to men who had established themselves as nomadic buffalo hunters. The Cheyennes who had boycotted the distribution of goods remained in the Republican River country, where buffalo was plentiful, and vowed to defend their precious land to the death.[12]

This erosion of loyalties assailed the very core of the Cheyenne system of justice and conduct—the unity of the Council Chiefs. The power of Maheo flowed through this sacred circle of the Forty-four, and it could only mean disaster for the People if this body was torn apart by infighting.[13]

There can be no doubt that Black Kettle viewed the dissident faction of his tribe with understanding and sympathy, but perhaps he also experienced a sense of nostalgia. He could close his eyes and relive those idyllic days of yesteryear when the circle of lodges rested on a verdant blanket of green beside a pleasant stream within a stand of glorious cottonwoods, and all around them the solitude of an endless prairie faded away to the horizon. He could hear the laughter and the merriment from those days when the People had celebrated each moment of life with a sense of fulfillment and freedom. Those joyous shouts of the men returning from a successful hunt or a raiding party. The aroma of buffalo meat cooking over the fire. The chatter of the women as they scraped clean the hairy hides. The comforting rhythm of drum beats and whispering flutes and children's happy calls as they grew strong playing warrior games.

But, sadly, those days were a thing of the past. Now, hunger, disease, and weeping pervaded every camp. Those comforting sounds had been replaced by creaking wagon wheels, axes striking trees, water running through sluice boxes, and the angry shouts and taunts of people with habits and behavior that would never be compatible with the Cheyennes.

Black Kettle desired to embrace that freedom again, to whatever measure was attainable, and knew that only the U.S. government could guarantee them a place of their own away from the white man.

He could no longer think with the individualism of a warrior, for he was a chief and, by virtue of his position, must make decisions to ensure the health and the welfare of the whole tribe. Perhaps the words that he had spoken about this radical lifestyle change had left a bad taste in his mouth. But even if the others were blind to the danger that closed around them like a strangling noose, his eyes were wide open. There was no other choice but to cast their lot with the white man and hope for the best.

By late summer, most of Green Russell's prospecting party had departed the area in disgust over not finding enough of the golden metal to pay for their day's work. The remaining miners were panning gravel worth from one to ten cents a panful but had been unable to find the source of this loose gold. With winter looming on the horizon—as evidenced by a severe early August snowstorm—Russell established a small settlement at the confluence of Cherry Creek and the South Platte River, which he called Auraria, after his hometown in Georgia.

In September, the Lawrence, Kansas, group moved about five and a half miles upriver from the mouth of Cherry Creek and Russell's Auraria—well off the beaten path—and organized a town company, plotted out the land, and built permanent cabins for a townsite they called "Montana." That location, however, was not acceptable to some members of the party, who returned to the mouth of Cherry Creek and founded their own town of St. Charles.[14]

Black Kettle and his fellow peace chiefs could not have predicted, when goods were distributed that summer, that a gold rush was imminent. But these chiefs, in what would prove to be a crucial time, had managed to reassert their supreme authority over the militant faction of the tribe. Any contemplated mutiny had been at least temporarily thwarted, and, in the face of the most threatening intrusion yet, the warriors heeded the warning of the chiefs and gave the white man a wide berth. Near Fort Atkinson, Colonel Sumner remarked on how he had happened upon "a party of Cheyennes, who were perfectly humble."[15]

In spite of outward appearances, Black Kettle and the Council Chiefs were quite concerned that their land and resources were being systematically ravished by the white invasion. On their behalf, William Bent wrote to the Indian Bureau in October, saying that the Cheyennes were "molesting me very mutch. They wish you to do something for them concerning their contry. The whites are abought taking posesion of it. The whites I am told are abought laying off town lots or towns, I am yousing all of my influence to keep the Indians quiet and I have suxceded in doing so."[16]

But the building on Cheyenne-Arapaho land only expanded. In mid-November, another party from Kansas, headed by General William Larimer, a banker and a real estate promoter, arrived in Auraria.

Larimer and his thirty-two men were accompanied by eight wagons that were loaded with six months' worth of supplies. In addition, Larimer had in his possession signed commissions from James W. Denver, the Kansas territorial governor, authorizing him to form a town and set up a local government. Larimer chose the present location of St. Charles, simply helped himself to the townsite, and began staking out and building "Denver City," named after the Kansas territorial governor.[17] Kansas territory at that time included Colorado.

Russell, Larimer, and the other real estate speculators, however, were aware that they were occupying land that had been awarded to the Cheyennes and the Arapahoes by treaty. The Iowa representative and future general Samuel R. Curtis was petitioned by the white squatters to help secure title for land. Curtis, whose son was working at Cherry Creek, wrote to James W. Denver and suggested that the removal of Indian rights to the area "would be the surest if not the only course to insure friendly relations between the miners & settlers and the Indian tribes."

The presence of the white man thus far had not been greeted with a violent reaction by the native inhabitants and the rightful owners of this land. Nonetheless, plans were already underway to find a manner in which to remove any claim the Cheyennes and the Arapahoes might have to this valuable parcel of real estate. The greed of the white man would not allow him to entertain the prospect of sharing this land. There was no talk of assimilation. The Indians must be either placed on out-of-the-way reservations, left to starve to death, or eliminated.[18]

By the time Black Kettle and the Southern Cheyennes emerged from winter hibernation in the spring of 1859, rumors of a major gold strike in Colorado had spread east. Newspapers in the Missouri River Valley reported embellished versions of the facts and made it appear that a bonanza of gold had been discovered. This story was picked up by big-city newspapers and touched off a stampede of miners, merchants, and fortune hunters from across the country.

The People were astonished by this influx of white men and regarded them as insane for the way they lusted after the yellow metal—the same soft substance from which the Plains tribes had for years made bullets. They watched with amazement as a steady stream of newcomers traveled across the plains toward Denver City and the mining camps.[19]

This migration intensified to a frenzied pitch when several areas of valuable gold deposits were discovered in what would become Boulder, Clear Creek, and Gilpin Counties—as well as in the rich placers found along Cherry Creek near Denver City. During that summer, an estimated 150,000 gold-seekers flooded into the mining camps.

The "Pike's Peak or Bust" gold rush was similar to the 1849 California gold rush—with one important exception. Most of the Colorado miners—perhaps as many as 40,000—unlike those on the West Coast, intended to remain in that region once the gold played out and to inhabit the permanent settlements that had been established around the mining districts.

Word of the gold strike not only encouraged novice and professional miners and adventurers to journey into the region but also brought a diversified workforce of merchants, blacksmiths, and other tradesmen—not to mention saloons, gaming halls, and brothels—that set up shop in the various towns. Almost overnight, this influx of "fifty-niners" transformed the vicinity of Larimer's fledgling Denver City into a thriving trade center and an important destination for emigrant wagon trains and stagecoaches.[20]

The newcomers, for the most part, traveled into the region on two main trails, both of which cut directly across the territory of the Cheyennes and the Arapahoes. To the north, the South Platte Trail, which followed the old Oregon Trail, brought emigrants westward along the Platte River. Farther south, the Cherokee Trail traced the Santa Fe Trail as it wound along the Arkansas River to Bent's Fort, where it continued to the front range of the Rocky Mountains, north at Old Pueblo through the area that now encompasses Colorado Springs, and on to the gold fields. To make matters worse, the Leavenworth and Pike's Peak Express Company soon began running coaches up the Republican River, directly through the heart of prime hunting grounds.[21]

The Cheyennes and other tribes often peacefully approached these travelers to trade. One such group of Cheyennes came upon a stagecoach that had overturned, scattering the baggage about. This particular coach carried as passengers two famous Eastern journalists, Albert D. Richardson of the *Boston Journal* and Horace Greeley of the *New York Tribune*. The journalists, without provocation, reportedly pulled their revolvers and held these curious Cheyennes, whom they called "instinctive thieves," at bay until the baggage was securely stored.[22]

These two notable men were perhaps the exception, because the Southern Cheyennes and the Arapahoes must have engendered some sense of mutual trust with the white travelers to have permitted them

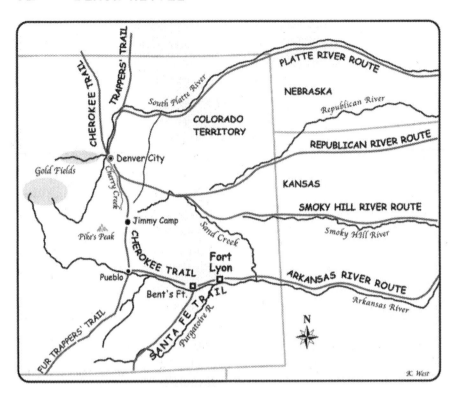

Overland routes to the Pike's Peak or Bust Gold Rush

to pass unmolested through their territory. There were even documented occasions when the Cheyennes encountered white prospectors wandering around the foothills or on the barren prairie in a delirious condition from the heat or lack of food and water. These white men were without exception taken to the village and nursed back to health.[23]

William Bent had made certain that A. M. Robinson, the superintendent of Indian affairs who was based in St. Louis, was kept abreast of the temperament of the Cheyennes and the Arapahoes, whose mood had darkened with the arrival of every new emigrant. The gold rushers had chased away most of the buffalo and chopped down every substantial stand of cottonwoods along the streams, as well as the pine and the cedar found in the foothills. By their very presence, the invaders had denied the tribes access to their favorite haunts. Many proud warriors had been reduced to begging food from miners, and the People were quite destitute. Bent urged that a treaty be made without delay, or he could not guarantee that the chiefs could, or would, restrain the young warriors from retaliating against those who had created their misery.

Robinson had great respect for the opinion of William Bent—enough, in fact, to recommend that the trader be appointed the new Indian agent for the Upper Arkansas tribes. The superintendent assigned Bent to the post that summer, and President Buchanan finally signed the commission on April 27, 1860. William Bent now found himself in an ideal position to assist his adopted tribe. His first official act was to press the government for a new treaty with the Cheyennes and the Arapahoes.[24]

In July, Bent set up the distribution of annuity goods at a campsite near the confluence of Beaver Creek and the South Platte and dispatched runners to seek out the various bands. While waiting, he contemplated the threatening circumstances that his charges presently endured. Bent concluded that with game becoming scarce, due to the pressures of the exploding population, the Cheyennes and the Arapahoes really had no choice but to turn to farming in order to survive. And the only way to prevent bloodshed between the two races was to move the two tribes to a location where contact with the white man would be kept to a minimum.

Inasmuch as the Southern bands, including his own family, were within closer proximity to Bent's trading post, much of William Bent's focus applied to only that particular faction. That summer, as he moved about the countryside to locate the various bands, he wrote a series of letters to Superintendent Robinson that outlined his educated opinion:

> The Cheyans and Arrapahos have took my advice to them last Winter and this last Spring. I am proud to say they have behaved themselves exceedingly well. . . . Their will be no trouble settling them down and start farming. They tell me they have passed theair laws amongst themselves that they will do anything I may advize. It is a pitty that the Department can't send Some farming implements and other necessarys this fall Sow as they could commence farming this Coming Spring.

Bent warned, however, that "a smouldering passion agitates these Indians, perpetually fomented by the failure of food, the encircling encroachment of the white population, and the exasperating sense of decay and impending extinction." The Southern Cheyennes and the

Arapahoes had been "pressed upon all around by the Texans, by the settlers of the gold region, by the advancing people of Kansas, and from the Platte, and are already compressed into a small circle of territory. A desperate war of starvation and extinction is therefore imminent and inevitable, unless prompt measures shall prevent it."[25]

Robinson shared Bent's concerns and authorized his new agent to inform the Cheyennes and the Arapahoes that the government was desirous of making a treaty. In September, Bent held a council with the Southern People to discuss the terms of an agreement. Attendance at this important meeting, however, was not what the agent had expected. The Southerners were fairly well represented, but the Northerners had boycotted the council. Bent was not necessarily surprised, for it had become apparent throughout the summer months that the division between the two factions of Cheyennes—Southern and Northern—was even more distinct than the gradual separation that had occurred over the last decade.

In addition to ongoing philosophical differences, the presence of well-beaten migration trails had placed what amounted to a physical barrier between the two groups. The Northerners—the fierce Dog Soldier society, in particular—were content to wander around the land between the North and the South Platte rivers and around the Smoky Hill in Kansas, while the Southerners remained farther south within the boundaries of the South Platte and the Arkansas rivers. The Northerners had allied even closer with the Lakota Sioux, hunting together and occasionally marrying into each other's tribe.[26]

Fewer Northerners were traveling south through this moving mass of white humanity to visit, which may have assisted Black Kettle and the Council Chiefs to better control the young men. Without the daily influence of their more warlike brethren from the north, the Southern warriors, although without question provoked by the growing presence of the white man, grudgingly obeyed the chiefs and avoided any conflict.

Perhaps another, more practical, reason that the Northern Cheyennes remained around the headwaters of the Republican and the Smoky Hill rivers was that the pressure from white travelers in that area had not been quite as intense as it had in the southern territory. Herds of buffalo and wild horses still grazed on northern grasslands, and these Cheyennes were decidedly not in as desperate a state as their southern kin. The favorable conditions, no matter how temporary, had persuaded many Southerners to head north and seek refuge.

These bands, consisting of the tribe's most aggressive warriors, were determined to defend this country against the encroachment of the white man.

Why Black Kettle and the Arkansas River bands did not simply move permanently to the northern land of plenty cannot be adequately explained. It could be speculated that the spiritual attachment to their traditional territory and the fear that, if abandoned, it would become completely overrun by the white man had discouraged a mass exodus north. Also, it was likely that the Southern peace chiefs had counseled their people that the defiant and unyielding attitude of the Northerners eventually would place them at odds with the U.S. Army, and that mistake, as Colonel Sumner and General Harney had proven, could be most disastrous.[27]

Therefore, the chiefs present at William Bent's treaty council— Black Kettle, White Antelope, Old Little Wolf, and Tall Bear—did not by any means represent the entire tribe but were the leading advocates of peace.

It was a foregone conclusion to these Southern chiefs that the only way to save their beleaguered people was to negotiate with the white man. Otherwise, the future of the People would hold nothing but disease, hunger, and bloodshed, which could lead to extermination. They did not intend to stand idly by and allow the vocal warmongers— those who ignored the truth—to place the entire tribe in peril. Once they had touched the pen to a treaty, they hoped to convince their militant and vacillating brethren that the best policy was to abide by its terms.

The chiefs patiently outlined their treaty demands to their friend William Bent. First of all, the tribes must be compensated for the land that the whites had, for all intents and purposes, already stolen by building their settlements and mining camps. Also, they wanted the right to choose the location of their new reservation and declared a preference for the area between the Arkansas River and the Raton Mountains. They expected the government to give them all the supplies necessary to establish them on their new reservation and annuities that would sustain them as they learned to grow crops.

The meeting concluded with Black Kettle and the other Council Chiefs agreeing to meet representatives of the government on the Arkansas River the following spring when their annuities were distributed. The Cheyennes then scattered into smaller bands and embarked on their fall buffalo hunts.

William Bent submitted his report to Superintendent Robinson, encouraging the government to accept the treaty demands without delay.[28]

The wheels of government, however, were known to turn painstakingly slow, and Bent continued his efforts throughout the winter of 1859–1860 to convince the Bureau of Indian Affairs that a new treaty was vital if peace was to be maintained. Before the year was over, he had sold Bent's New Fort to the War Department, built a new stockade across the river on the south side, and resumed his trading business at that location.

The army garrisoned Bent's former trading post with troops and renamed it Fort Fauntleroy. That name would be changed twice. First it was named Fort Wise, in honor of the Virginia governor Henry A. Wise. At the outbreak of the Civil War, Wise joined the Confederacy, and his name was removed and replaced by that of Brigadier General Nathaniel Lyon, the first Union general to die in the war.[29]

By the fall of 1859, Denver City, which had been competing for dominance with Auraria, swallowed up its rival from across the creek. The presence of Cheyennes and members of other tribes on the streets of this rapidly growing population center became commonplace. In fact, one of the most frequent visitors was the Arapaho chief Little Raven, who had "pledged his word for the preservation of peace and law and order by his people." He was said to have been "a very sensible and friendly disposed man" who "handles a knife and fork and smokes cigars like a white man."[30]

This was not to imply that incidences of violence did not occur between the races. One example was the night when drunken "bummers," which was the name associated with those too lazy to work but not to steal or cause trouble, entered a camp of Cheyennes, Arapahoes, and Apaches who were visiting Denver to trade buffalo robes. These white men raped and beat old and young women alike and stole several mules. The Indians had been the guests of the legendary mulatto mountain man Jim Beckwourth, who persuaded the aggrieved parties not to take revenge. Beckwourth vented his anger at the atrocity in the *Rocky Mountain News:*

> The Indians are as keenly sensible to acts of injustice, as they are tenacious of revenge, and it is more humiliating to them to be recipients of such treatment upon their own lands, which they have been deprived of, their game driven off and they made to suffer by hunger, and when they pay us a visit, abused more than dogs. . . . All of our Indian troubles are produced by imprudent acts of unprincipled white men.[31]

The Cheyennes and the Arapahoes may have established a tenuous coexistence with the white man, but that was not the case with the Kiowas and the Comanches. Texans had encroached on the land traditionally occupied by these tribes, which forced them to move north toward the Arkansas River. The angry Greasy Wood People and the Rattlesnake People, who were under the jurisdiction of William Bent, were spoiling for a fight.

This warlike posture displayed by their former enemies did not sit well with the People, who worried that any aggression might be interpreted that they, too, were preparing for war. The Cheyennes volunteered to ride against the Kiowas and the Comanches, a suggestion that William Bent considered "the cheapest plan to get rid of the Kiowa." In the end, Bent, who was hesitant to start an intertribal war, dismissed the idea.

In the spring of 1860, when Kiowa and Comanche warriors began raiding into Texas, Bent encouraged the War Department to take immediate action. Two columns of army troops subsequently were dispatched, with intentions of severely punishing the militant tribes. Major John Sedgwick led one column on a five-hundred-mile arc south of the Arkansas but failed to locate any enemy. The other column, under Captain Samuel D. Sturgis, engaged about six to eight hundred Kiowas and Comanches—with a handful of Cheyenne warriors—on the Solomon River. This running battle proved to be less than decisive, and the army finally withdrew, with each side losing four killed.

Although the renegades were not exactly punished to the extent that the government had planned, the action did serve as a reminder to the various Plains tribes that the army would not tolerate any threat to peace on the frontier.[32]

The government continued its procrastination about a new treaty with the Cheyennes and the Arapahoes. William Bent understood the desperate situation of the tribes and relentlessly badgered the Bureau of Indian Affairs to take action. Finally, his efforts paid off.

On September 8, 1860, Commissioner of Indian Affairs A. B. Greenwood and a group of his friends, his relatives, and other dignitaries, including his son, his brother-in-law, a nephew, the son of the secretary of the interior, and Albert G. Boone, Daniel's grandson, arrived at Bent's New Fort, leading a caravan that consisted of thirteen wagons loaded with trade goods intended as treaty presents.[33]

The Arapahoes, the Cloud People, were anxious to talk and were waiting at the fort when Greenwood and his entourage arrived. The

Cheyennes, however, were said to be 250 miles away, hunting buffalo with the Dog Soldiers in the northern territory.

Messengers were dispatched, and on September 18 Black Kettle, White Antelope, and several other Southern chiefs, called "sub-chiefs" by Greenwood, rode alone into Bent's New Fort. These chiefs told Greenwood that their bands could not possibly reach the fort for at least twenty days. The commissioner, however, was not about to waste his time waiting and called for an immediate council with the Cheyenne and Arapaho chiefs who were present.[34]

The conference opened with Greenwood and the chiefs passing around the pipe—the symbol that everyone was honor bound to speak the truth. Greenwood then commenced flattering the chiefs, telling them how pleased it made the Great Father that they had demonstrated such good conduct in the midst of hostilities and that they had chosen to enter into a treaty. Medals bearing the likeness of President James Buchanan were awarded to each chief as a token of appreciation and friendship. The commissioner then distributed a third of the treaty goods—tobacco, sugar, coffee, clothing, bacon, flour, shirts, blankets, scissors, knives, and other desirable items—and promised the remainder when the treaty was signed.[35]

Black Kettle and the chiefs most likely were overwhelmed by this deferential treatment and bedazzled by the display of the white man's wealth that was there for the taking. They responded to Greenwood by stating that they were proud that their good behavior had come to the attention of the Great Father, and they once again expressed their desire to live peaceably with the white man as farmers, if the government would teach them how to work the land.

According to the local newspaper, skeptical frontiersmen at the fort privately scoffed at the idea that rambunctious young warriors would settle down and transform themselves into farmers, although cynically adding that they were "fast becoming civilized. They get drunk as readily as white men and swear with great distinctiveness."[36]

Greenwood reviewed the terms of the 1851 Horse Creek Treaty, the one that the entire Council of Forty-four had agreed upon, and was impressed that the chiefs were so well-versed about its provisions. He wrote that they "exhibited a degree of intelligence seldom to be found among the tribes, where no effort has heretofore been made to civilize them."[37]

The commissioner then outlined the articles of the new treaty. He told them that the tribes must agree to relinquish the territory that they had been awarded in the Fort Laramie Treaty (i.e. the Horse Creek Treaty) of 1851. In return, they would be given a much smaller but agriculturally suitable tract of land, described in the new treaty as:

> Beginning at the mouth of the Sandy Fork of the Arkansas River and extending westwardly along the said river to the mouth of the Purgatory River; thence along up the west bank of the Purgatory River to the northern boundary of the Territory of New Mexico; thence west along said boundary to a point where a line drawn due south from a point on the Arkansas River, five miles east of the mouth of the Huerfano River, would intersect said northern boundary of New Mexico; thence due north from that point on said boundary of the Sandy Fork to the place of the beginning.

In addition, the government would reward them with annuities of $30,000 ($15,000 for each tribe) a year for fifteen years, to be used for the purchase of livestock, farming implements, and other items necessary to successfully work the soil. The tribes would also receive a sawmill, various workshops, and assistance from interpreters, millers, farmers, and mechanics for a period of five years. Each member of the tribe would receive forty acres of land, "to include in every case, as far as practicable, a reasonable portion of timber and water."[38]

Black Kettle and the chiefs heartily agreed to this generous proposal and professed their confidence that the treaty would be accepted by the People as a whole. But, they told Greenwood, in order to avoid any conflict with members of the tribe who were not present, they needed to speak with the other chiefs before signing. Apparently, Greenwood was satisfied that the chiefs would convince their brethren to abide by the treaty and agreed to postpone the signing to a later date. The council was concluded, and the Cheyenne and the Arapaho chiefs departed.

Meanwhile, William Bent requested that he be relieved of his duties as the Indian agent for the Upper Arkansas Agency. Nothing can be found to suggest that Bent resigned in protest or whether he simply believed that his work had been completed, but he must have had some inkling that the treaty would eventually prove to be unworkable.

Bent would have known—as did the government—that this new reservation consisted of a desolate patch of prairie on the upper Arkansas River in southeastern Colorado Territory that was nothing more than dry, sandy, barren, almost gameless land. It was so worthless that

Southern Cheyenne–Arapaho Territory, Fort Wise Treaty of 1861

an experienced farmer would have had difficulty raising a crop on it—
so pitiful that whites would never consider settling on it.

Whether Bent had argued for a better situation for his adopted
tribe and was rebuffed cannot be documented. Therefore, it cannot be
stated that William Bent betrayed or assisted the Cheyennes. But he
certainly would have been consulted by Black Kettle and the others
before they had agreed to the terms, which raises questions about
either his integrity or the circumstances surrounding his resignation.
To give Bent the benefit of the doubt, perhaps he heard the same
promise that Black Kettle would later argue that he understood to be
true—that the People would live on this reservation but could hunt
buffalo in other areas of their choice. Regardless, Bent recommended

that his former business associate Albert Boone be appointed as his replacement, which was accepted.

Boone, Daniel's grandson, had been born in St. Charles, Missouri, on October 4, 1806, and first explored the Rocky Mountains in the mid-1820s while working as a bookkeeper for an Ashley Fur Trapping Expedition. Later, with a partner, he operated an outfitting concern in Westport, Missouri, that bought and sold goods with William Bent, who became his friend. During that period of time, Boone served as a guardian for Bent's children, who were attending school in Westport. Boone headed for Denver at the height of the gold rush in 1860 and opened a store. Upon his appointment as Indian agent, he founded the town of Booneville (present-day Boone) on the Arkansas River at the mouth of Haynes Creek, about twenty miles east of Pueblo, where he operated a store.

On September 20, Commissioner A. B. Greenwood departed Bent's New Fort, leaving Special Agent F. B. Culver in charge of the treaty goods, and Albert Boone, the newest Indian agent, with the responsibility to affect the signing of the treaty.[39]

Black Kettle returned to his people and led them south into Kiowa country to camp for the winter around the Cimarron River, where, unlike their homeland between the South Platte and the Arkansas rivers, buffalo were plentiful and the white man was relatively scarce.[40]

It was February 1861 when Black Kettle and the other chiefs who had petitioned for peace were summoned to Fort Wise, the new military post that had been recently built near Bent's New Fort on the Arkansas. Interpreters Robert Bent and Jack Smith, who, curiously, were each compensated with a section—640 acres—of prime agricultural land in the Arkansas River Valley for their work, explained the treaty provisions to the Cheyenne and the Arapaho chiefs.

On February 18, Black Kettle and the other chiefs who were present agreed to sign the document and did so by making their marks. First Black Kettle, then White Antelope, Starving Bear (Lean Bear), Little Wolf, Tall Bear, and Lone Bear for the Cheyennes. Little Raven, Storm, Shave Head, and Big Mouth signed for the Cloud People. One of the witnesses was First Lieutenant Jeb Stuart, the future Civil War hero who had been severely wounded by the Cheyennes four years earlier at Solomon's Fork.[41]

Six Cheyenne chiefs from the Council of Forty-four had signed, which meant that the majority of the People had not authorized this treaty. Those who did sign, however, were elevated in status to head chiefs by Albert Boone and other government officials, who were ignorant of the political structure of those tribes.

In fact, Black Kettle, whom Agent Boone claimed was the only one who could fully comprehend the details of the matters under consideration, became known, unfairly, as the head chief of the entire Cheyenne tribe, when he actually represented just one band. Great resentment within the tribe was directed at the six signers, their actions regarded as a slap in the face of the Council of Forty-four.[42]

To be fair, Black Kettle and the others who signed had witnessed the suffering of their people and understood the need for relief. They had, however, likely been misled at some point during the proceedings, and each later stated so. What was explained to them and what was actually written into the treaty may have been quite different—especially when it came to surrendering so much territory for so little in return.

It would stand to reason that they envisioned this reservation as a much-needed sanctuary for their desperate people but never intended to relinquish traditional hunting grounds. The idea of owning land away from the white man on which to farm may have been viewed as compensation for no longer being able to travel about the territory and gather roots, vegetables, and fruits in season. The harvest from farming would take the place of those supplements to their diet of wild game.

It would also be logical to assume that Black Kettle and the five other chiefs believed that they were signing for their bands alone and had no intentions of obligating any other band.

Perhaps George Bent put it best when he wrote, "It was the old, old story of the white man with plenty of fine presents and a paper which he wished the Indians to sign."[43]

Another hint that skullduggery and deception may have been employed can be evidenced by Article 11 of the treaty, which demonstrated the influence of the Denver business community. This provision permitted land speculators to purchase city lots on the reservation for $1.25 an acre. Fortunately, Article 11 was disallowed by Congress and struck from the treaty when it was ratified.[44]

The government, however, had signatures on what it believed was a legal and binding document that was very favorable to its interests, one of which was removing the Cheyennes and the Arapahoes from the pathway of progress.

Due to the misunderstanding or perhaps resentment of the provisions, a majority of the two tribes chose to ignore the boundaries stated in the treaty and shunned this new reservation. Instead, these Cheyennes and Arapahoes continued their age-old custom of following the buffalo herds within their traditional hunting grounds between the Platte and the Arkansas rivers.

And this act of perceived defiance would place them in direct conflict with the government's interpretation of the treaty. The days of wandering the plains, moving or camping whenever and wherever they pleased, were about to end for Black Kettle and the People.

Black Kettle and other chiefs at Camp Weld Council, September, 1864. *Seated from left to right,* One-Eye, Black Kettle, Bull Bear, White Antelope; *standing,* Neva, Heap of Buffaloes

Black Kettle and other chiefs and dignitaries at Camp Weld Council, September, 1864. *Kneeling in front row,* Edward Wynkoop and Captain Silas Soule; seated directly behind Wynkoop, Black Kettle; *third from left, standing,* John S. Smith.

William Bent

George Bent, *right*, and his wife, Black Kettle's niece, Magpie

Major Edward
"Ned" Wynkoop

Fort Lyon, Colorado Territory

Colonel John
M. Chivington

Colorado Territorial
Governor John Evans

5

IN THE WAY OF PROGRESS

W HILE THE TOUCHING OF THE PEN TO THE FORT WISE TREATY WAS taking place in February 1861, President Buchanan was signing paperwork in Washington that officially recognized Colorado as a U.S. territory. The region had been initially organized by local citizens in 1859 as "The Provisional Territory of Jefferson," to honor the country's third president. That designation was scrapped when Congress balked at naming a territory after a man. Idaho, Montana, and several other names were proposed before officials finally settled on Colorado.[1]

Shortly after Abraham Lincoln took the oath of office as president in March, he nominated the forty-seven-year-old Missourian William Gilpin as governor of this new territory. William Larimer had been the local favorite for the nomination, but, inasmuch as Missouri was a border state, the appointment of Gilpin was viewed as politically expedient.

Gilpin, who has been described as a romantic visionary and an adventurer, was born into a wealthy Quaker family on October 4, 1813, probably on the Revolutionary War Brandywine Battlefield southwest of Philadelphia—some sources list his year of birth as 1822 and his birthplace as Wilmington, Delaware. He was educated by private tutors, studied in England for several years, attended the University of Pennsylvania, and spent eight months at the United States Military Academy at West Point before dropping out. At the outbreak of the Seminole War, Gilpin received a commission as a second lieutenant and served primarily as a recruiter in Missouri. He remained in Missouri after the war, worked as a newspaper editor, and was admitted to the bar, then in 1843 joined the Fremont Expedition and explored Oregon, staying long enough to assist settlers in the Willamette Valley in organizing a government. Gilpin subsequently rejoined the service, and distinguished himself as an army officer in the Mexican War.[2]

William Gilpin was an army lieutenant colonel and commanded a battalion of 1,200 Missouri volunteers that was stationed in Colorado during a portion of the years 1847 to 1848. At this time, his unit camped much of the time in the vicinity of Bent's Fort, and he became well-known to the trader William Bent, as well as to the Indian agent Thomas Fitzpatrick, with whom he may have become acquainted on the Fremont Expedition. Accounts vary widely with respect to whether he and his troops experienced any action against the Plains Indians—they could have fought a number of skirmishes or merely carried out routine patrols.

At that time, however, Gilpin had fanciful notions about the Cheyennes and the Arapahoes who had recently inquired about the prospect of the government setting them up as farmers—the idea set forth by the Cheyenne chief Yellow Wolf in 1847. Gilpin proposed that these Cheyennes be taught how to farm, then settled at the Cimarron cutoff of the Santa Fe Trail, where they could provide food for travelers and act as an armed buffer to prevent their allies the Comanches from raiding along the trail. This naive idea to establish what could be termed a "Cheyenne Till and Kill Cafe" was ridiculed by Fitzpatrick, which touched off a winter-long feud between the two men.

Gilpin, to the ire of Fitzpatrick and Bent, who had expended considerable effort to maintain peace, also claimed that only the presence of his dragoons had managed to pacify the Cheyennes and the Arapahoes. Gilpin's troops, however, had failed to discourage the Comanches from terrorizing travelers along the Santa Fe Trail, a job that, Fitzpatrick quipped, five hundred "properly led men" could have accomplished.[3]

While Gilpin was en route to Colorado Territory to assume his new position as governor, Fort Sumter was fired upon and relations between the North and the South had flared into a Civil War. Up to that point, Federal troops had garrisoned both Fort Garland in the San Luis Valley and the new Fort Wise. By the time that first salvo of the war had been fired, most of these soldiers had been transferred back East to defend Washington, which left the defense of Colorado mainly in the hands of common citizens and local militias.

Segments of the Native American populace, perhaps taking advantage of the absence of regular army troops, were reported to have been raiding around the vicinity of Denver City. On April 25, Agent

Albert Boone wrote to Superintendent Robinson, "Daily and hourly I am receiving complaints of burning ranches, killing stock as well as many cases of outrages of the gravest character perpetrated on white women."

There was no way of determining exactly which tribe, or if any of those in the southern region—the Cheyennes, the Arapahoes, the Kiowa, or the Comanches—were responsible for the raids, but Boone asked that Major John Sedgwick, with his depleted cavalry at Fort Wise, be prepared to ride at a moment's notice. Boone also noted in his message that he had heard rumors to the effect that the Cheyennes and the Arapahoes were preparing for war against the Pawnees.[4]

It would appear from Boone's perspective that the territory was a powder keg ready to explode into violence, but that was not by any means the case. The Southern Cheyennes and the Southern Arapahoes, in particular, remained outwardly friendly to the whites and had no intentions of going to war with the Pawnees that spring. Although the daily living conditions of these tribes had continued to deteriorate, Black Kettle and the other peace chiefs were able to discourage most of their young warriors from taking to the warpath—except for the occasional raid against the Utes, the Black People.

Perhaps one reason that the Cheyennes and the Arapahoes did not cause mischief was that circumstances had afforded them an opportunity to return for the time being to their traditional ways—albeit with less freedom than in the past. With few troops patrolling the vicinity, they ignored their new reservation and were content to wander around their territory without the threat of military intervention.[5]

Of course, there were always some tribal members who frequented Denver City and other communities and could be found begging on the streets or staggering about in a drunken state. In some cases, their presence in town was quite menacing. The Denver resident Susan Ashley recalled,

> One beautiful Sunday morning, during my first year in Denver [1861], I remember being startled by a most weird and unfamiliar sound, which sent me to the door to learn its source. From there I saw a band of Indians coming up our street, and a minute later thirty or more Cheyennes and Arapahoes passed by, holding aloft on poles five freshly-taken Ute scalps.[6]

Also, groups of intoxicated Cheyennes and Arapahoes were known to roam about the countryside, accosting travelers and occasionally

bullying their way into the occupied dwellings of settlers to steal whatever they could lay their hands on.

As might be expected, the whites around Denver had little regard
for their red neighbors. The pioneer rancher Richens "Uncle Dick"
Wootton summed up the prevailing sentiment of the citizenry when
he said that the Indians

> are about as wild by nature as any other animal found roaming through
> the forest or jungle. They have never recognized any law but the law of
> force and the difference between a "wild Indian" and a "civilized Indian"
> is about the difference between the tiger at large, and the tiger in a cage.[7]

Governor William Gilpin assumed his office in May 1861, without
funds or written instructions, and served with a promise to President
Lincoln that he would keep Colorado Territory loyal to the Union.
On April 24 a Confederate flag had been unfurled over a storefront in
downtown Denver City, but it was quickly ripped down by angry
Union loyalists and destroyed. The Union partisans, who comprised
the vast majority—likely, two-thirds—of the local citizenry, then held
a spirited political rally in conjunction with like gatherings in other
towns and the territory demonstrated its allegiance to Lincoln and the
United States.[8]

Gilpin's first order of business was to implement his plans for a
strong and everlasting territorial government—regardless of the fact
that this foundation was being laid on what was arguably land owned
by the Cheyennes and the Arapahoes. The new governor personally
visited the various mining camps and settlements to assess the needs
of his growing territory—a census showed a population of 25,331, a
figure approximately equal to the number of Native Americans in the
region. Gilpin appointed district federal judges, which in many cases
replaced justice meted out by vigilante committees or people's courts.
He devised a twenty-two-member legislature, which would be elected
by the citizens, and scheduled the first convention for Denver in September. This body, which would use law books available from various
states, would at that time compile the basic codes for both civil and
criminal law.

Gilpin's most pressing concern, however, was the military defense
of his territory, inasmuch as regular troops were few and far between.
He was nagged by the real possibility that the attraction of gold for the
taking could lead to an invasion by the Confederates, and an Indian

uprising certainly was not out of the question. Gilpin understood the need to prepare without haste to combat either threat.

The governor, in a bold and highly questionable move, issued $375,000 in drafts on the federal treasury—without bothering to obtain official approval from anyone in Washington. These drafts were used to purchase equipment and supplies from local businesses that were necessary to organize and maintain a militia. This controversial act was unpopular with many merchants, who were skeptical about the future worth of these paper chits. Most businessmen, who were also wary that armed conflict from within or without could erupt at any moment, however, went along with the governor's wishes, believing that the drafts would be honored by the U.S. government.

The 1st Regiment of Colorado Infantry, ten companies strong, was organized and went into training near Denver City at the newly constructed Camp Weld—named after Lewis L. Weld, the territorial secretary. The unit was commanded by Colonel John Slough, a local lawyer, with Lieutenant Colonel Samuel F. Tappan serving as second in command.

This militia was composed of a variety of diverse characters—a handful of solid citizens, men who had become tired of mining, bored ranch and farm hands, and an assortment of ne'er-do-wells, scalawags, and hooligans. Right from its inception, these troops gained a reputation for drinking to excess, brawling, stealing from local merchants, and generally raising all kinds of hell around Denver City.

In fact, a special police task force was activated by city officials to deal specifically with these uniformed troublemakers, but this effort had no real effect. The undisciplined troopers wanted to fight—either Indians or Confederates, it made no difference to them—and had no regard for proper military behavior. It was said of them that "they deserted at will and cussed out their officers with impunity. Taps was merely a signal to head for the fleshpots in town. They only came to camp to get their meals."[9]

Meanwhile, that summer of 1861 was extremely hot and dry, and Southern Cheyenne and Southern Arapaho territory along the Arkansas River was parched into dust by the interminable heat and lack of moisture. The great buffalo herds that once grazed in that area had gradually drifted away over time, due to the pressures of civilization, and the tribes were hungry and restless. Governor Gilpin had instructed the Indian agent Albert Boone to withhold annuities, which were stored at Fort Wise, from the tribes until the fall. If the goods were handed out in the summer, he deduced, perhaps correctly, there would be little remaining to satisfy the need over the winter.

By September, however, conditions had deteriorated to the point that some three thousand angry Cheyennes, Arapahoes, Kiowas, and Comanches assembled around Fort Wise, demanding that they be paid their annuities within ten days or war would be declared. Captain Elmer Otis, the post commander, distributed only a small amount of provisions, but it was sufficient enough to quiet the clamor for the time being.[10]

The Fort Wise Treaty had been signed by the six Southern Cheyenne and four Southern Arapaho chiefs that spring, but this document had only been ratified by Congress on August 6 and now required that the chiefs touch the pen to the amended version. When Boone approached Black Kettle and the other chiefs with this request, he was told that they had vowed to never again sign a treaty with the white man and intended to abide by that decision.

Albert Boone, however, spent two difficult days in late October—the month when the water begins to freeze on the edge of the streams—conjoling, demanding, pleading, pledging, and assuring before the chiefs grudgingly agreed to sign. In the end, Boone promised, likely among other incentives, that the Cheyennes would receive thirty-six sets of military uniforms—six with epaulets—and that he would schedule a visit to Washington for the chiefs.[11]

Boone had been replaced as the Indian agent for the Upper Arkansas Agency on August 21, but word of the appointment of Samuel G. Colley was not received until mid-November. One of Boone's final official acts as Indian agent was to complete a census of his charges. He reported that 1,380 Southern Cheyennes lived in 250 lodges and included 425 men, 480 women, and 475 children.[12]

In his letters and reports, Boone also revealed his opinions and recommendations about the native people whom he had been paid to oversee. He believed that they had a "natural want of intellect and hatred & jealousy to the white race" and professed that most of their problems, as well as those on the frontier, could be attributed to the illegal whisky trade. Boone recommended that the Indians could be more easily supervised if the government would remove the "low depraved beings" who intermarried with the tribes and then peddled them whisky. He also noted that the "swarm of petifogging traders" who descended upon the Indians when the annuities were paid out and traded whisky for government goods should be banned. In describing the men of the Upper Arkansas tribes, Boone wrote that they

> abhor labor, the women do all the drudgery; they are an indolent community, lay around, pilfer & beg, great lovers of whisky, sugar and think it very strange that I have not allowed it to be brought and traded for such commodities as they have to sell, often offering a good Pony or mule for one Bottle. They are very licentious, they worship the Sun, Earth and Smoke and swear by the Pipe.[13]

Boone was correct in his assessment of the effects that whisky had on the various tribes. At one point, officials asked that Black Kettle and the Arapaho chief Little Raven lead their people far out onto the plains, away from any settlement and every source of whisky, which, it was believed, was the only way in which to calm tensions created by drunken warriors.[14]

During that fall season, the Southern Cheyennes and the Southern Arapahoes were afforded an opportunity to bite the hand that fed them. The tribes were contacted by Comanche messengers on behalf of a man named Albert Pike. This native of Boston, who was now a prominent Arkansas lawyer, planter, and journalist, had been dispatched by the Confederate government in Richmond to win over the tribes in Indian Territory (present-day Oklahoma) for the South. He had successfully negotiated treaties with the Five Civilized Nations—Cherokee, Chickasaw, Choctaw, Creek, and Seminole—mainly due to the fact that the Union had abandoned that territory and had not fulfilled treaty obligations. These tribes, as part of the bargain, organized military units that would fight for the Confederacy in battles against Federal troops.[15]

Albert Pike had now set his sights on expanding his Confederate Indian fighting force by recruiting the Southern Cheyennes and the Southern Arapahoes. His runners told the tribes that the Texans—which was what the Plains tribes called all Southerners—were planning to head north in the spring and, with the alliance of Cheyennes and Arapahoes joining them, they would wipe out every fort along the Arkansas River and then attack Denver City and the other white settlements.

Black Kettle and the other Council Chiefs must have been quite intrigued and tempted by this promise of treaty presents and the opportunity to gain revenge against the whites who had invaded their territory. By accepting the South's offer, they could also repudiate this recent treaty of Fort Wise, which had caused such dissention within the tribes. They were, however, confused about which side might prevail in this great war, and about whether or not Albert Pike could be trusted to deliver on his promises. Before responding to the South's entreaty, the peace chiefs decided that they would seek council from the one man whom they believed had their best interests at heart. They paid a visit to William Bent at his stockade at the mouth of the Purgatorie River.

One word from William Bent encouraging the tribes to accept a treaty with the South could have dramatically changed the course of history in Colorado. The trader, however, told the chiefs that they would be best served by staying clear of this white man's war and having nothing to do with Pike or his Texans.

This was an interesting position taken by Bent, who hailed from Missouri, a state torn apart by the war, particularly when his son George had enlisted in a Confederate cavalry unit and had already seen action at Wilson's Creek.[16]

Regardless of the reasons for Bent's loyalties, this advice from a man whom the Cheyennes respected convinced them to rebuff Pike. They went into winter camps while the white man was settling his differences on eastern battlefields. The two factions of Cheyennes—Northern and Southern—likely did not share winter quarters that year to the extent of previous years, as had been the custom. The Northern bands were bitter about the cession of lands by the six Southern peace chiefs—and probably were envious of the annuities paid to the Southerners for their betrayal. Every band, however, abided by the decision of the chiefs and kept clear of the white man and his war.

During the summer of 1861, a Confederate army of Texans under Brigadier General Henry Hopkins Sibley had invaded New Mexico Territory and captured Albuquerque and then Santa Fe. In March 1862, the 1st Colorado Volunteers—1,340 strong—were ordered to march south and reinforce the undermanned Union troops in New Mexico, in an effort to repel Sibley's troops.

On March 26, the advance guards of the two armies happened upon each other at La Glorieta Pass, east of Santa Fe. The Rebels and the Yankees battled for most of the day, with the Confederates holding the field at the end.

Two days later, reinforcements arrived for the Confederates, which brought their strength to about 1,100, and another vicious battle of charges, countercharges, and artillery duels commenced. By late afternoon, the Confederates had chased off the Union forces and believed that they had gained a smashing victory for the South.

While the main battle had taken place, however, a flanking movement by Colorado volunteers under the command of Major John Chivington raided the ranch where the Rebel wagon train was stored. Chivington and his men overpowered the guards, captured seventeen prisoners, and destroyed eighty-five wagons that contained vital supplies and ammunition—as well as killing five to six hundred horses and mules.

This heroic action by Major Chivington was a crushing blow to the Confederates. The victory on the battlefield meant little when supplies necessary to sustain the army had been lost. General Sibley had no choice but to retreat back down the Rio Grande Valley and return to Texas, his ambitious plans to capture New Mexico for the Confederacy thwarted by the lack of provisions.[17]

It could have been assumed that this major victory by the Coloradans over the invading Confederates would have vindicated Governor William Gilpin for his controversial decision to issue the treasury drafts that were used to organize and outfit his troops. That, however, was not the case. The territory was in dire financial straits, and when the merchants who had accepted the drafts requested compensation, the federal government refused to honor them.

Gilpin was denounced by the citizenry, and a petition for his recall was circulated. In an effort to save his job, the governor traveled to Washington to straighten out the matter. By April, however, President Lincoln had concluded that Gilpin was guilty of mismanagement, extravagance, and exceeding his authority and ordered him removed from office. The drafts were eventually paid by the U.S. Treasury, but not before many merchants had sold them at a fraction of their original worth.

William Gilpin devoted the rest of his life to land speculation in the Southwest, eventually purchasing over one million acres of real estate in New Mexico, which he sold to accumulate a fortune. He died in Denver on January 20, 1894, from injuries suffered in a carriage accident, and was buried in Mount Olivet Cemetery.[18]

As the replacement for Gilpin, the president turned to Dr. John Evans, an old friend. Evans, a forty-eight-year-old Ohio native, had studied medicine at Pennsylvania's Claremont Academy and enjoyed great renown in that profession. He had pioneered the humane treatment of mental patients and discovered the contagious nature of cholera, the "cramps" that had devastated the Cheyennes and other Plains tribes years earlier.

In addition, Evans was a wealthy man, who boasted profitable ventures in railroading—he was a director of the newly organized Union Pacific Railroad—and as a real estate investor. He had also been involved in the founding of Northwestern University, as well as the city of Evanston, Illinois, which was named after him. He had turned down the position as governor of Washington Territory before accepting the Colorado appointment.

Evans arrived in Denver in May 1862 with ambitious plans for the territory, one of which was making Denver a major hub for the first transcontinental railroad. This achievement would ensure the growth and the prosperity of the region and would likely result in statehood for Colorado and the election of Dr. John Evans to the United States Senate.[19]

The new governor was not overly concerned about the possibility of a Confederate invasion of his territory but became quite disturbed when the chilling news of the Sioux uprising in Minnesota reached him. In August 1862 the Santee Sioux protested their concentration camp-like conditions by rampaging throughout the Minnesota countryside on one of the most brutal reigns of terror and carnage ever recorded in the annals of warfare between whites and Native Americans. Perhaps as many as eight hundred white settlers and soldiers, and countless Sioux, lost their lives before hostilities were brought under control.[20]

This indiscriminate mass slaughter of whites in Minnesota raised an immediate loud, almost hysterical, cry of alarm throughout the Plains. Colorado, with Denver City the largest population center in the region, was gripped with fear, as rumors that this bloody trail of destruction and death would lead to their unprotected doorstep.

Although the nearby Cheyenne and Arapaho tribes remained at peace, it was noted that Colorado Territory was virtually defenseless against an Indian attack, inasmuch as the 1st Colorado Infantry was still stationed in New Mexico. Therefore, Governor Evans raised another regiment, the 2nd Colorado Volunteers, which was commanded by Colonel Jesse H. Leavenworth. Leavenworth's men had initially garrisoned Fort Lyon, the former Fort Wise—the name had been changed in June 1862 in honor of General Nathaniel Lyon, the first Union general to die in the war—but they subsequently were transferred to Fort Larned, Kansas, leaving only a small detachment behind.[21]

This force, however, was bolstered when the soldiers from New Mexico were recalled, and Evans could report, "Now that the War Department has ordered the Colorado troops home, and mounted one regiment, giving us ample military protection, we have but little danger to apprehend from Indian hostilities"[22]

By this time, Colonel John Slough had resigned as the commander of the Colorado volunteers in a dispute over not being permitted to pursue Sibley's fleeing Texans after the La Glorieta battle. Slough was replaced as the commanding colonel of the newly created Military District of Colorado by John Milton Chivington, the hero of that fight, who had reaped national accolades for his actions.[23]

Chivington was a huge, imposing man—standing six-foot, five-inches tall and tipping the scales at about 260 pounds—and was said to be as "strong as a bull elephant." He had been born into a farming and lumbering family of three sons and a daughter on January 27, 1821, in Warren County, Ohio. Chivington's father had died when the boy was five, and his older brother assumed responsibility for the family businesses. John attended school whenever an itinerant teacher happened to pass through the area, but most of his education was received at home from his mother.

When Chivington was about thirteen, he went to work in the woods, wielding an axe beside his two brothers. By age eighteen, he had taken over the marketing of their wood products. On one of his sales trips to Cincinnati, Chivington was introduced to Martha Rollason, a refined, well-educated Virginian whose family owned a plantation. Martha had left home with a small inheritance after the death of her mother and her father's remarriage to a woman with whom she had a contentious relationship. She had her heart set on becoming a teacher but could find work only as a domestic. After a whirlwind courtship, the two were married and had one son and two daughters.

Chivington's life dramatically changed in 1843 when he attended a series of Methodist revival meetings and became a "born again" Christian. He voraciously studied everything he could find about his new faith, a religion that stressed conversion, holiness, and social welfare. In September 1844, he was ordained a minister in the 3-million-member Methodist-Episcopal Church and subsequently moved his family around the Midwest, as he was sent on various preaching assignments in Ohio, Illinois, Missouri, Kansas, and Nebraska. In 1854, Chivington and several others organized the first Masonic lodge in Kansas Territory. Two years later, he was appointed as presiding elder of the Omaha District of the Methodist Church.

John Chivington was said to have been quite conservative and essentially humorless and became known for his gentlemanly behavior and kindly nature. He was a strong-willed man who was fervently opposed to slavery. One example of many that best portrays his pertinacious character when professing his beliefs occurred in Ohio. The reverend had preached an antislavery message in a church whose congregation was, for the most part, proslavery. He was warned that if he ever again spoke against slavery, he would be tarred and feathered and run out of town. The following Sunday morning, Chivington stepped to the pulpit, placed two pearl-handled Colt revolvers on either side of his Bible, and railed about the evils of slavery. His message was greeted without protest, and there were no repercussions. This episode gained him recognition within the church and propelled him into a leadership role.

Chivington believed that the rush of prospectors to Colorado presented a perfect opportunity for him to spread the gospel in that region. He arrived in Denver with his family in May 1860 and accepted the position as presiding elder of the fledgling First Methodist Episcopal Church. Chivington organized a Sunday School in his church and traveled as a circuit rider to the outlying mining towns to preach the gospel. It was said that he possessed such a powerful voice that his sermons could be heard three blocks away.

Chivington had initially been tendered a commission as chaplain of the 1st Colorado Regiment, but he requested a "fighting" commission, rather than a "praying" one, and was appointed a major. His heroism at La Glorieta Pass had earned him regional and national attention as Colorado's "Fighting Parson." This notoriety encouraged him to set his sights on higher political ambitions, such as becoming the first congressman from Colorado when the territory was granted statehood.[24]

Chivington and Governor Evans were of like mind when it came to handling affairs with Indians. Both held to the view that the red man was an obstacle in the pathway of Colorado's progress—as well as of their ambitious political plans, which depended on gaining statehood. This realization, coupled with the bloody uprising in Minnesota, made Evans recognize that the Cheyenne and the Arapaho tribes, which had not abided by the provisions of the 1861 Fort Wise Treaty, must be convinced to comply.

Black Kettle and most of the other bands had ignored the boundaries of their reservation and continued to follow the buffalo. A number of isolated incidences of conflict between whites and Indians had occurred—harassment of traffic on the overland trails and occasional livestock stealing—but the Southern Cheyennes and the Southern Arapahoes, although their condition was deteriorating due to hunger and disease, remained peaceful as the year 1863 arrived.

In November 1861, Samuel Gerish Colley had succeeded Albert Boone as the Indian agent for the Upper Arkansas Agency, headquartered at Fort Lyon (Fort Wise). The fifty-four-year-old native of Bedford, New Hampshire, had in recent years resided in Beloit, Rock County, Wisconsin, where he had served in that state's legislature from 1848 to 1850. He had spent a year prospecting for gold in California before arriving in Colorado. Colley had no doubt gained his office through nepotism, inasmuch as he was appointed shortly after his cousin William P. Dole became commissioner of Indian Affairs.

It had not taken long for Samuel Colley to use his position to establish a thriving family business, albeit corrupt, on the side. Along with his son Dexter, Colley introduced the practice of coercing the tribes into handing over presents of horses, robes, and other valuable trade items for the privilege of receiving their own annuity goods. Dexter, who first arrived in Colorado with about thirty head of cattle, had by now reportedly amassed at least $25,000 by selling the wares meant for the tribes on the black market. Colley's wife also participated in the family enterprise by baking pies with flour appropriated from annuity supplies, which she sold to the troops at Fort Lyon.

Colley and his son allegedly recruited John Simpson Smith to assist with these underhanded dealings with his charges. Smith, a white man who had arrived in the territory from St. Louis in 1830, had married into the Cheyenne tribe and was known to them as "Gray Blanket." It has been noted that no one, not even William Bent, knew the Cheyenne or their language better than John S. Smith did. Jack, Smith's son by a Cheyenne wife, had served as an interpreter for the reading of the Fort Wise Treaty of 1861 and had received 640 acres of land for his work.[25]

In March 1863, Colley followed through on the promise made by Albert Boone at the treaty talks that certain chiefs would pay a visit to Washington. The published purpose of this trip was billed as an effort by Colorado and Washington officials to strengthen the strained relationship between the two races. In truth, the visit was intended to expose these chiefs to the wealth, the population, and the achievements of the white man, as well as to demonstrate the strength of the army, which would discourage any idea of an uprising.

John S. Smith carried the invitation to the various Cheyenne bands, but only three chiefs accepted the offer—War Bonnet, Standing in the Water, and Starving Bear (also called Lean Bear), the latter being the only one of them who had signed the Fort Wise Treaty.

It has been mentioned in certain biographical texts that Black Kettle made this journey as a representative of the Cheyennes, but, for whatever reasons, he had declined the opportunity and remained at home with his people.

Colley's delegation of chiefs from the Cheyennes, the Arapahoes, the Caddoes, the Comanches, and the Kiowas—with John Smith acting as interpreter—passed through Fort Leavenworth, Kansas, then traveled by train from St. Louis to Washington. On March 26, the chiefs had an audience with President Lincoln at the White House.

Starving Bear, who had been designated the spokesman for the Cheyennes, declined to bow and scrape to the Great White Chief, instead addressing Lincoln as if he were an equal. The chief told the president that the Cheyennes desired to live in peace with the white man and stated that Lincoln must counsel his white children to live in harmony with the Indians and put a stop to the violence against them.

Lincoln responded to the chiefs by saying that although the whites were engaged in a war against each other, they were not a warring race that wished to fight the red man. He told the chiefs that the whites were strong and prosperous because they depended on farming, rather than on hunting, for subsistence and added, "I really am not capable of advising you whether, in the providence of the Great Spirit, who is the Great Father of us all, it is for you to maintain the habits and customs of your race, or to adopt a new mode of life. I can only say that I can see no way in which your race is to become as prosperous as the white race except by living as they do, by cultivation of the earth."[26]

Meanwhile, conditions on the Plains were growing increasingly worse. Tension mounted as a severe drought dried up the grasslands that supported the huge buffalo herds. As a result, these herds migrated farther north—as much as two hundred miles away from the Southern Cheyennes and the Southern Arapahoes—and the People and the Cloud People were on the brink of starvation. This dilemma was exacerbated

by the fact that Agent Colley and his son had been systematically stealing a portion of the annuities.

Black Kettle and the Cheyennes, in spite of the desperate conditions, had been trying to maintain their traditional way of life. Therefore, when the Dog Soldiers called for a Sun Dance that June, Black
Kettle and the other bands made their way to the headwaters of the
Republican River, in the heart of Dog Man country, to take part in the
ceremony. This great village of the Cheyennes was shaped in the customary half moon, with the opening facing toward the east, where the
sun would rise to flood its rays into the circle. The Lakota Sioux, who
had been invited as guests, formed their circle of lodges within four
hundred yards of their allies.

A special lodge with a sacred pole in the center had been erected
for this renewal ceremony. While attached to this pole by rawhide
ropes imbedded in the flesh of their chests, the warriors danced in a
self-torture ritual, offering their own blood as a sacrifice intended to
bless all of the people.

When the ceremony concluded, the Cheyenne bands all moved to
a new camping place, which symbolized a new beginning and a new
life. They did, however, remain in the vicinity and attend the Lakota
Sun Dance. Then, when that ceremony concluded, the village broke
up and the individual bands scattered across the Plains to find fresh
grazing for their pony herds.[27]

It should be noted that the Southern Cheyennes welcomed a tribal
member back into their fold at this Sun Dance. George Bent, the Confederate cavalryman and the son of William, had been captured by
Union forces during the October 1862 siege of Corinth, Mississippi.
He was eventually taken to St. Louis and paraded through the streets,
where he was recognized by a former schoolmate, who notified Robert Bent. Robert interceded on his brother's behalf with a Union
acquaintance. George was paroled, on the condition that he promise
to return home and take no further part in the war. After a ten-year
absence, George arrived in Colorado Territory and joined the Cheyennes that spring, just in time to participate in the Sun Dance festivities as a member of his military society, the Dog Soldiers. The
Cheyennes bestowed upon him the nickname "Tex." This was probably a shortened version of "Texan" and alluded to Bent's service with
the South's forces, whom the Cheyennes called Texans.[28]

By August, the month when the cherries were ripe, Black Kettle
and the Cheyennes became aware that representatives of Governor

Evans were traveling through their country, seeking out every band. Evans and his military commander, Colonel John Chivington, were adamant that the Southern Cheyennes and the Southern Arapahoes—as well as other tribes—who were scattered in small bands around the territory should be made to adhere to the Fort Wise Treaty and submit to their reservations. Bands of Indians wandering around Colorado Territory, where they might engage in petty mischief or worse, could no longer be tolerated. Evans decided that he would arrange a peace council and personally impress upon the minds of the tribal leaders that they must obey the provisions of the treaty and move onto their assigned land.

One of the governor's emissaries was Elbridge Gerry, a trader and a rancher who had married into the Lakota Sioux tribe and was generally respected by the Cheyennes. Gerry was described by Evans as a grandson of the Elbridge Gerry who had signed the Declaration of Independence, as well as a scholar and a man of very good mind.

Gerry, accompanied by a wagonload of presents, traveled about 600 miles in his search for the various Cheyenne and Arapaho camps, which were widespread throughout the territory. He managed to locate a few camps, including one consisting of 150 lodges at the head of the Smoky Hill River, and invited all the chiefs to a council with the governor on September 1 on the Arikara Fork of the Republican River, east of Denver.

Gerry's request for this parley, however, was met by mild resistance. The tribes were in the midst of their fall buffalo hunt, which was vital to their survival that winter, and declined the invitation to meet with Evans. Finally, with some reluctance, most bands agreed to parley with the governor.[29]

Governor John Evans and his entourage arrived at the appointed place on time, but there was no sign of the Indians and he finally departed for home. Elbridge Gerry was ordered to scour the area, in an effort to learn why the Indians had snubbed Evans.

By this time, Black Kettle had moved his band to Beaver Creek to join a Dog Soldier village that was reported to be some 240 lodges in size. When Gerry arrived, Black Kettle reportedly refused to meet with him, choosing instead to remain inside his lodge.

White Antelope and several other chiefs, however, smoked the pipe with Gerry around the sacred circle within the lodge. Gerry asked them why they had not attended the meeting with Governor Evans. The chiefs offered various excuses, such as the buffalo hunt was going too well to quit for a parley, the bands were too widely scattered to assemble at that particular location, or children were sick with whooping cough and needed attention. Then, finally, the main reason for their snub was revealed—dissatisfaction with the Fort Wise Treaty.

The chiefs told Gerry that they considered the treaty a fraud, a swindle, that the government had taken advantage of them, that they had not understood the provisions—all of which was probably true. There were no buffalo on this new reservation, they argued, and the presence of that animal was a necessity for survival. They denied that they had agreed to cede their land at the headwaters of the Republican and the Smoky Hill Rivers and vowed to never relinquish it to the white man.

In addition, a warrior named Little Heart had recently been shot and killed by a sentry at Fort Larned. Agent Colley had given the man's relatives gifts to compensate for his death, but that had not appeased many in the tribe. The chiefs told Gerry that "The white man's hands are dripping with our people's blood, and now he calls for us to make a treaty!"

Furthermore, and perhaps most surprising, White Antelope denied having signed such a treaty, and it was stated to Gerry that Black Kettle, who, he was told, was present in the village but was ill, also did not make his mark to approve a treaty with those provisions.

During the course of the discussion, Gerry told them that the whites were planning to build a railroad through their country. The chiefs responded by saying that such an act was of little concern to them—the whites, however, would never be permitted to establish settlements along the route of this railroad.[30]

It seems curious that Black Kettle, who was always receptive to a parley with the white man, did not smoke the pipe with Elbridge Gerry and at least listen to what the emissary had to say. The chief would presumably have been interested in learning exactly what was being discussed and in assessing the remarks of Gerry and his peers for future reference. He would have had to be deathly ill not to attend, which, without any evidence of his health at that point in time, renders that excuse questionable.

There is another conceivable reason for Black Kettle's absence. The Fort Wise Treaty was a delicate topic to the Dog Soldiers, who had vehemently opposed it, and this camp was a Dog Man camp. Perhaps Black Kettle did not attend as a mild protest—a show of solidarity meant to heal and unify the tribe—which would have served him well in the eyes of that militant soldier society. Although he continued to speak for peace, his act of ignoring Gerry—as well as the Evans council—would have gained him great admiration from the faction of the tribe that had disapproved of his signing the treaty.

There does exist the distinct possibility, however, that Elbridge Gerry or the Dog Soldiers could have lied about Black Kettle saying that he had never signed the treaty. This statement was not a firsthand account, inasmuch as Gerry did not personally hear the words directly from the chief, and it was never repeated in the future by Black Kettle. Perhaps Black Kettle was not even in that village at the time of Gerry's visit or was in some manner discouraged from attending the meeting— which is not to imply that the strong-willed Black Kettle could have been intimidated into remaining out of sight had he desired to meet with Gerry.

Regardless, Elbridge Gerry reported to the governor that the attitude of the Cheyennes was hostile, and they were opposed to peace with the whites. Naturally, this negative, threatening response was quite disturbing to Evans and Chivington. Evans, who was accustomed to getting his own way, was said to have been bitter, rather than simply disappointed, about being rebuffed by the Indians at his proposed council but, for the time being, was unable to do anything about it.

And apparently, in his estimation, although he remained resolute about adherence to the treaty, there was no reason to take immediate action. In October, the governor informed Washington that except for a few depredations by "single bands and small parties," his territory was relatively peaceful.[31]

On November 10, however, Evans received a dubious report from a man who has been described as the "murderous white chief of an outlawed band of the Northern or Big Horn Arapahoes" and was said to be insane. Robert North informed the governor that all the Plains tribes had formed a secret alliance and pledged to go to war against the whites "as soon as grass was up in the spring."[32]

Without questioning the credibility of this report, and it would prove to be a lie, Evans—as well as Chivington—had a major change of heart with respect to their attitude toward the Southern Cheyennes and the Southern Arapahoes. Both men were convinced that Colorado was in imminent danger of a surprise attack, and the only way to prevent it was to force the Indians onto their assigned reservations by use of military might.[33]

The War Department, however, had been drawing Colorado volunteers for assignments in the East, and Evans was short on troop strength. The 1st Colorado Infantry had been converted into a cavalry regiment, and thus far, Colonel Chivington had prevented that unit from being transferred away from Denver and the surrounding area.

Governor Evans made a trip to Washington in December 1863 to plead his case for the return of Colorado troops, as well as to request that other Federal soldiers be dispatched along the Platte and the Arkansas supply routes. The War Department, however, did not share Evans's concern about the threat of the Plains Indians and was not about to transfer troops away that were needed for the fighting in the East. Evans returned home determined to prove in some manner that he was not simply crying wolf—perhaps even if it meant provoking a war.[34]

The winter of 1863–1864 was extremely hard on the various Plains Indian tribes. The buffalo had wandered far away from traditional hunting grounds, and other wild game had become scarce. Black Kettle and the People were starving, racked with smallpox, and compelled to visit trading posts to exchange anything of value that they possessed for food. Unscrupulous traders took advantage of their desperate clients and paid lower than normal prices for buffalo robes and other items. Many tribe members drowned their sorrows in watered-down rot-gut whisky. Some traders went as far as to suggest to these alcoholic Indians that they steal livestock from ranches and farms to trade for whisky. How many thefts can be blamed on this devious encouragement cannot be determined, but it was known to have happened.[35]

Agent Samuel Colley reported that "most of the depredations committed by them are from starvation. It is hard to make them understand that they have no right to take from them that have, when in a starving condition." Quite a sanctimonious statement from a man who was becoming wealthy by stealing from them that had—namely, the annuities that belonged to the Southern Cheyennes and the Southern Arapahoes.[36]

In spite of their present poor condition, most of which could be blamed on the presence of white invaders, there was no indication that the Indians were anything but peaceful toward whites during this desperate period that the Southern Cheyennes and the Southern Arapahoes called "the year of hunger."[37]

That fact did not deter Evans and Chivington from the conviction that they must create a situation that would justify removing the Indians far from any settlement or pathway of progress. Regardless of the enormity of the crime, the two men viewed each infraction as another piece of damning evidence that added to their case for the war that they believed would, with a little prodding, flare up in the near future.

The plans to use force against the Indians that were being concocted by the governor and his military commander, however, suffered a severe blow on March 29. Major General Samuel R. Curtis, the commanding officer of the Department of Kansas, notified them that he was obliged to draw every available trooper from the Plains to meet the threat of a Confederate invasion of Kansas.

But, to the relief of the two men, this setback proved to be only temporary. Within a week and a half, before their troops were officially ordered away, evidence of the Indian war that Evans and Chivington had predicted presented itself.[38]

The Plains were about to erupt in flames, and Black Kettle and his Southern Cheyennes would find themselves at the center of this tragic firestorm.

6

THE PLAINS ERUPT
IN FLAMES

IN MARCH 1864, THE SAME MONTH IN WHICH GENERAL CURTIS HAD made his demand for Colorado volunteers, Black Kettle and several other Southern chiefs visited Agent Samuel Colley at Fort Larned. To protect themselves from reprisals due to mistaken identity, the chiefs passed on the information to Colley that the Lakota Sioux were planning to raid settlements along the Platte and the Arkansas rivers that spring and summer. The Lakota had sent down a war pipe to the People and the Cloud People, which was a request for them to join in the raids, but both tribes had refused to smoke it.

Colley reported that news to Governor Evans and added that the Cheyennes and the Arapahoes could be regarded as peaceful, that there was no danger of them causing any trouble in the foreseeable future. Evans, however, had already made up his mind that a war was inevitable, and that the Cheyennes and the Arapahoes had lied to Colley about not participating with the Sioux. The governor instructed the Indian agent to recruit spies to gather information with respect to the intentions of these Southern tribes, which he believed would confirm his suspicions.[1]

On April 5, near the headwaters of Sand Creek, several Cheyenne men were riding through the sand hills and noticed a number of grazing cattle. These animals were part of a herd totaling about 175 that was being wintered in that location by the government contractors Irwin, Jackman, and Company. The Cheyennes, perhaps with the idea that they could gain a reward, herded these stray cattle to their camp. Rounding up this stock was likely a relatively innocent act. Had the men and their families been starving, the cattle surely would have

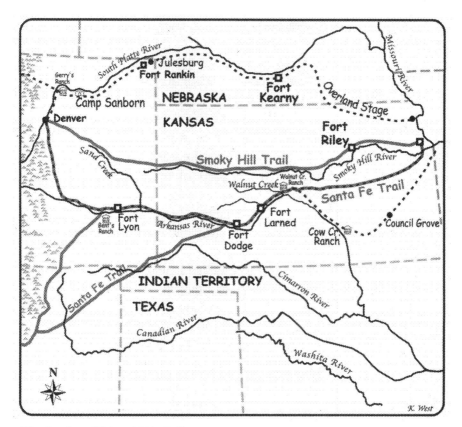

The Southern Plains, 1864–1865

been taken for food. These Cheyennes, however, had bellies full of buffalo meat and were not interested in eating "tame meat."[2]

The herders reported this alleged theft by the Indians to authorities—overstating the total number taken as the entire herd of 175. It was common practice among unattentive herdsmen to blame Indians, when in some cases the stock had merely wandered off. Regardless, this information made its way up the chain of command to General Samuel Curtis at Fort Leavenworth. Orders were relayed from that headquarters to Colonel John Chivington not to let "district lines prevent pursuing and punishing" the thieves. In other words, Chivington had permission to overstep the boundaries of his district, if necessary, to pursue these Indians.

On April 8, Lieutenant George S. Eayre, commanding a detachment of 54 troopers and two 12-pound mountain howitzers, set off to track down the thieves, recover the cattle, and, if possible, punish the guilty parties.[3]

While Lieutenant Eayre was on the march, another episode occurred on the South Platte River that Black Kettle later noted as perhaps the primary spark that eventually ignited all-out war.[4]

In early April, the Southern Cheyenne camp on Beaver Creek received word that its Northern brothers were forming a war party against the Crows to avenge the killing the previous summer of a fellow warrior named Brave Wolf. A party of fifteen Dog Soldiers decided to head north toward the Powder River country to assist their brethren in hunting down the assailants. Along the way, on April 11, the Cheyennes happened upon four stray mules near the South Platte River and rounded up the animals.

That evening, a Bijou Creek rancher named W. D. Ripley rode into the Cheyenne camp and demanded that they hand over his mules. Bull Telling Tales told Ripley that he and another brave had spent considerable time catching the ornery mules, and a gift for their return would be appropriate. Ripley promised nothing and departed.

The rancher rode up the river to Camp Sanborn, a temporary post on the Platte River trail. He reported that Indians were running off all the stock along Bijou Creek, knocking down telegraph poles, and terrorizing local ranches, and that he had been fortunate to escape a confrontation with them with his life.

The following morning, Lieutenant Clark Dunn and forty men of the 1st Colorado Cavalry, with W. D. Ripley as guide, were dispatched by Captain George L. Sanborn with orders to recover these animals—and to disarm the perpetrators. Dunn decided to divide his command, sending more than half the men toward Ripley's ranch, while he and fifteen troopers remained on the trail of the alleged mule thieves. The soldiers marched sixty miles before pausing to water their horses on the Platte River near Fremont's Orchard, in present-day Morgan County.

The Cheyenne war party, herding the mules, had already crossed the Platte and was riding toward the northern hills when the Cheyennes noticed Dunn and his troopers. Apparently, these Cheyenne warriors were under the impression that the soldiers had come to discuss on friendly terms the return of the mules and rode to the river to meet them. The Cheyennes and the soldiers greeted each other across the shimmering waterway, but any friendliness on either side was about to disappear.[5]

At this point, the sequence of events becomes quite contradictory and wide open to interpretation.

One version of the Cheyenne side of the story was provided later that year by Black Kettle to Lieutenant Joseph A. Cramer, when the two met on the Smoky Hill River. The chief contended that the Indians had happened upon some loose stock and were in the process of delivering them to Elbridge Gerry's ranch when they were overtaken by the soldiers, who appeared friendly. The chief of the soldiers demanded that they return the animals, to which the Indians agreed, except for one mule that one of them had out hunting. It was promised that this animal would be returned as soon as possible. Cramer, repeating Black Kettle's story at a congressional hearing, continued,

> The chief of soldiers still demanded the mule, at the same time taking from the Indians their arms, which the Indians supposed were merely to look at. One of the Indians refused to let him take his arms, when he undertook to take them by force. I am not positive that the Indians fired first, but my impression is that [Black Kettle] said the Indians fired first after the attempt to take arms by force. I think that the Indians stated that there were three killed or wounded.[6]

Another Cheyenne account, recorded by George Bent, added that the troops charged into the Dog Soldiers without warning or provocation and commenced firing. Bull Telling Tales shot a soldier in the chest with an arrow and cut off the man's head, and three other whites were shot from their saddles. The rest of the frightened troopers ran away. Three Dog Men were wounded in the encounter. The Cheyennes aborted their trip north and returned to their camp on Beaver Creek, carrying with them the soldier's head, jacket, field glasses, and watch. These items were said to have been later shown to a trader named May Gilman, who, for the most part, confirmed the Cheyenne side of the story.[7]

Lieutenant Dunn, in his official report, wrote that he dismounted, stepped forward, and made signs for the Indians to send someone out to parley. Eventually, all the Indians approached to shake hands with the soldiers. Dunn, in accordance with his orders to disarm the Indians, reached out to take away a weapon held in the hands of one warrior. This affront apparently surprised and outraged the Indians, who responded by opening fire. The soldiers answered by discharging their own weapons, which resulted in a running battle between the two parties over a distance of fifteen miles. Dunn's command suffered four men wounded, two of whom later died. The lieutenant claimed to have killed eight or ten Indians and wounded as many as fifteen more—certainly an exaggeration.[8]

Another version of this episode was provided by Colonel John Chivington. He reported that when Dunn spoke with the leader of the Indians, the lieutenant was told that the Indians would rather fight than simply hand over the livestock. The Indian leader then gave the signal for his warriors to open fire, and the battle commenced.[9]

In any case, one point was clear to both sides: The Indians would not stand idly by and permit the army to disarm them under any circumstances. Word of this attempt by Lieutenant Dunn to take away their weapons reverberated throughout Indian country and predictably engendered ill feelings toward the government and the soldiers around every tribal fire. Any bond of trust between the two races had been shattered, and the Indians vowed to fight to the death before relinquishing their weapons to the soldiers.

While Dunn was contending with the alleged Cheyenne mule thieves, Lieutenant George Eayre, who had been delayed by a snowstorm, was presently moving along a fresh trail that in his opinion had been made by at least a hundred cattle. On April 14, scouts returned to report that they had located a village up ahead. Eayre divided his command into squads, with orders to search the countryside for hostile warriors.

This unsuspecting village of about seventy lodges was occupied by the Crow chief's band. At daylight, a warrior named Antelope Skin had headed out to hunt buffalo when he spotted the approach of the soldiers and galloped back to give the alarm. Every man, woman, and child dashed for the horse herd, leaped astride a mount, and fled, often two or three on one pony. The Cheyennes were escaping from one end of the village as the soldiers entered the other end. Antelope Skin loosed several arrows at the invaders but failed to hit anyone, then dashed away to catch up with the others. One old woman, however, was too weak to ride and was inadvertently left behind.

Eayre and his men halted in the village and commenced looting the possessions of the Cheyenne families—robes, dried meat, blankets, cooking utensils, and other necessities vital to survival. The soldiers then set fire to the lodges and discarded camp equipment and rode off, loaded with plunder, on the trail of the fleeing Indians.

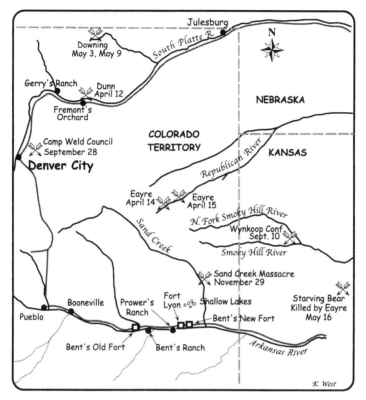

The Cheyenne War of 1864

Later, the family of the old woman who had been abandoned went back to search for her but found no sign. Her family presumed that she had crawled off into the bushes and starved to death.

Lieutenant Eayre's column next came upon the remnants of a small, temporary village. Chief Raccoon's band had been afforded enough warning of the soldiers' approach, which enabled the villagers to pack most of their belongings and flee prior to Eayre's arrival. The soldiers entered this deserted village, found little to loot, but did locate nineteen head of cattle nearby that were part of the missing Irwin, Jackman, and Company herd. The authorities now had, in their opinion, sufficient evidence that the Cheyennes had indeed rustled the herd. Eayre reported "that the Cheyenne Indians are the ones who stole the cattle; that they meditate hostilities against the whites, from the fact of their having first fired upon the command."[10]

Meanwhile, Lieutenant Dunn responded to a report that a herd of cattle had been stolen by Cheyennes from a ranch on Beaver Creek, and in the process two men had been killed. Dunn and thirty troopers rushed to the location where this atrocity was alleged to have taken place but found no evidence of any deaths. The patrol did, however, follow a trail and recovered about forty head of cattle that they surmised had been bypassed by the renegade Indians, who, in their estimation, were probably heading toward the Arkansas River. Dunn returned to Camp Sanborn on April 16, after having ridden 250 miles in 60 hours.[11]

Captain Sanborn forwarded Dunn's report to Colonel Chivington, who responded by ordering additional troops into the saddle to intercept the Indians, who presumably were headed for the Arkansas, and saying to "be sure you have the right ones, then kill them."[12]

On April 18, Eayre gave up his chase, turned about, and marched his column back toward Denver. The lieutenant implied in his report that he had scored a glorious victory by destroying two large Cheyenne villages. And Colonel Chivington, with great embellishment, reported to General Curtis that Eayre's troops had recovered a hundred head of cattle.[13]

These unprovoked attacks on the Cheyennes caused great anxiety within the various camps, with the Dog Soldiers in particular concerned for the safety of the People. Several Dog Men visited Elbridge Gerry's ranch and told him about the actions of the U.S. troops. Gerry notified Major Jacob Downing, who now commanded Camp Sanborn, that the Arkansas River bands had no intention of going to war against the whites and were in fact camping peacefully in their winter grounds. Downing, who was under orders to move against the Indians, if necessary, and see to it that "they are appropriately chastised for their outlawry," was unimpressed. He informed Gerry in no uncertain terms that he intended to attack any Indians whom his unit happened upon, whether they professed peace or not.[14]

At the same time, Agent Samuel Colley wrote to Governor John Evans that his charges had demonstrated their commitment to peace by not accepting the war pipe that had been sent down from the Lakota Sioux. In addition, the Cheyennes had expressed their apprehensions that the trouble on the South Platte River would bring retaliation on their innocent bands.[15]

This nonaggressive posture displayed by the Southerners was the result of the strong influence of Black Kettle and the other peace chiefs. These chiefs exerted great effort to assure that the young, mischievous warriors in their bands were not involved in any endeavors that could be construed as depredations against the white man.

That, however, was not the case up in the Platte River country.

On April 19, a party of drunken Indians—said to be Cheyennes—had chased off some settlers from their ranch and commenced taking whatever they pleased. Major Jacob Downing mounted his troops and pursued the raiders but was unable to overtake them. This brazen intrusion terrified ranchers and settlers along the Platte, who feared that an Indian war had broken out that would threaten travel along the Platte Road.

Downing requested that more troops be placed in the vicinity of these atrocities, on account of the delayed response time from Camp Sanborn, which was some distance away.[16]

Shortly after the ranch invasion, a Cheyenne raiding party ran off a horse herd—said to be worth $800—from the Moore and Kelly Overland Stage station, west of Julesburg. A patrol of soldiers was dispatched to recover the horses and punish the guilty parties. During their pursuit, the troops came upon a Cheyenne camp of eleven lodges and destroyed everything, including many fresh buffalo robes. No Indians were killed, however, and no horses were found.[17]

By this time, Major Jacob Downing was itching for a fight and sent out scouts with instructions to locate a Cheyenne camp—any Cheyenne camp. Downing, riding with forty men, eventually caught up with his scouts, who had captured a half-Cheyenne, half-Sioux man. Downing demanded that this man guide them to any nearby Cheyenne camp. When he refused, the major had an inclination to kill him but reconsidered and resorted to torture to encourage his prisoner to talk. The man was tied up, and the troopers "toasted his shins over a small blaze" until he agreed to serve as guide.[18]

By daylight on May 3, Downing's prisoner had guided the army column to a small Cheyenne camp of five lodges near Cedar Canyon, about sixty miles north of the South Platte. The inhabitants of this particular village—primarily women and children; most of the young men were out hunting—had no idea that there had been recent trouble between the Indians and the U.S. soldiers.

Without warning, Major Downing ordered his men to attack the unsuspecting Cheyennes and commence killing them. The troops advanced, firing their weapons, and cutting the Indians off from their horse herd, which prevented any chance of escape. The old men, women, and children fled into the nearby rock-strewn canyon, which afforded a defensible position. In the ensuing battle, this handful of older Cheyenne men who had once been distinguished warriors bravely held off the soldiers for three hours. Finally, the frustrated Major Downing and his men ran out of ammunition, and the Indians took advantage of this lull to flee.

Downing claimed to have killed at least twenty-five warriors and wounded anywhere from forty to seventy-five—quite an exaggeration— and no prisoners were taken. He later denied that any women and children had been harmed. One soldier had been killed and another wounded. The village was destroyed, and about a hundred horses were confiscated. Downing divided the Cheyenne ponies "among the boys," which was forbidden by law but was more often than not practiced to reward the troops.

The major reported, "Though I think we have punished them pretty severely in this affair, yet I believe now it is but the commencement of war with this tribe, which must result in exterminating them."[19]

The word of this latest unprovoked attack infuriated the Arkansas River bands. It was only with the utmost skill and persuasion that Black Kettle and his fellow peace chiefs managed to calm the warriors enough to keep them from going on the warpath. Black Kettle understood, however, that every village would be on guard, and, if the soldiers chose to attack, the People would certainly defend themselves.

Another testament to the peaceful intentions of the Southerners came from Major Edward W. "Ned" Wynkoop, the new commanding officer at Fort Lyon, who would play an important role in the near future.

The twenty-eight-year-old Wynkoop had been born in Philadelphia, the youngest of eight children in a family engaged in pig iron smelting. He emigrated to Kansas in the mid-1850s and arrived in Colorado during the 1858 gold rush. Wynkoop was one of the early residents of Denver City but saw little riches from panning gold or speculating in real estate and mainly worked at the Criterion Saloon as a bartender. Ned Wynkoop served as the sheriff of Arapahoe County in 1859 and Jefferson Territory in 1860 but was known more for his association with vigilante organizations. In August 1861, he married Lois Wakely, a noted actress on the mining camp theater circuit, with whom he had acted in benefit performances. That same year, Wynkoop received a commission as second lieutenant in the 1st Colorado Volunteers and by 1862 had risen to the rank of major. He fought against the Confederates as a company commander in the 1862 New Mexico battles of Apache Canyon and La Glorieta Pass, afterward remaining on active duty, pursuing hostile Indians and commanding Camp Weld. Wynkoop had been designated the commander of Fort Lyon on May 2, 1864.[20]

Major Wynkoop informed Colonel Chivington on May 9 that he had not heard of any depredations committed by the bands in the Upper Arkansas Agency, and, as far as he could determine, relations were peaceful. Chivington, who had no proof of any Southern involvement in the recent incidents, told Wynkoop to keep a close watch on the Cheyennes in his vicinity.

The major was also ordered, if possible, to arrest George Bent, the former Confederate soldier who had joined the Cheyennes, and place him in irons in the guardhouse. Apparently, Chivington feared that Bent, a member of the Dog Soldier society, would convert that militant faction of Cheyennes into Confederate sympathizers.[21]

Wynkoop may have thought that he had been assigned to an uneventful tour of duty at Fort Lyon, but that was about to change.

Black Kettle's band, along with other Southerners, had wintered on Ash Creek, sixty miles north of Pawnee Creek. By the middle of May, the chief became concerned about that location, due to the nearby attacks by the army. He decided to move his people—250 lodges—and join the bands that were camped on the Smoky Hill River. Black Kettle and Starving Bear (Lean Bear), the head chiefs, rode at the front of this lengthy procession, which halted after a day's march and made camp for the night.

Some men had gone out hunting and, to their surprise, observed a column of soldiers. The Crier made his rounds through the camp to announce the news that soldiers with cannons were heading their way. The People were wary about the motive of these troops, but Chief Starving Bear decided to greet the soldiers in peace. He placed around his neck the medal that President Lincoln had presented to him in 1862 and held the papers from Washington that proved that he was friendly. Chief Starving Bear, accompanied by a number of warriors, rode out to parley with the soldiers.[22]

These army troops were a detachment of eighty-four men, supported by two mountain howitzers, under the command of Lieutenant George Eayre. The lieutenant had received orders from Denver to "kill Cheyennes whenever and wherever found," and he was determined to carry out his instructions to the fullest extent possible.[23]

Starving Bear and his entourage rode to a hilltop, where they were immediately noticed by the soldiers. Eayre formed his troopers into a battle line and waited to discern the intentions of those whom he regarded as hostile warriors.

Starving Bear advised his people to remain behind, while he rode down alone to present his papers and profess peace. Eayre calmly watched the approach of the chief, who was making signs of peace as he rode toward the soldiers. Suddenly, the lieutenant shouted an order. The troopers instantly opened fire at Starving Bear, as well as at the warriors assembled on the hill.

The chief was cut down from his horse by a fusillade of bullets and fell to the ground, where he was repeatedly shot as he lay helpless. Starving Bear, one of the six peace chiefs who had signed the Fort Wise Treaty and a man who had personally professed his desire for peace to President Lincoln, had been killed in cold blood.

The shocked and enraged warriors on the hilltop, led by Wolf Chief, the Southerner, quickly returned fire and raced their ponies down the slope to close with the soldiers. Before long, the field was the scene of mass chaos as the two sides furiously filled the air with bullets and arrows. The soldiers brought the howitzers into play, raining grapeshot in the direction of their enemy, but the hastily fired guns could not be accurately aimed at the speedy, darting ponies and had little effect.

Within moments, small groups of aroused warriors dashed from the main camp to reinforce their comrades on the battlefield. Eventually, as many as five to six hundred Cheyennes and Arapahoes arrived to engage Eayre's detachment of only eighty-four men.

The soldiers were without question in danger of annihilation, when, through the smoke and dust, Black Kettle appeared, riding his pony into the midst of the fray, shouting to the warriors, "Stop the fighting! Do not make war on the whites! Stop the fighting!"

The chief, without regard for his own safety, exposed himself to the rifles of the soldiers and rode into the thickest of the fighting, exhorting his warriors to cease firing and return to the camp. Within a short time, Black Kettle was able to influence most of the Cheyennes and the Arapahoes to leave the field.

Lieutenant George Eayre was savvy enough to know that his men were caught in an extremely precarious position. He likely watched with puzzlement as the warriors gradually broke contact and faded away, perhaps wondering if army reinforcements were approaching or if it was some trick and the Indians had other treachery in mind. The reason for his good fortune, however, was of no consequence to him at that moment. He viewed this lull in the fighting as an opportunity to flee. The lieutenant and his men spurred their horses and retreated as fast as they could ride in the direction of Fort Larned—with one band of incensed warriors, who either had not heard or had ignored Black Kettle, nipping at their heels for some miles.

This act by Black Kettle, which could be called nothing less than intrepid, proved not only that his influence with the warriors was great but that his perception was even greater. He had risked his life, as well as perhaps the wrath of his people, by preventing a slaughter that assuredly would have brought severe reprisals against every band of Cheyennes and Arapahoes in the territory. It also demonstrated how committed he was to peace with the white man, inasmuch as he was willing to die to stop the bloodshed.

Starving Bear had been murdered, however, and Cheyenne custom dictated that vengeance was appropriate. Black Kettle, the warrior, had led and participated in expeditions against enemy tribes to exact revenge for the killing of fellow Cheyennes, and he understood and empathized with the anger and the emotions that burned within the hearts of the warriors who had watched Starving Bear fall. He was also aware, however, that the white man was a far more powerful adversary than any Plains tribe—as evidenced by General Harney in 1854 at Ash Hollow—and it was now the white man who controlled the territory. Any hope for peace, and the survival of the People, would have vanished had Eayre and his eighty-four soldiers been slain by the Cheyennes. This news certainly would have brought more troops than the People had ever encountered, and then peace would have likely come only after every Cheyenne man, woman, and child were dead.

The Cheyennes said that four or five of Eayre's soldiers had been killed and fifteen horses captured during the skirmish. Starving Bear and two other Cheyennes had lost their lives, and countless warriors had been wounded.[24]

Eayre never reported that he had instigated the battle by his ruthless act, and he claimed that at the end of the fight, twenty-eight Indians lay dead—including Black Kettle, who had apparently been mistaken for Starving Bear, and two other chiefs—and an undetermined number had been wounded. Four soldiers had been killed and three wounded.[25]

Later testimony by a soldier who had participated in the skirmish—
as well as by the interpreter John S. Smith—confirmed that Starving
Bear had approached Eayre's troops alone and had been shot down.
Colonel John Chivington, however, was impressed enough with the
fight to commend Eayre. He wrote that "the colonel commanding
district is highly gratified at the conduct of yourself and command,
and will so speak of you in his report to department headquarters."[26]

Black Kettle may have been able to stop the warriors from wiping
out Eayre's command, but he and the other peace chiefs could no
longer restrain all of their young men, the Dog Soldiers in particular,
from raiding the stage road from Fort Larned to Fort Riley, as well as
striking isolated ranches in retaliation for the murder of Starving Bear.

The chiefs assembled in their Council Lodge and discussed the
prospects of a war against the white man. Once again, most of them,
including Black Kettle, spoke for peace.

The Dog Soldiers, however, could not be pacified. They had made
an effort to keep the peace, but the soldiers had violated their trust
with attack after attack on innocent Cheyennes and now they had
killed Starving Bear. Perhaps most important, the soldiers had already
attempted to disarm some Cheyennes, and that would never be tolerated. Tall Bull, White Horse, and Bull Bear informed the chiefs that
they were taking their bands north, to the Republican River country,
where they would smoke the war pipe with the Lakota Sioux. The Dog
Men had declared war on the white man.[27]

Black Kettle and the other bands moved their camp south, across
the Arkansas River, to the Salt Plain on Medicine Lodge Creek, a short
distance from Fort Larned. These Cheyennes and Arapahoes would
remain at that location during May and June and were quiet and at
peace with the whites—even maintaining a cordial relationship with
Major Scott J. Anthony, the commandant at the fort.

It was a different story to the north, however. The Dog Soldiers
and the warriors from Starving Bear's band sought revenge for the
murder of the respected chief and for the lodges and possessions that
had been put to the torch. The Fort Riley-Fort Larned Road was a
scene of massacres and murders as the riled warriors swept across the
territory, striking at any whites whom they happened to find.

Governor Evans wrote to General Curtis on May 28 with a plea
not only to allow the Colorado troops to stay put, but he requested
the authority to raise a militia and receive assistance from federal
troops:

They [the Indians] are in strong force on the Plains. . . . and if the U.S. troops are withdrawn I feel confident that they will wipe out our sparse settlements in spite of any home force we could muster against them. . . . Unless a force can be sent out to chastise this combination severely and at once the delay will cost us a long and bloody war and the loss of a great many lives, with untold amounts of property. . . . In the name of humanity, I ask that our troops now on the border of Kansas may not be taken away from us.[28]

Curtis responded by authorizing Evans to recruit a militia, which commenced immediately, and said he hoped that Federal troops would soon be available.[29]

George Bent summarized the likely motives of Evans and Chivington when he wrote,

I never could understand why the soldiers made those attacks on the Cheyennes in April, 1864. There was no reason for it. One of Colonel Chivington's political enemies once hinted that there was politics behind the whole business. . . . If Chivington did not wish to obey the order to go east, the easiest way out of his difficulty was to attack the Indians and stir them up. The troops would then be needed in Colorado, and the officers would have a splendid chance to make reputations as Indian fighters. On the frontier this was the shortest road to the people's hearts; give the Indians a whipping and the voters would give you any office you asked of them.[30]

Perhaps the Indians by now had been provoked to a greater degree of violence than either Evans or Chivington had originally planned. The governor and his military henchman had likely envisioned a manageable conflict with a few skirmishes and villages burned and, in the end, the two of them emerging as heroic protectors of the people. Now, they faced an aroused Indian populace that threatened not only Colorado Territory but surrounding states and territories. Chivington was nearly buried under an avalanche of reports of hostile Indian movements and ordered every available soldier into the field.

On June 11, an event occurred that struck fear into the hearts of every resident of Colorado Territory. As it was initially reported, four Cheyenne braves had visited a ranch some thirty miles southeast of Denver, where Ward Hungate, his wife, and his four-year-old and infant daughters lived, and left behind a horrifying scene. The body of Ward Hungate was found on the road, riddled with arrows. His wife's nude body showed evidence of torture and multiple violations. The children had also been tortured—throats slashed, heads nearly severed, entrails torn out. They had all been scalped.

Robert North, a white man who had married into the Arapaho tribe, informed Evans that John Notee, an angry Arapaho who was forced to return some stock that he had stolen, was probably behind the murders. Notee vehemently professed his innocence. He was aware, however, that Evans wanted the Cheyennes blamed and therefore hedged when he stated to the governor that he was uncertain as to which tribe members might have committed the atrocity but believed that they very likely were Cheyennes.

Later that year, the Arapaho chief Neva admitted that the Hungate murders had in fact been committed by the Northern Arapaho Roman Nose, also known as Medicine Man, and three of his fellow Arapahoes.[31]

The identities of the actual guilty parties were of little consequence to Evans, who perhaps viewed the atrocity as a manner in which to enlist public outcry as an ally in his quest to reinforce his military presence.

The mutilated bodies of the Hungate family were carried by wagon into Denver and, as one witness stated, were

> placed in a box, side by side, the two children between their parents, and shown to the people from a shed where the City Hall now stands. Everybody saw the four, and anger and revenge mounted all day long as the people filed past or remained to talk over Indian outrages and means of protection and reprisal.[32]

The citizens were not only outraged but panic-stricken. People from outlying ranches and settlements fled to Denver, and, when the rumor spread that the Indians were preparing to attack that city, a general alarm was sounded. Women and children huddled in the Mint and other downtown buildings, while the men built fortifications on the outskirts of town.

Governor Evans appealed directly to Secretary of War Edwin Stanton for assistance and called on every ablebodied man to enroll in the home guard. Although the immediate threat of an attack on Denver soon subsided, preparations continued for war.[33]

At about this time in the conflict, Black Kettle sent messengers to locate William Bent. The chief told Bent about the recent unprovoked attacks on his people and wanted the trader to visit him. One week later, Bent rode out to Black Kettle's village on Coon Creek, and the two men discussed the situation. Black Kettle expressed his desire for peace, a position that he thought was well-known to authorities. He asked Bent why the soldiers had taken to the field against his people, beginning in April, for no apparent reason—and why they had felt the need to disarm the Indians. He was concerned that the retaliation of the warriors for these attacks and the killing of Starving Bear had harmed any chance his people might have for peace.

William Bent could not answer Black Kettle's questions, but he knew who could. He returned to Fort Lyon in time to meet with the visiting Colonel John Chivington. Bent told the colonel about his parley with Black Kettle and that the Cheyennes desired an end to this war. He pointed out that the Plains were teeming with white travelers, and that there was not an adequate force of soldiers to protect every wagon train on every trail. Peace was the practical solution.

Chivington was not moved by Bent's portrayal of Black Kettle's professions of peace, nor was he interested in the suggestions of the trader with the Cheyenne wife and the half-Cheyenne, half-white family, including one son who had served in the Confederate army. The colonel stated that he was not authorized to make peace and was personally "on the warpath." As for the travelers—they would have to protect themselves.

William Bent returned to his ranch, troubled by his conversation with this man who apparently had little knowledge of the Indians and even less of a desire to learn. It was evident that Chivington viewed force—punishment, or perhaps annihilation—as the only manner in which to bring about the end of hostilities.[34]

By this point, Governor John Evans perhaps realized that he had been influenced by Chivington's militant attitude to the point that all control over the Indians had been lost. On June 27, Evans decided to take the initiative away from the military for the moment and issued a proclamation that was intended to separate the friendlies from the hostiles. "The object of this," wrote Evans, "is to prevent friendly Indians from being killed through mistake." At the same time, he vowed to wage a vigorous war against the hostile elements "until they are all effectually subdued." The proclamation read,

Colorado Superintendency Indian Affairs
Denver, June 27th, 1864
To the Friendly Indians of the Plains:

AGENTS, INTERPRETERS, and TRADERS, will inform the friendly Indians of the Plains that some members of their tribes have gone to war with the white people. They steal stock and run it off hoping to escape detection and punishment. In some instances they have attacked and killed soldiers and murdered peaceable citizens. For this the Great Father is angry, and will certainly hunt them out and punish them. But he does not want to injure those who remain friendly to the whites. He desires to protect and take care of them. For this purpose I direct that all friendly Indians keep away from those who are at war, and go to places of safety.

Friendly Arapahoes and Cheyennes, belonging on the Arkansas River, will go to Major Colley, U.S. Indian Agent at Fort Lyon, who will give them provisions and show them a place of safety.

Friendly Kiowas and Comanches will go to Fort Larned, where they will be cared for in the same way.

Friendly Sioux will go to their Agent at Fort Laramie for directions.

Friendly Arapahoes and Cheyennes of the Upper Platte, will go to Camp Collins on the Cache-la-Poudre where they will be assigned a place of safety, and provisions will be given them.

The object of this is to prevent friendly Indians from being killed through mistake. None but those who intend to be friendly with the whites must come to these places. The families of those who have gone to war with the whites must be kept away from among the friendly Indians.

The war on hostile Indians will be continued until they are all effectually subdued.

JOHN EVANS
Governor of Colorado, and Superintendent of Indian Affairs[35]

Emissaries, including William Bent, were dispatched to inform the Indian tribes that those who were friendly should go to the places of safety listed or face an uncertain future at the hands of the Colorado militia.

This appeal by Evans, however, had perhaps come too late. The unprovoked attacks by the soldiers had undermined any faith in the white man's promises, and many Indians who once were friendly chose to join their hostile comrades in a general uprising. Others moved away in order to avoid any contact with whites and were beyond the reach of the emissaries.

Black Kettle's Cheyennes were one of the bands that was unaware that Governor Evans had offered peace and protection to friendly Indians. The Southerners had moved with the Cloud People to the Solomon Fork in central Kansas and gathered in one of the largest villages ever seen on that waterway.

It was here that the tribes offered their renewing ceremonies. After the Sacred Arrows were renewed, it was time to renew the Council of

Forty-four. With the current turmoil that swirled around the tribe, the Council "was careful not to let go of any man who possessed wisdom, bravery, and holiness of special quality." Black Kettle, who had served as chief for nine winters, was formally seated, as were most of the previous chiefs.[36]

Although the Council called for peace with the white man, young men from the various military societies—mainly, the Dog Soldiers—had not, in their opinion, exacted sufficient revenge.

Throughout July and into August, vicious attacks by Cheyenne Dog Soldiers and their allies resulted in many incidents of bloodshed across the region, which, except for several minor reprisals, troops from Colorado, Kansas, and Nebraska were virtually helpless to prevent. Indian war parties had, for all intents and purposes, stopped any movement on the Overland Trail along the South Platte River, and for a period of about six weeks, Denver was cut off from its main supply route.[37]

On August 11, Evans, who had been unable to gain assistance in the form of troops from higher authority and was becoming desperate, issued another proclamation, stating that

> All citizens of Colorado, either individually or in such parties as they may organize, to go in pursuit of all hostile Indians on the plains, scrupulously avoiding those who have responded to my said call to rendezvous at the points indicated; also, to kill and destroy, as enemies of the country, wherever they may be found, all such hostile Indians. And further, as the only reward I am authorized to offer such services, I hereby empower such citizens, or parties of citizens, to take captive, and hold to their own private use and benefit, all the property of said hostile Indians that they may capture, and to receive for all stolen property recovered from said Indians such reward as may be deemed proper and just therefor. . . . The conflict is upon us, and all good citizens are called upon to do their duty for the defence of their homes and families.[38]

How many citizen Indian-hunting expeditions were actually formed cannot be accurately calculated, but, nonetheless, this effort by Evans to subdue his enemy had little effect—raids by large parties of Indians on whites intensified. In one instance, a general attack on a number of settlements by a force of a thousand Apache, Comanche, Cheyenne, and Arapaho warriors was averted when friendly Indians informed the trader Elbridge Gerry, who rushed to Denver to spread the alarm. The hostiles learned that their plans had been revealed and, other than stealing some stock, chose not to attack.

On the Wyoming-Nebraska border, eighty covered wagons were attacked on August 12, with 9 whites killed and about seventy-five horses and mules taken. Three days later an Overland stage with five occupants vanished, and that same day ranches within thirty miles of Denver were looted and burned. At least three more wagon trains were attacked that month, and two white trappers were captured, tortured, and killed near Fort Lyon. Marauding bands of hostile Indians were attacking at will on the trails up the Arkansas, the Platte, and the Smoky Hill—wagon trains, stagecoaches, ranches, and stage stations—with dozens of people killed, women and children carried off, and hundreds of head of horses, mules, and cattle stolen.[39]

By the end of August, however, Black Kettle had exerted every ounce of his authority and persuasive abilities and had successfully called in most of the Cheyenne raiding parties. His efforts, combined with the fact that it was time for the fall buffalo hunt, had a dramatic effect in reducing the number of incidences of violence between Indians and whites.

Now that hostilities had diminished, Black Kettle, ever hopeful that he could convince the white man of his intentions before retaliation such as that administered by General Harney threatened the People, sought a manner in which to express his desire for a lasting peace.

That opportunity was about to present itself at his doorstep.

In late August, William Bent finally found Black Kettle and other Southern chiefs in their camp, which was populated by about two thousand Cheyennes and Arapahoes, with forty lodges of Lakota Sioux nearby, at Hackberry Creek on the south branch of the Smoky Hill River. Bent informed them about the governor's June 27 overture to make peace and strongly urged them to accept.[40]

The chiefs gathered in the Council Lodge, passed the pipe around the sacred circle, offered a prayer for guidance from Maheo and the Sacred Powers, and commenced debate on this most important issue.

The prospect of peace in the eyes of Black Kettle, after this summer of turmoil and violence, could be likened to the sight of his comfortable lodge following a long, arduous journey. He understood that he must make every effort to convince the Council that there was no alternative but to respond favorably to the governor's entreaty. After all, the chiefs had been placed in their positions of authority to make decisions for the good of the tribe—and further hostilities could only cause much weeping and anguish in the camps.

Black Kettle, along with most members of the Council, spoke in favor of making peace with the white man, the exceptions being several Dog Soldier chiefs, who argued for continuing the war. In the end, however, the peace chiefs prevailed. It was decided to send letters to white officials, relaying their willingness to accept this offer of peace and protection and promising to hand over white captives who had been captured during the summer raids.

George Bent and his brother-in-law Edmond Guerrier, both of whom were proficient in English, were asked by Black Kettle to write two identical letters that would be delivered to Agent Samuel Colley and Major Edward Wynkoop, the commander at Fort Lyon.[41]

Wynkoop later said that the letters were in fact addressed to Colley and William Bent.[42]

The text of Black Kettle's letter to Colley, which was written by George Bent, is as follows:

Cheyenne Village Aug 29/64
Maj. Colley:

We received a letter from Bent wishing us to make peace. We held a council in regard to it. All come to the conclusion to make peace with you providing you make peace with the Kiowas, Comanches, Arapahoes, Apaches and Sioux. We are going to send a messenger to the Kiowas and to the other nations about our going to make peace with you. We heard that you [have] some prisoners at Denver. We have seven prisoners of yours which we are willing to give up, providing you give up yours. There are three war parties out yet, and two of Arapahoes. They have been out some time, and expected in soon. When we held this council, there were a few Arapahoes and Sioux present. We want true news from you in return, that is a letter.

Black Kettle &
other Chieves.[43]

The olive branch had been offered by Governor Evans, and Black Kettle and the People had accepted. In the minds of the Cheyennes and the Arapahoes, it would now be a matter of the white man demonstrating his sincerity in bringing about an end to hostilities and making a lasting peace.

7

SEEDS OF BETRAYAL

COUNCIL CHIEF ONE EYE (LONE BEAR) AND EAGLE HEAD, A BOW-string leader, accompanied by One Eye's wife, were chosen to deliver the letters that had been dictated by Black Kettle. On September 4, the three Cheyennes were within several miles of Fort Lyon when they encountered an army patrol. The soldiers took them prisoner, and they were escorted to the fort, where they were presented to Major Edward "Ned" Wynkoop.

Wynkoop accepted the letters and, when assured by Dexter Colley that the messengers were friendly, began questioning the two men with respect to the sincerity of Black Kettle and the other chiefs. One Eye responded that he would guarantee the forthrightness of the chiefs with his life, which was good enough for the major.[1]

Two days later, Major Wynkoop, who was eager to liberate the captives, mounted 127 men, accompanied by two howitzers and John S. Smith—Gray Blanket—as interpreter, and rode out of the fort. One Eye and Eagle Head, who were treated like hostages, guided the way toward the Cheyenne camp on Hackberry Creek.

The column marched for four days, covering about 140 miles, before arriving in the vicinity of the village. On the fifth day, Wynkoop and his troops approached within several miles of the camp when their way was blocked by a battle line of as many as eight hundred painted Cheyenne and Arapaho warriors, who displayed a warlike presence.

Wynkoop, in anticipation of an attack, formed his own troops into a line. He then dispatched One Eye to let the chiefs know that he had received their letter and had come in peace. The major judiciously held back the wife of One Eye and a Cheyenne man who lived near Fort Lyon as hostages in case of trouble. Wynkoop then ordered his men to move slowly forward in battle formation.

The warriors watched this advance, their rifles poised, arrows notched in their bows, apparently ready to engage the soldiers.

Wynkoop feared that a fight was imminent and, inasmuch as his command was outnumbered by at least five to one, realized that they likely would be annihilated.

At that moment, Black Kettle appeared on the field and ordered the People to hold their fire, that the soldiers had come in peace, at his request, and they should be permitted to safely pass.

The Cheyennes and the Arapahoes lowered their weapons but closed in on all sides to surround the soldiers and in that manner escorted them the remaining miles toward their camp. Wynkoop eventually halted his column in what he considered a favorable defensive position and ordered the men to bivouac for the night.[2]

The next morning, September 10, Black Kettle, White Antelope, and other chiefs, including the Arapahoes Little Raven and Left Hand and the Dog Soldier chief Bull Bear, visited the soldiers' camp to parley with Major Wynkoop. A number of warriors had also entered the camp, and before long, one of them attempted to borrow some of a soldier's tobacco without asking, which was a common practice among the Cheyennes. Another warrior was rudely pushed away from inspecting one of the howitzers. Insults were hurled from both sides. One warrior armed his bow with an arrow; one trooper drew his revolver. Black Kettle was summoned and quickly soothed tempers.

The council began with the customary smoking of the pipe, with John S. Smith interpreting and George Bent on hand at Ned Wynkoop's request to make certain that Smith's words were true.

Bent was a fugitive whom Colonel Chivington had earlier ordered Wynkoop to arrest on sight and throw into the Fort Lyon guardhouse. Evidently, Wynkoop had placed his faith in William Bent's son, perhaps from a past or a present family friendship. The major, of course, was in no position to apprehend Bent, but his use of Bent as an interpreter perhaps indicated that he had no intention of doing so anyway. Wynkoop, who was on friendly terms with Chivington, likely did not share his commander's paranoia that Bent, the former Confederate soldier, was a threat to convince the Indians to align with the South. Bent had left his service behind and was now a member of the Cheyennes, his mother's tribe, and apparently posed no threat to incite sympathies for the Confederacy.

It might also be noted that Wynkoop did not share the philosophy of genocide concerning the Indians that was embraced by Chivington and many of his fellow Coloradans. He believed that hostilities could and should be prevented—a position that for obvious reasons he did not readily advertise. Wynkoop had, however, demonstrated his earnestness to do his part in that process by boldly marching into the midst of hostile territory for this peace parley.

Major Wynkoop presented the letters that One Eye had delivered, and, inasmuch as they bore the name "Black Kettle"—who ever since the Fort Wise Treaty had been viewed by the whites as *the* prominent Southern Cheyenne chief—the major addressed his remarks primarily to Black Kettle.

Wynkoop read aloud the letter that Black Kettle had dictated and assured the chiefs that he believed that they were acting in good faith and truly wanted peace. He then read the June 27 proclamation written by Governor Evans. The major told them that he was not a big enough chief to negotiate terms of peace but would arrange a meeting for the chiefs with the governor of Colorado Territory. The chiefs, however, must demonstrate their peaceful intentions by handing over to him the white captives whom they held. Wynkoop stated that he had not been aware that any Cheyenne prisoners were being held in Denver. If that was true, however, he admitted that he could not guarantee that they would be released, that the decision was not his to make but that of the authorities in Denver. But, the major said, it would serve the tribes well with respect to receiving their prisoners back if they would release their white captives to him.[3]

The chiefs were not well deposed to the idea that they should release their prisoners but receive nothing in return. They argued among themselves and vehemently chastised Wynkoop for trying to take advantage of them, accusing him of treating them like fools or children for asking them to hand over their prisoners with no guarantee of reciprocation.

One chief demanded that the major tell them why he said that he had come in peace but had brought along armed men and powerful guns. Wynkoop candidly responded that he was aware that some militants may oppose his presence, and he was prepared to fight, if necessary. He added that he did not want trouble and hoped that they could come to an understanding that would permit him to return with the white captives.

The chiefs then took turns hurling a verbal barrage at Wynkoop—many airing grievances, threatening him, or taunting him, while several others encouraged peaceful relations. Finally, One Eye stepped forward and began apologizing to Wynkoop for the behavior of his peers.[4]

Wynkoop described Black Kettle, while the chiefs were speaking, as "one who had stamped on every lineament, the fact that he was born to command, he while all the balance of the council were snarling like wolves, sat calm, dignified, immovable with a slight smile on his face."[5]

Black Kettle was also keenly aware of Wynkoop's demeanor. The chief had been intently listening, as well as studying and assessing Wynkoop's reaction to this most intimidating situation. When One Eye had finished his apology, Black Kettle mumbled a few words, waved his hand, and the Council Lodge became silent.

The chief rose to his feet, gathered his blankets around him, and addressed Ned Wynkoop. He summarized the tragic events of the past several months: how he had made efforts for peace but had been rebuffed; how his people had been treated badly by the whites; how he had convinced most of the war parties to come in and how the whites were the aggressors; and how he was now encouraged by the governor's words of peace in William Bent's message and the fact that Major Wynkoop had responded to his letter by coming to talk.

Black Kettle then moved to Wynkoop's side, took the major's hand in his own, and led the white man to the center of the circle. His voice was commanding as he spoke to the assembled chiefs.

> This white man is not here to laugh at us, nor does he regard us as children, but on the contrary unlike the balance of his race, he comes with confidence in the pledges given by the Red man. He has been told by one of our bravest warriors, that he should come and go unharmed, he did not close his ears, but with his eyes shut followed on the trail of him whom we had sent as our messenger. It was like coming through the fire, for a white man to follow and believe in the words of one of our race, whom they have always branded as unworthy of confidence or belief. He has not come with a forked tongue or with two hearts, but his words are straight and his heart single. Had he told us that he would give us peace, on the condition of our delivering to him the white prisoners, he would have told us a lie. For I know that he cannot give us peace, there is a greater Chief in the far off Camp of the White Soldiers; who must talk to one even still mightier, to our Great Father in Washington, who must tell his Soldiers to bury the hatchet, before we can again roam over the Prairies in safety and hunt the Buffaloe. Had this white soldier come to us with crooked words, I myself would have despised him; and would

have asked whether he thought we were fools, that he could sing sweet words into our ears, and laugh at us when we believed them. But he has come with words of truth; and confidence, in the pledges of his red brothers, and whatever be the result of these deliberations; he shall return unharmed to his lodge from whence he came. It is I, Make-ta-va-tah that says it.

Black Kettle concluded by telling Wynkoop that he should "return upon the trail on which you came with your soldiers, until the sun has kissed the prairie, there camp and remain until another sun has gone; before that time passes you will have news from Make-ta-va-tah [Black Kettle]; our Chiefs will spend the night in Council."

Ned Wynkoop remarked that as Black Kettle spoke,

I noticed that the cloud upon the countenances of the stern looking chiefs surrounding me was gradually dispelled. And I frequently caught their eloquent eyes from which all suspicion had fled, fastened upon me with a kindly expression. And upon the close of his remarks, they arose and each and everyone advanced, shook me by the hand exclaiming with their usual gutteral expression of satisfaction: "How."[6]

There can be no question that Black Kettle had, at least for the present, assumed the role as the principal chief of the Southern Cheyennes, not only in the eyes of the whites but in the hearts and the minds of the People. His steadfast stand for peace, based on his extraordinary perception and understanding of the political climate, had convinced the People that his wisdom and guidance would be of utmost importance if they were to be successful in achieving the goal of harmony with the white man.

Major Wynkoop heeded Black Kettle's words and marched his troopers away from the Cheyenne camp to a place about twelve miles distant, where a defensive position was formed. The major, wary but having no choice other than to honor the promise made by Black Kettle that they would not be harmed, would wait in that location for the decision of the chiefs and the possible return of the white captives. Many of his troops, however, did not share Wynkoop's confidence in Black Kettle's ability to restrain the warriors and demanded that they march without delay for the fort. The consensus opinion of the soldiers was that the "savages" intended to initiate a surprise attack that would surely overwhelm them. Major Wynkoop refused to leave and endured a sleepless night as he contended with this internal rebellion, all the while knowing that he was surrounded by thousands of Indians, most of whom were hostile toward whites.[7]

Meanwhile, the Council Chiefs discussed their parley with Wynkoop, and, although the Dog Soldiers were defiant, the majority counseled for peace. Black Kettle immediately set in motion the difficult task of procuring the white captives, several of whom were with the Sioux. Tribal custom dictated that these captives could not be simply taken away from the owners but must be purchased.

The first captive delivered to Wynkoop, sixteen-year-old Laura Roper, was brought into the soldier camp by the Arapaho chief Left Hand at about noon the following day. This young lady, who was married, told Wynkoop that she had been treated well and had been promised all along that she would be released as soon as the whites made peace.

Black Kettle demonstrated his personal commitment to the peace process by securing three white captives in exchange for trading his own valuable ponies to the captives' owners. The day after Left Hand's visit, the Cheyenne chief rode into the soldier camp with Isabelle Eubanks or Ewbanks, a five-year-old whose mother had hanged herself while in captivity; Daniel Marble, age seven or eight, who was disappointed that he could not keep his Indian pony; and Ambrose Usher or Archer, a seven- or eight-year-old, who told Wynkoop that he would just as soon stay with the Indians.

The other three captives, Black Kettle told Wynkoop, were located quite a distance away up on the Republican River and would be delivered as soon as possible.

Ned Wynkoop was so overcome by emotion that he had to separate himself from the others in order to hide the fact that tears had welled in his eyes.[8]

Black Kettle announced to Wynkoop that he and a delegation of chiefs and their families would return with the soldiers to Fort Lyon, then travel with the major to Denver for an audience with Governor John Evans. Accompanying Black Kettle would be the Cheyennes White Antelope and Lone Bear and the Dog Soldier Bull Bear, as well as the Arapahoes Left Hand, Neva, Heap of Buffalo, and Knock Knee.

Upon arrival at Fort Lyon, Agent Samuel Colley distributed annuities to the chiefs, and Major Wynkoop supplemented those supplies with army rations. The goods were then transported back to the village on Hackberry Creek, with word that the chiefs were safe and would soon be going to Denver for the peace council.

When the annuities were received at the village, the various bands, which were under the impression that they were now protected from an attack by the army, scattered about the countryside and headed for their traditional hunting grounds.

The Cheyenne bands of Black Kettle, White Antelope, and War Bonnet, as well as several Arapaho bands, had moved south, camping on the night of September 23 near the head of Ash Creek, a tributary of the Pawnee Fork that flowed into the Arkansas River. Word had been passed to them by the Lakota Sioux that the Pawnees were hunting on the Republican, and six men, including White Leaf and Wolf Robe, decided to leave camp and raid the hated Wolf People.[9]

They were not the only ones, however, who were traveling in that vicinity. On September 22, Major General James G. Blunt had left Fort Larned with four hundred men and two mountain howitzers, remarking that he wanted to "steal a march on the red devils and give them a chastising, which is the only thing that will do them good—a little killing."[10]

White Leaf, who carried the pipe, and his Cheyenne war party had halted for the night about ten miles from the main camp. The next morning, they awoke to observe soldiers galloping toward them. The alarm was given, and the six men dashed to mount their ponies— five succeeded, but White Leaf was left to run on foot behind the others as they fled in the direction of the main village.

These soldiers were members of General Blunt's advance guard, fifty-nine men under the command of Major Scott J. Anthony, and ahead of the column was a detachment of Delaware scouts, who commenced firing at the fleeing Cheyennes. White Leaf, still on foot, bravely held off the pursuers as he trailed the others.

The sound of rifle shots soon could be heard at the main camp. Warriors quickly gathered up their weapons and ponies and raced off in small groups to assist their beleaguered brethren.

When the Cheyennes and the Arapahoes arrived at the scene of the firing, they assembled into a larger force and managed to surround Major Anthony and his command. The soldiers moved into a defensive position on a small hill and exchanged fire with the warriors who circled around them. White Horse, an Arapaho, brazenly charged into the soldiers but was killed, then scalped by the Delaware scouts.

Before long, however, the warriors became aware that General Blunt and his column—more than three hundred troops strong—were charging toward the battlefield. Just like in the movies, the cavalry had arrived in the nick of time to save a stranded detachment.

The Cheyennes and the Arapahoes, realizing that they could not defeat the soldiers now that reinforcements had arrived, wisely broke contact and pulled back toward their camp. The warriors delayed the troops long enough for the women to tear down the lodges and pack their possessions, and the bands hastily retreated. Blunt and his troopers chased them for some time but gave up when their horses played out.

General Blunt reported that he counted nine dead Indians on the field and speculated that others had been killed but were carried away by their comrades. Army losses were reported as two soldiers killed and seven wounded. The Cheyenne narrative by George Bent noted that only one warrior, the Arapaho White Horse, had been lost.

This skirmish, however, served as notice to the Cheyennes and the Arapahoes that peace might be at hand, depending on Black Kettle and the others at their parley in Denver, but until a truce had been confirmed, it would be prudent to avoid the army. These bands had been planning to winter at Fort Larned but instead camped at the mouth of Running Creek, in the Smoky Hill River country, to await word from Black Kettle and the other chiefs.[11]

On September 28, 1864, Black Kettle and his fellow chiefs were granted an audience with Governor John Evans at Camp Weld. Also in attendance were Colonel John Chivington, commanding the district of Colorado; Colonel George L. Shoup, 3rd Colorado Volunteer Cavalry; Major Edward Wynkoop; U.S. Indian Agent Simon Whitely, who would act as clerk and record the proceedings; John S. Smith, who would serve as interpreter; and an unknown number of private citizens and army officers.

Evans and Chivington were not particularly pleased about the appearance of the Indians. Chivington in particular had become quite overbearing. He was contemptuous of legal, ethical, or military authority, and behaved as if he could do whatever he pleased without being accountable to anyone. The two men were unyielding in their opinion that the Indians had declared war and no peace could be made until the guilty parties had been punished.[12]

Black Kettle and the chiefs were escorted into the room of dignitaries and made it a point to shake hands with everyone present. The chiefs then offered the pipe, which was smoked as a symbol that they would speak the truth.

Evans then told John Smith to ask the Indians why they were there.

Black Kettle, who was the presumed head of the delegation of chiefs, was the first to speak.

> On sight of your circular of June 27, 1864, I took hold of the matter, and have now come to talk to you about it. I told Mr. Bent, who brought it, that I accepted it, but that it would take some time to get all my people together, many of my young men being absent; and I have done everything in my power since then to keep peace with the whites.
>
> As soon as I could get my people together we held a council and got a half-breed who was with us to write a letter to inform Major Wynkoop, or other military officer nearest us, of our intention to comply with the terms of the circular. Major Wynkoop was kind enough to receive the letter, and visited us in camp, to whom we delivered four white prisoners—one other, Mrs. Snyder, having killed herself. There are two women and one child yet in our camp, whom we will deliver as soon as we can get them in.
>
> We have come with our eyes shut, following his handful of men, like coming through the fire. All we ask is that we may have peace with the whites; we want to hold you by the hand. You are our father; we have been travelling through a cloud; the sky has been dark ever since the war began. Those braves who are with me are all willing to do what I say. We want to take good tidings home to our people, that they may sleep in peace. I want you to give all the chiefs of the soldiers here to understand that we are for peace, and that we have made peace, that we may not be mistaken by them for enemies.
>
> I have not come here with a little wolf's bark, but have come to talk plain with you. We must live near the buffalo or starve. When we came here we came free, without any apprehension, to see you, and when I go home and tell my people that I have taken your hand and the hands of all the chiefs here in Denver, they will feel well, and so will all the different tribes of Indians on the plains, after we have eaten and drunk with them.

Governor Evans apparently was not impressed by Black Kettle's speech and coldly replied,

> I am sorry you did not respond to my appeal at once; you have gone into an alliance with the Sioux, who were at war with us; you have done a great deal of damage, have stolen stock, and now have possession of it. However much a few individuals may have tried to keep the peace, as a nation you have gone to war; while we have been spending thousands of

dollars in opening farms for you and making preparations to feed, protect, and make you comfortable, you have joined our enemies and gone to war. . . . your people went away and smoked the "war pipe" with our enemies.

Black Kettle answered, "I don't know who could have told you this."

"No matter who said this," Evans responded. "But your conduct has proved to my satisfaction that such was the case." Evans had in fact been told just the opposite by Agent Samuel Colley on more than one occasion.

"This is a mistake," Black Kettle and several others chiefs protested. "We have made no alliance with the Sioux or anyone else."

This denial was so emphatic that Evans was compelled to explain that smoking the "war pipe" was a figurative term, but their conduct had been such as to show that they had an understanding with other tribes.

Several chiefs said, "We acknowledge that our actions have given you reason to believe this."

Evans said through the interpreter, "So far as making a treaty now is concerned, we are in no condition to do it; your young men are on the warpath, my soldiers are preparing for the fight. You so far have had the advantage, but the time is near at hand when the plains will swarm with United States soldiers. I understand that these men who have come to see me now have been opposed to the war all the time, but that their people have controlled them, and they could not help themselves. Is that so?"

"It has been so."

Evans continued,

The fact that they have not been able to prevent their people from going to war in the past spring, when there was plenty of grass and game, makes me believe that they will not be able to make a peace which will last longer than until winter is past. . . . The time when you can make war best is in the summer time; the time when we can make war best is in the winter. You so far have had the advantage; my time is fast coming.

I have learned that you understand that as the whites are at war among themselves, you think you can now drive the whites from this country, but this reliance is false. The Great Father at Washington has men enough to drive all the Indians off the plains, and whip the rebels at the same time. Now, the war with the whites is nearly through, and the

Great Father will not know what to do with his soldiers, except to send them after the Indians on the plains.

My proposition to the friendly Indians has gone out. I shall be glad to have them all come in under it. I have no new proposition to make. Another reason that I am not in condition to make a treaty is, that war had begun, and the power to make a treaty of peace has passed from me to the great war chief. My advice to you is to turn on the side of the government, and show by your acts that friendly disposition you profess to me. It is utterly out of the question for you to be at peace with us while living with our enemies and being on friendly terms with them. The only way you can show this friendship is by making some arrangement with the soldiers to help them.

Black Kettle spoke. "We will return with Major Wynkoop to Fort Lyon; we will then proceed to our village and take back to my young men every word you say. I cannot answer for all of them, but think there will be but little difficulty in getting them to assent to help the soldiers."

Major Wynkoop addressed Black Kettle. "Did not the Dog Soldiers agree, when I had my council with you, to do whatever you said, after you had been here?"

"Yes," Black Kettle replied.

Governor Evans explained that if the Indians did not have an arrangement with the soldiers, they would all be treated as enemies.

White Antelope, who wore the medal that he had been given on his trip to Washington, rose to speak.

I understand every word you have said, and will hold on to it. I will give you an answer directly. The Cheyennes, all of them, have their ears open this way, and they will hear what you say. I am proud to have seen the chief of all whites in this country. I will tell my people. Ever since I went to Washington and received this medal, I have called all white men as my brothers, but other Indians have since been to Washington and got medals, and now the soldiers do not shake hands, but seek to kill me. What do you mean by us fighting your enemies? Who are they?

"All Indians who are fighting us," Evans said.

White Antelope asked, "How can we be protected from the soldiers on the plains?"

"You must make that arrangement with the military chief."

"I fear these new soldiers who have gone out may kill some of my people while I am here."

"There is a great danger of it."

"When we sent our letter to Major Wynkoop, it was like going through a strong fire, or blast, for Major Wynkoop's men to come to our camp; it was the same for us to come to see you. . . . When Major Wynkoop came, we proposed to make peace. He said he had no power to make peace, except to bring us here and return us safe."

"Whatever peace you make," Evans repeated, "must be with the soldiers, and not with me."

White Antelope attempted to explain that this war had been initiated by the soldiers, and other chiefs wanted to tell their side of the story, but Evans cut them short. Instead, the governor began interrogating White Antelope, Neva, and Bull Bear about which tribe was responsible for specific attacks and raids that had occurred in the recent past, as well as about the present locations of these tribes. The chiefs answered each question until late in the day.

It was then that the huge, dominating figure of Colonel John Chivington rose to tower over the chiefs. Chivington had said nothing all day, apparently content to allow the governor to conduct the meeting. It was as if he had no interest in hearing what the chiefs had to say about their role in the conflict or in learning the identities of those who were the true perpetrators. His mind had already been made up with respect to the Indians, and he could not be swayed at this late hour by what he would have perceived as baseless pledges of peace from untrustworthy sources.

Chivington said, "I am not a big war chief, but all the soldiers in this country are at my command. My rule of fighting white men or Indians is, to fight them until they lay down their arms and submit to military authority. You are nearer Major Wynkoop than anyone else, and you can go with him when you get ready to do that."

The Camp Weld council then adjourned.

Black Kettle embraced both Governor Evans and Major Wynkoop, then shook hands with everyone else. He told John S. Smith that he was satisfied that peace for the People was at hand. The chiefs then posed for the photographer, which produced the only two known photos of Black Kettle.[13]

Smith later testified with his overview of the meeting:

He [Governor Evans] told them he had nothing to do with them; that they would return with Major Wynkoop, who would reconduct them in safety, and they would have to await the action of military authorities.

Colonel Chivington, then in command of the district, also told them that they would remain at the disposal of Major Wynkoop until higher authority had acted in their case. The Indians appeared to be perfectly satisfied, presuming that they would eventually be all right as soon as these authorities could be heard from, and expressed themselves so.[14]

The chiefs departed the meeting in high spirits about what had been said, with one exception. They were puzzled by the closing statement that had been made by Col. John Chivington and were uncertain about its meaning.

Black Kettle and the other chiefs would soon learn that Chivington's intentions were anything but honorable—and the Cheyennes would suffer the tragic consequences.

The Council Chiefs returned with Major Wynkoop to Fort Lyon. Wynkoop, with nothing mentioned otherwise, worked under the assumption that the proclamation that Evans had issued on July 27, offering military protection to any tribe that chose to surrender, remained in effect. He advised the Cheyennes and the Arapahoes that they should move their people to the vicinity of Fort Lyon and camp there until word regarding their disposition had been received from the big chief.

Black Kettle professed his faith in Ned Wynkoop's words through the interpreter John Smith. Then he and the other chiefs, encouraged that peace was within their grasp, rode to their village in the Smoky Hill country.

The People tore down the lodges, packed their possessions, and prepared to move closer to Fort Lyon.[15]

Major Wynkoop sent a dispatch to General Samuel Curtis, outlining his plans for peace: "I think that if some terms are made with these Indians, I can arrange matters so, by bringing their villages under my direct control, that I can answer for their fidelity."[16]

Black Kettle led the Southern people to Sand Creek, known to them as Dry Creek, about forty miles northeast of Fort Lyon.

Bull Bear, the Dog Soldier chief, meanwhile, headed up to the Republican River to relay the news from the Camp Weld council. The Dog Soldiers were not impressed by Bull Bear's summary of the talks and refused to—what they termed—surrender to the white man. Instead, they would move deeper into the heart of their hunting grounds and continue the war. Even as Black Kettle and the People headed toward Sand Creek, the Dog Soldiers raided along the Platte

Road and were chased by Colorado cavalrymen, who rode under Colonel Chivington's orders: "Kill all the Indians you come across."[17]

When the People were situated at the Smoky Hill Crossing of Sand Creek, Black Kettle, White Antelope, War Bonnet, and several Arapaho chiefs returned to Fort Lyon. Major Wynkoop distributed rations and reiterated his promise that they would be safe under army protection while department headquarters decided where to permanently locate them.

The relationship between the visiting chiefs and the soldiers, especially the officers, was quite friendly, which encouraged Little Raven to immediately move his 113 lodges—about 650 Arapahoes—to the fort. These people were welcomed by Major Wynkoop, food was distributed, and the Arapahoes acquired additional supplies by trading buffalo robes.[18]

By mid-October, General James Blunt heard rumors that Major Wynkoop had been issuing rations to hostile Indians. This word was passed on to Colonel John Chivington, and Wynkoop became the target of his wrath. The colonel was in no mood to make peace with Indians or tolerate those who did.

On October 17, Special Order No. 4 stated that Major Edward W. Wynkoop was relieved of his command at Fort Lyon and would be replaced by Major Scott J. Anthony. Furthermore, Major Anthony would "investigate and report on the rumor in regard to the treaty made at Fort Lyon" and "investigate and report upon unofficial rumors that reached headquarters that certain officers had issued stores, goods, or supplies to hostile Indians in direct violation of orders from the general commanding the department." Ned Wynkoop had been relieved of duty in favor of Anthony, who was a confirmed Indian hater. Chivington had placed his man in charge, replacing one who advocated peace.

Anthony took command of Fort Lyon on November 2 under strict orders from Major General Samuel R. Curtis "not to permit or allow any agreement or treaty with the Indians without his approval . . . [or] allow any Indians to approach any post on any excuse whatsoever."[19]

Anthony faced a dilemma with the presence of the Arapahoes. He fed them for ten days—in disobedience of orders—then told the Cloud People to leave and go hunt buffalo. Little Raven had no choice but to follow the major's orders, and he moved his band down the Arkansas, fifty-five miles below Fort Lyon. Chief Left Hand and a few Arapaho lodges decided to join Black Kettle's Cheyennes at Sand Creek.

Ned Wynkoop had remained at the fort and made certain that Anthony was aware of the promises that he had given the Indians, the details of which were common knowledge to the fort's other officers. Wynkoop also was present when Black Kettle rode into the fort to visit with the new commander. Wynkoop spoke first at this meeting and assured Black Kettle that Major Anthony would abide by the promises between them.

The Cheyenne chief then addressed Major Anthony, telling him that the People desired peace and did not want to fight the white man anymore. Black Kettle also asked Anthony whether he had the authority to make peace with them.

Anthony answered that he was under orders not to have anything to do with the Indians and could not personally make peace. This order applied to Black Kettle in particular, due to the depredations that were being committed along the Platte that were being blamed on his band. Anthony added, however, that he now realized that reports that Black Kettle's people were involved were not true, and that he would immediately inform headquarters of that fact. Anthony advised Black Kettle that he had no objection to the Cheyennes camping at their present location on Sand Creek, and that he would let them know as soon as he heard anything from headquarters. He also apologized that he could not issue them any rations but gave permission for the young men to go out and hunt buffalo. In so many words, Anthony had pledged to continue Ned Wynkoop's policy of peaceful coexistence.[20]

Wynkoop remembered that Anthony told Black Kettle "that though acting under strict orders, under the circumstances, he could not materially differ from the course which I had pursued, and allowed them to remain in the vicinity of the post, with their families, assuring them perfect safety until such time as positive orders should be received from headquarters in regard to them."[21]

Black Kettle had been apprehensive about this change of command at Fort Lyon. The chief and Ned Wynkoop, who had been given the name "Tall Chief," had established a friendship based on mutual respect and trust in the days since the Camp Weld council. Black Kettle's doubts were removed at this meeting, however, and he stated that he was perfectly satisfied with what had been said by Major Anthony. He had intended to move his tribe to the Purgatorie River but would abide by Anthony's wishes that they remain at Sand Creek.

Black Kettle spent that night as a guest of John Prowers. Prowers, who had married the daughter of Chief One Eye, was viewed as a trusted friend and an adviser by the Cheyennes. He had worked for William Bent, until buying some land and operating his own ranch near Fort Lyon, which raised government stock.

Black Kettle told Prowers that he was happy about what had transpired in the meeting with Anthony and hoped that peace would soon come to the People. He lamented about Ned Wynkoop's removal from command but believed that Scott Anthony would carry on the policies of the Tall Chief. Prowers was asked his opinion and responded that from what he had heard, everything looked good for the peace process. His words pleased Black Kettle, who again voiced his hope for a swift end to hostilities.

In the morning, John Prowers presented Black Kettle with gifts of coffee, sugar, rice, flour, and bacon. He also gave the chief a quantity of tobacco, which had been supplied by the officers at the post as a special gift to the chiefs. In fact, several of the officers were on hand for this presentation, and Black Kettle personally shook their hands and thanked them. In Cheyenne culture, tobacco was a sign of peace, and this gesture by the officers further bolstered Black Kettle's belief that peace was at hand.

Major Anthony had promised to visit before Black Kettle departed but instead sent John S. Smith. Anthony relayed his apologies, duty had called him elsewhere, but he instructed Smith to let the chief know that he was welcome any time at the post and could remain camping at Sand Creek, where he would have nothing to fear from the soldiers.[22]

Unquestionably, Black Kettle's heart soared as he and the others rode away from Fort Lyon to their camp on Sand Creek. He had put forth great effort, at personal risk, and now the white man had spoken the words that he had wanted to hear.

Perhaps a wave of nostalgia engulfed him as he envisioned a village reminiscent of the old days, when the People had been free to celebrate the simple pleasures of daily life. Never again did his ears wish to capture the present sounds of outraged warriors calling for war, women weeping for lost loved ones, and the mournful cries of hungry babies. The People would survive as a tribe, and he would do everything within his power to bring about that glorious day when peace prevailed.

What Black Kettle did not know was that Major Scott Anthony was a deceitful man, who apparently did not regard promises made to those he considered savages as binding. The assurances that Anthony had made from the time Black Kettle arrived until his departure had been outright lies, intended to keep the Cheyenne camp at Sand Creek quiet until he could obtain reinforcements and take to the field.

In the days following the parley with Black Kettle, Anthony sent a flurry of dispatches to General Curtis at headquarters that revealed these intentions. He informed Curtis that additional manpower would be required to mount an effective attack on the Cheyennes. Anthony did not worry about his capabilities against the small band that was camped on Sand Creek, but he would need a stronger force if troops were to attack the larger Dog Soldier and Sioux camps on the head-waters of the Smoky Hill River.[23]

On November 23, Governor John Evans conveniently embarked on a journey to the nation's capital. He was on a mission to convince the War Department that he would require additional troops and equipment if he were to succeed in keeping the western trails free of hostiles. Evidence clearly reveals that Evans left Denver with the knowledge that Colonel Chivington was planning to mount a major campaign against the Cheyennes.[24]

Major Ned Wynkoop finally realized that he had made a tactical error in his quest for peace. According to the chain of command, the person who could grant treaty conditions was not Chivington but the department commander, General Samuel Curtis. Wynkoop should have secured pledges from the general before making promises based on offhand remarks made by Evans and Chivington.

With that in mind, Wynkoop departed Fort Lyon on November 26 and headed for Fort Leavenworth, Kansas, in an effort to both clear his name of any wrongdoing with respect to issuing rations to the Indians and to promote his peace policy. He carried in his posses-sion two letters testifying to support for his recent promises to Black Kettle and the Southerners.

One of the letters had been written by Lieutenant Joseph A. Cramer and had been signed by every officer at Fort Lyon—as well as by the Indian agent Samuel Colley—with an endorsement by Major Anthony, which bore "testimony to the fact that the course adopted and carried out by you was the only proper one to pursue."

The other letter had been signed by twenty-seven residents of the Arkansas River Valley, indicating a "desire to express to you [Wyn-koop] our hearty sympathy in your laudable efforts to prevent further danger and bloodshed, and sincerely congratulate you in your noble efforts to do what we consider right, politic, and just."[25]

That same day, Major Anthony dispatched John S. Smith, a teamster named Watson Clark, and a trooper, Private David Lauderback, to Black Kettle's Sand Creek village. The publicized purpose of this trip was for the men to engage in their normal business of trading for buffalo robes. All three, however, had agreed to spy on the People and inform Anthony and Samuel Colley about the size of the camp, what was being planned by the inhabitants, and any other information that might be of interest to the army.

The three white men were not the only source that Anthony had placed in that camp. Cheyenne Chief One Eye, the man who had delivered Black Kettle's letter to Fort Lyon to begin this peace process, had signed on as a spy for $125 a month and rations. This chief was also expected to travel to the Dog Soldier and Sioux camps at the headwaters of the Smoky Hill and report any movement by those warriors. One Eye, a trusted member of the Council of Forty-four, had agreed to betray his own people.[26]

On November 28, Ned Wynkoop was overtaken by a messenger from Black Kettle, who warned him that he was riding on a collision course with a war party of two hundred Sioux warriors. The major cautiously continued on his journey and arrived safely at Fort Larned to learn that this war party had indeed been sighted in the location that Black Kettle had indicated.[27]

That night of November 28, 1864, Black Kettle and his people retired to their lodges on Sand Creek and heard nothing but a reassuring silence, the sound of peace, that engendered a sense of security.

Out in the bitter cold night, some forty miles away, that silence was being interrupted by the more ominous sound of a multitude of horse's hooves crunching against the ice-crusted prairie of eastern Colorado Territory. A group of determined men, led by a Methodist minister turned diabolical militia commander, was riding toward a rendezvous with infamy.

8

THE SAND CREEK MASSACRE

The frosty pre-dawn of november 29, 1864, brought the promise of another tranquil day to the Southern Cheyenne camp nestled within the arcing north bank of Sand Creek, at a point known as Big South Bend. The buffalo-hide lodges—more than 100, which were home to about 500 of Black Kettle's people, and 10 lodges with 50 Arapaho under Chief Left Hand—were arranged in the traditional circle that spread over a half mile in diameter, broken only by an opening that faced the rising sun. Nearby, beyond a scattering of cottonwood and willow that grew along the bend, grazed a sizable horse herd, in addition to another smaller herd below the camp.[1]

The People had been reassured by Black Kettle's recent trip to Fort Lyon that they would be safe and secure in this remote place, far away from the militant Dog Soldier camps on the Smoky Hill, where the soldiers were more likely to attack. After months of living with the fear that soldiers would appear without warning and, at the least, destroy all their possessions and the stores that had been gathered for the winter, they could now seek contentment and raise their families in peace.

The men remained inside the lodges, wrapped snugly in warm buffalo robes on this chilly morning, while the women went about their morning chores. Campfires had been kept burning throughout the cold night and were now replenished in preparation for the morning meal. The women paid a visit to the creek to draw fresh water—yesterday's water was dead and was emptied out in favor of living water. Pleasant greetings and children's chatter could be heard as they dipped their containers into the faint trickle of flowing water or into one of the small, ice-crusted puddles in this mostly dry creek bed.

The serenity of the moment ended abruptly when the natural rhythm of the day was interrupted by a rumbling noise that emanated from beyond the eastern horizon. The startled women hurried back to camp to spread the word—buffalo! That distinct pounding of hooves must indicate that a herd of buffalo was approaching. The entire village was roused. Men, women, and children burst from the lodges with great anticipation of viewing this welcome sight.

Those oncoming hooves, however, did not belong to buffalo but to cavalry horses, about 750 strong, and they carried soldiers to the threshold of Black Kettle's camp.

The Cheyenne initially watched with great curiosity as this large force of horsemen materialized within the distant haze. Curiosity gradually changed to apprehension, although no one shouted an alarm for them to flee or encouraged the warriors to retrieve their weapons and prepare to fight.

John S. Smith and his son Jack, Ed Guerrier, Watson Clark, and Private David Lauderback, who were camped upstream from Black Kettle's lodge, were roused and asked to go find out what the soldiers wanted. The women, however, had driven the horses away from camp at first sight of the soldiers. So the Smiths and Lauderback walked down toward the lower part of the village, the direction from which the soldiers approached.

Black Kettle had called for someone to bring him the longest lodge pole in the camp. He then hurried inside his lodge and emerged with a large American flag. This particular flag had been presented to him four years earlier by Commissioner of Indian Affairs A. B. Greenwood, who had told the chief to display it should soldiers approach, that it would be respected as a symbol of peace. The chief attached the flag to the top of the pole and for good measure added a smaller white flag beneath. Black Kettle hoisted the lodge pole as high as possible so that "Old Glory" rose well above the tops of the lodges. He waved it back and forth to make it highly conspicuous to the soldiers.[2]

By this time, many interested people from within the camp had congregated around Black Kettle's lodge, perhaps seeking safe haven under the American flag. These soldiers must merely be passing by in their search for hostiles, Black Kettle told them, and they would go away after determining that this was the place that the officers at Fort Lyon had designated that friendly Indians remain under military protection. The chief stood holding the sturdy pole, the flags rustling gently in the cool breeze, high in the air, where they could be seen for some distance.[3]

In spite of Black Kettle's assurances, the calm and the contentment of the camp were replaced by a shroud of anxiety, as this potential storm of violence loomed on the horizon. Within moments, the troops would reveal the reason for their presence, and life for Black Kettle and his peaceful Southern Cheyenne band would never be the same.

These particular troops that were assembled within a mile of Black Kettle's camp were primarily members of the 3rd Colorado Cavalry, with elements of the 1st Colorado Cavalry, commanded by Colonel John M. Chivington. The unit could best be described as a ragtag group of farmers, miners, shopkeepers, ranchers, gamblers, adventurers, and assorted ruffians. Many of these men had signed up after the August 11 plea by Governor Evans for recruits. They had been called the "Bloodless Third" because it was assumed that the term of their enlistment would expire before they had engaged in a meaningful battle with hostile Indians. The colonel, however, did not intend to disappoint his men, who were anxious to prove themselves in battle.

Chivington, under a cloak of secrecy to conceal his movements from the Indians and their sympathizers, had mustered his troops under Colonel George L. Shoup and issued marching orders for November 14. His intended destination for the 3rd Cavalry, revealed to only a handful of trusted subordinates, was Fort Lyon to the southeast—and the nearby Southern Cheyenne camp at Sand Creek.

Colonel Shoup had led the 3rd Cavalry, plus two companies of the 1st Colorado, from Bijou Basin eastward through bitter cold and drifting snow until reaching the Arkansas River, where the ground was nearly bare. Chivington, who had brought along four additional companies of the 3rd and 1st Colorado, assumed command on November 23 at Spring Bottom near Booneville (present-day Boone), twenty miles east of Pueblo. The column was also met at that point by Jim Beckwourth, the renowned sixty-nine-year-old mulatto trapper and hunter, who would serve as guide.[4]

The overbearing Colonel Chivington, contemptuous of any authority other than his own, had not even informed Brigadier General Curtis at headquarters in Kansas of his campaign, perhaps for fear of being denied permission. Curtis, however, would have certainly applauded the colonel's secret mission. Without knowing of Chivington's plans, Curtis had written to his aide stating that even if the Southern

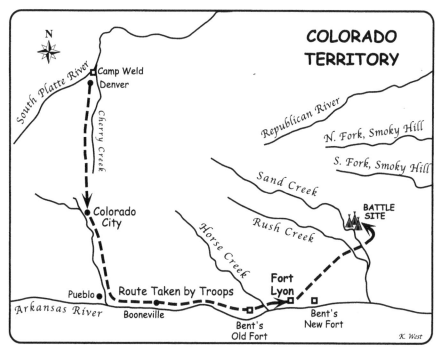

Chivington's march to Sand Creek

Cheyennes and the Southern Arapahoes presented themselves at Fort Lyon seeking peace, the military was not obligated to accept them. "At the proper time," Curtis wrote, "a campaign would be undertaken against the hostiles, and to assure its success, the march of the troops would be masked from the view of the public."[5]

Chivington, as if reading the mind of General Curtis, was aware that most major operations failed due to the Indians gaining knowledge that the army had taken to the field, which enabled them to escape before the troops arrived. He was determined not to make that mistake.

Patrols were dispatched along the way to visit outlying ranches, where the soldiers, without explanation, disarmed and detained the occupants to ensure that no one could warn the Indians about Chivington's march. These innocent people were placed under guard for up to three days, not even being permitted to tend to their livestock, many of which wandered off. Travelers and stagecoaches were stopped, until the only movement along that stretch of the Arkansas River was the Colorado cavalry.[6]

Chivington, therefore, was furious when on the morning of November 28 a detail from Fort Lyon under Captain Silas Soule rode out to meet him when his cavalry had ventured to within about ten miles of the fort. Soule assured Chivington that his arrival at Fort Lyon had not been expected, and that the captain had only learned about the presence of the troops a few minutes earlier from an old mule skinner who had been riding ahead of Chivington's column, close enough to recognize the colonel but without being observed by the troops.[7]

Chivington was concerned that the mule driver would alert others along his route or those camped around the fort. The colonel and Major Jacob Downing, his aide, raced ahead of the column to take measures that would prevent any security lapses. The two officers arrived at the fort, pleased that they had indeed caught everyone by surprise, and Chivington immediately issued orders for a perimeter to be established around the entire area. No one, without exception, could leave, and those who dared disobey would face death.

The cavalry column arrived near Fort Lyon at about noon and bivouacked a half mile away. The soldiers were given strict orders to stay in camp, fires after dark were prohibited, and anyone who contacted the Indians would be considered a spy and shot.[8]

Chivington informed Major Scott Anthony, the post commander, that he intended to march that night and attack Black Kettle's camp at Sand Creek, some forty miles to the northeast. Anthony enthusiastically supported the plan but recommended that friendly Indians and three white men—Smith, Clark, and Lauderback—who were present in the camp be spared. Anthony also stated that Chief One Eye, who was on the payroll as an informant, as well as the friendly chiefs Left Hand and Black Kettle, should be removed from the camp before the attack.[9]

The colonel bristled when the name "Black Kettle" was mentioned. He said,

Black Kettle is the principal chief of the Cheyenne nation, which has been engaged in bloody war with the whites since April. His claim of friendship seems to have arisen with the ending of the summer season and the approach of cold weather when Indians fight at a disadvantage. However, it is not my intention to attack without warning. Actual operations must, of course, depend on conditions which we find on arrival, but I propose to first immobilize the Indians, if possible, and then to offer them a parley on terms of surrender. Such terms would include the delivering up for punishment of all savages guilty of hostilities, the return of all stolen property, the surrender of all firearms and the giving of hostages to insure against further hostilities.[10]

This statement contradicted remarks that Chivington had made on the ride to Fort Lyon, when he had said, "Scalps are what we're after," and "I long to be wading in gore."[11]

Apparently, Anthony was satisfied with Chivington's explanation, and the conversation concluded with the major promising his services and that of a battalion from the fort consisting of 125 officers and men.

Marching orders were issued for eight o'clock that night. Each man was given several pounds of bacon and sufficient hardtack to last three or four days and was instructed that only gear that could be packed into saddlebags could be taken along. This would be a quick march—the supply train would remain at the fort—and it was imperative that they travel as light as possible.

While preparations for the march were under way, behind-the-scenes opposition to the campaign was mounting. Not every officer at the fort agreed with Chivington and Anthony that an attack on Black Kettle's village was justified under any circumstances. A number of these officers had accompanied Major Edward Wynkoop into hostile Cheyenne territory to arrange Black Kettle's peaceful surrender, and all of them had signed the letter that the major was delivering to headquarters, attesting to the fact that Black Kettle's Southerners desired peace. Now they were being told that they would be obliged to attack this friendly camp.

Wynkoop, although subsequently deposed as the commander of Fort Lyon, had guaranteed the safety of these Indians at Sand Creek until the time when General Curtis would provide provisions for a peace treaty. Black Kettle and his band had acted in good faith and were peacefully camped at Sand Creek, awaiting Curtis's decision. That being that case, it appeared that Chivington had taken matters into his own hands without consulting a higher authority, which was contrary to the pledge of safety given Black Kettle. This pending betrayal was an affront to the honor of each officer who had been with Wynkoop.

Throughout the day, the discussion around Fort Lyon was dominated by officers who voiced objections to this campaign. The only course of action for honorable men, it was decided, would be for the officers to attempt to dissuade Chivington from making this grievous mistake. No one, however, had as yet summoned the nerve to directly confront the intimidating colonel.

Captain Silas Soule sought an audience with Major Scott Anthony. The twenty-six-year-old Soule reminded his commander that both he and the major had promised to carry out Wynkoop's pledge. Soule had expected that Anthony would support the objections of the officers and speak with Chivington. Instead, Soule was surprised and disappointed when Anthony responded by saying that "he was in for killing all Indians, and that he was only acting or had been only acting friendly with them until he could get a force large enough to go out and kill all of them."

Word of this conversation reached Chivington, who predictably became livid with anger. Soule had fought beside the colonel at La Glorieta Pass and had been one of his most trusted officers, as well as a personal friend. That relationship, however, was now in the past. Chivington went as far as to make indirect threats against the life of Captain Soule for questioning the legitimacy of this campaign. Soule was warned by several fellow officers to stay away from the colonel, but he would not be completely deterred from trying to make his feelings known. He sent a note to Chivington, but it was returned unopened.[12]

Another of the more outspoken officers was Lieutenant Joseph Cramer. The lieutenant told Major Anthony that he believed that the officers who had accompanied Wynkoop to Smoky Hill and had signed the letter would perjure themselves as both officers and men if they participated in an attack and, furthermore, that it would be murder to kill the Indians in Black Kettle's camp.

Anthony assured Cramer that "Black Kettle would not be killed; that it was a promise given by Colonel Chivington that Black Kettle and his friends would be spared; that the object of the expedition was to surround the camp and take the stolen stock and kill the Indians that had been committing depredations during the last spring and summer."[13]

Cramer was not convinced that this was an accurate portrayal of Chivington's intentions. The lieutenant decided that the only way to settle the matter was to confront the quick-tempered colonel. The courageous Cramer did just that, stating to Chivington that killing

Black Kettle would be nothing less than murder and that "you are placing us in a very embarrassing circumstance."[14]

Chivington listened to the lieutenant in silence, then exploded in anger, waving his meaty fist and shouting, "The Cheyenne nation has been waging bloody war against the whites all spring, summer, and fall, and Black Kettle is their principal chief! I believe it right and honorable to use any means under God's heaven to kill Indians who kill and torture women and children! Damn any man who is in sympathy with them!" Chivington turned on his heel and, as he strode from the room, added that any officer or man who sympathized with the Indians should resign from the army.[15]

As evening approached, one final effort to reason with Chivington was made in person by Lieutenants C. M. Cossitt, J. S. Maynard, and W. P. Minton, the Indian agent Sam Colley, Captain Samuel H. Cook, and several civilians who lived at Fort Lyon. They argued that the consensus opinion was that these "Indians were recognized as friendly by all parties of this post." Colley, perhaps with a guilty conscience, pointed out that Black Kettle's Southern Cheyenne had been misrepresented and maltreated, and that it would be a crime to attack them after they had been promised protection. The others affirmed Colley's sentiments and respectfully requested that the colonel reconsider his plans.

Chivington had paced around the room during this tense meeting, glaring at those who dared to defy him, his temper escalating with each challenge to his supreme authority. He had not prepared his troops for battle and ridden all the way from Denver to be insulted by a bunch of whining Indian-lovers over a mission that he fervently believed was God's will. The colonel abruptly concluded the meeting by once again declaring, "Damn any man who is in sympathy with an Indian!"[16]

There would be no last-minute reprieve for Black Kettle and his Southern Cheyennes who were camped at Sand Creek. Their fate was now in the hands of John Milton Chivington, whose misguided ambition and absolute power gave him the authority to rewrite the rules of legal, ethical, and military propriety as he saw fit.

The Fort Lyon officers, however, rode with the understanding that the lives of Black Kettle and the other peace chiefs would be spared, that the mission of the operation was to surround the Sand Creek village, recover stolen stock, and arrest or perhaps punish the few inhabitants who may have been responsible for committing acts of violence against whites. With that accomplished, the column would head up the Smoky Hill River and attack the Dog Soldier village, which was known to be out raiding.[17]

At eight o'clock that night, Chivington formed his command for the march to Sand Creek. This column of Indian hunters consisted of about 700 to 750 troops—including the 125 officers and men from the post garrison—divided into 5 battalions under Lieutenant Colonel Leavitt L. Bowen, Major Scott J. Anthony, Major Hal Sayr, Captain T. G. Cree, and Lieutenant Luther Wilson. Four pieces of artillery—12-pound mountain howitzers—would be under the direction of Bowen. Major Jacob Downing and Captain A. J. Gill would serve as aides to Chivington.[18]

Private Irving Howbert of Company G, 3rd Cavalry, remembered the march to Sand Creek: "Each company was formed in ranks of fours, and we traveled rapidly from the start. It was walk, trot, gallop, dismount and lead, all night long. It was a bright, clear, starlight night, the air crisp and uncomfortably cool, as might have been expected at that time of year."[19]

Howbert's description of conditions that night was an understatement. In fact, the air was so cold during the march that the guide Jim Beckwourth became incapacitated and was replaced by Robert Bent, one of the mixed-blood sons of William Bent and Owl Woman. Black Kettle's village was home to Robert's brother George and three sisters. Accordingly, Chivington kept a close eye on his guide. At one point, when the colonel thought that Bent might have been leading the column astray, he warned, "I haven't had an Indian to eat in a long time. If you fool with me, and don't lead us to that camp, I'll have you for breakfast."[20]

At daybreak, Chivington and Shoup, riding in the advance, topped a rise and, about a mile away, observed Black Kettle's camp on the far banks of Sand Creek. The two officers could hear the sound of barking dogs and view a flurry of activity within the camp which indicated that their presence was known. Chivington understood that he must act without delay. This would be the victory that would elevate him to the status of national hero, and he was not about to let it slip from his grasp.

Contrary to his promise to surround the village and seek the surrender of the friendly Indians, which could have been accomplished by sending a detail into the camp with or without a white flag, the colonel did not waste any time deploying his troops into battle formation.

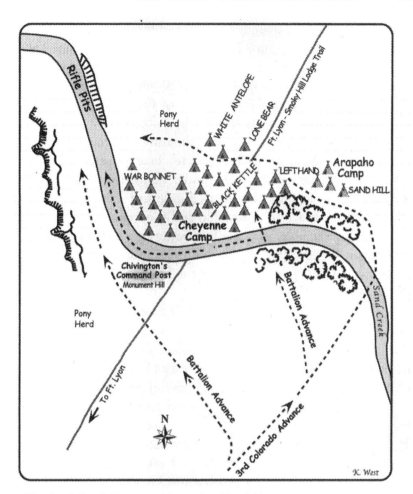

The Sand Creek Massacre, November 29, 1864

Lieutenant Luther Wilson, with Companies C, E, and F of the 1st Colorado, was sent by Chivington across the creek to the north to strike between the village and the large horse herd. When a number of warriors ran to save their horses, Wilson ordered his men to dismount and assume a position in the creek bed northeast of the camp. He gave the order to fire into the advancing Indians, and the ensuing fusillade successfully thwarted the attempt by the Cheyenne to reach the herd. These soldiers then formed a skirmisher line and fired at will into the village.

Major Anthony, with three companies, had thundered across the creek behind Wilson and halted just southeast of the camp to lay down a base of fire. Chivington positioned his artillery near the creek bank, and the powerful guns immediately began firing grape and canister shot into the helpless village. Several detachments in succession were dispatched in a maneuver to encircle and assault the camp from various directions, while the remainder of the men advanced on foot across the creek bed, directly toward their objective.

Chivington rallied his men by shouting, "Remember the murdered women and children on the Platte! Take no prisoners!"[21]

George Bent described these initial moments: "I looked toward the chief's lodge and saw that Black Kettle had a large American flag tied to the end of a long lodgepole and was standing in front of his lodge, holding the pole, with the flag fluttering in the grey light of the winter dawn. I heard him call to the people not to be afraid, that the soldiers would not hurt them; then the troops opened fire from two sides of the camps."[22]

Black Kettle, with the assistance of Chief White Antelope, stood by his lodge and continued to wave the American flag, resolute in his belief that their safety had been guaranteed. The barrage of bullets that poured into the camp, however, served as evidence that the army had no intention of honoring the promise of protection.

Finally, the people who had gathered around Black Kettle's lodge could no longer stand passively by in the face of the vicious onslaught. They scattered in utter confusion, not knowing which direction to run, the fire from the soldiers cutting off every avenue of escape.

One of those who ran for his life was George Bent, who said that at this point, "The women and children were screaming and wailing, the men running to their lodges for their arms and shouting advice to one another."

Black Kettle, however, remained standing in front of his lodge, waving the flag in a futile attempt to stop the bloodshed.[23]

The trader and interpreter John S. Smith, wearing an army overcoat and a broad-brimmed hat, had approached to within thirty yards of the soldiers with the belief that he would be recognized. He indeed was noticed and identified. Shouts from Chivington's men rang out, "Shoot the old son-of-a-bitch! He's no better than an Indian!" Smith dashed back to seek refuge from the wrath of the soldiers in Chief War Bonnet's lodge.[24]

Seventy-five-year-old Chief White Antelope, wearing around his neck a medal given to him by President Abraham Lincoln, had grown

anxious and headed toward the soldiers, waving his arms and exhorting them in English not to fire. Black Kettle called out to his friend,
telling him to come back, that his efforts would be in vain. But White
Antelope's heart was heavy with the realization that they had been
betrayed by the white man, and he no longer wanted to live. The
chief finally halted and stood at the creek bed, his arms folded across
his chest to signify that he did not want to fight, and chanted his
death song:

Nothing lives long
Except the earth and the mountains

White Antelope was cut down by a hail of bullets. The soldiers
scalped him and cut off his ears and nose—as well as his scrotum, from
which the violator was said to have bragged that he would make a
tobacco pouch.[25]

The soldiers poured murderous, indiscriminate fire into the panic-
stricken Indians, and cannon shells rained down on the village. Colonel
Shoup's men charged directly toward the lodges, shooting down the
vulnerable, fleeing Indians. A group of warriors armed mostly with
bows and arrows attempted to hold off Shoup but were soon routed
by devastating explosions of grape and canister shot.

The determined blue-clad troops, whose actions now resembled
a mob, then commenced a raid into the lodges, killing great numbers
of men, women, and children and riddling those who were already
dead with bullets. Wounded Indians, many of them women and children, crawled toward the creek, marking their trail with blood and
bodies, as one by one, the soldiers mercilessly put them out of their
misery.

The Arapaho chief Left Hand had vowed to never fight against
the white man and, true to his word, remained in front of his lodge in
the midst of the carnage, reminding anyone who would listen that he
was peaceful. Several reports indicated that the chief had been killed,
but his body was not found on the field. It has been speculated that
he escaped, then from that day forward vanished from the pages of
history.[26]

About a hundred Cheyennes—perhaps thirty men, the rest women
and children—raced from the camp in a desperate attempt to seek
refuge in the six- to ten-foot-high, almost perpendicular banks of the

dry creek bed about two miles above the village. The soldiers followed these people, and many of them were struck by bullets during this mad dash and fell dead or severely wounded. Those who managed to reach that point safely began scooping out the loose sand to make rifle pits for cover, with driftwood as barricades. The outnumbered warriors organized a stiff defense, while protecting the women and children who cowered nearby in the crude trenches.[27]

The soldier Amos Miksch, of the 1st Colorado Cavalry, recalled, "There were no rifle pits except what the Indians dug into the sand bank after we commenced firing. I saw them digging out sand with their hands, while the firing was going on; the water came into the trenches as they dug in this manner."[28]

Black Kettle had waited in front of his lodge until everyone else had fled, then, with wife, Medicine Woman Later, at his side, started northward up the creek bed to join those who were frantically digging defensive positions into the sandy banks. Groups of soldiers were rushing to attack that creek bank, and Black Kettle and his wife became prime targets for their rifles. The couple dashed through a gauntlet of bullets and an obstacle course of dead and dying bodies, until finally Medicine Woman Later fell to the ground and lay unmoving.

Black Kettle stopped and knelt beside his wife, but she appeared to be dead. Reluctantly, knowing that if he remained at her side he would die, Black Kettle continued up the creek, with the soldiers constantly firing at him, and took shelter in the pits where his people were fighting in a desperate attempt to keep the soldiers at bay.[29]

Most of the Cheyenne who had managed to reach the creek bank had been wounded along the way but refused to surrender their lives without a fight; they burrowed into their hastily dug holes to mount a fierce defense. For some of the wounded, the cold temperatures temporarily saved their lives by freezing their wounds, which kept them from bleeding to death. Black Kettle, whose eyes were failing him, accepted the task of reloading weapons for the younger warriors who were able enough to shoot.[30]

George Bent, who had been severely wounded by a bullet in his hip as he scrambled to the refuge in the creek bank, described events at this only organized line of defense: "The soldiers concentrated their fire on the people in the pits and we fought back as well as we could with guns and bows, but we had only a few guns. The troops did not rush in and fight hand to hand, but once or twice after they had killed many of the men in a certain pit they rushed in and finished up the work, killing the wounded and the women and the children that had not been hurt."[31]

While a great number of Chivington's troops assailed Black Kettle and the Cheyennes trapped in the creek bank, the village and the surrounding area had become the scene of the most heinous atrocities imaginable. Groups of soldiers roamed about in a state of frenzied bloodlust, killing and torturing the wounded and scalping and mutilating the dead—committing merciless acts on women and children, who screamed and pled for mercy, to the extent that many of their comrades became physically ill at the sight of this barbarity.[32]

Private David Lauderback eventually made personal contact with Chivington, who called the private by name and told him to join the command. Soon after, John S. Smith peeked out of War Bonnet's lodge and hailed the colonel. Chivington called out, "Run here, Uncle John; you are all right." Smith brought with him the teamster Watson Clark and Charles Bent, who also fell in with the soldiers as they moved up the stream. Smith would soon return to the camp in order to protect his wife and child, who were hiding in Chief War Bonnet's lodge. By this time, that chief, known for making the first raid into Mexico, had died at the hands of the bloodthirsty soldiers.[33]

Smith had observed the battle from several parts of the camp and attested to the atrocities committed by the soldiers: "All manner of depredations were inflicted . . . they were scalped, their brains knocked out; the men used their knives, ripped open women, clubbed little children, knocked them in the head with their guns, beat their brains out, mutilated their bodies in every sense of the word. . . . children two and three months old; all ages lying there, from sucking infants up to warriors."[34]

Testimony from other participants and eyewitnesses was equally as horrifying.

Major Scott J. Anthony, who later reluctantly admitted to seeing some bodies that were mutilated, also reported, "There was one little child, probably three years old, just big enough to walk through the sand. The Indians had gone ahead, and this little child was behind following after them. I saw one man get off his horse, at a distance of about 75 yards, and draw up his rifle and fired—he missed the child. Another man came up and said, "Let me try the son of a bitch; I can hit him." He got down off his horse, kneeled down and fired at the child, but he missed him. A third man came up and made a similar remark, and the little fellow dropped."[35]

First Lieutenant James D. Cannon related that "I did not see a body of man, woman, or child but was scalped, and in many instances their bodies were mutilated in the most horrible manner—men, women, and children's privates cut out, &c; I heard one man say that he had cut out a woman's private parts and had them for exhibition on a stick."[36]

Robert Bent, the brother of George, had been forced to guide Chivington's troops to Black Kettle's village. He later told government investigators about several instances that he had witnessed during the battle: "Some thirty or forty squaws and children collected in a hole for protection. [They] sent out a little girl about six years old with a white flag on a stick. She had not proceeded but a few steps when she was shot and killed. I saw a little girl who had been hid in the sand. Two soldiers drew their pistols and shot her, then pulled her out of the sand by the arm. I saw quite a number of infants in arms killed with their mothers."[37]

Robert Bent also related that he saw a pregnant woman, who fell behind the others as they ran for the stream bed. She was overtaken by the soldiers, who killed her, then cut open her stomach and yanked out her unborn baby, which was tossed down on the ground beside her.[38]

Robert's brother George wrote, "One old woman who had been scalped by the soldiers walked about, but unable to see where to go. Her entire scalp had been taken and the skin of her forehead fell down over her eyes."[39]

Remembrances of Cheyenne victims are equally troubling. One woman told about how when the soldiers attacked, she slung the cradle-board holding her baby onto her back and grabbed hold of her little boy's hand. She tried to escape the onslaught by running toward the creek bed, with bullets zipping all around her. Finally, this woman was struck in the shoulder but managed to hide herself and her children along the sandy bank. She removed the cradle-board from her back, only to discover that her baby had been shot through the body and was dead. Her husband also died that day.[40]

Another woman, Black Bear's wife, was struck by a bullet in the face, which damaged her appearance so badly that she was thereafter known as One Eye Comes Together. She lived, however, to tell about the soldiers killing women and children and grabbing women, who struggled to free themselves while the soldiers brutally raped them.

When the soldiers had finished raping a woman, they simply shot her in an attempt to conceal their crime. Yet enough women survived to testify that this practice was not isolated but quite common.[41]

These acts of brutality and outrage, too numerous to cite item by item, were rampant throughout the village. Other typical examples were: "A group of soldiers paused amid the firing to take turns profaning the body of a comely young squaw, very dead. Indians' fingers were hacked away to get their rings as souvenirs. One soldier trotted about with a heart impaled on a stick. Others carried off the genitals of braves. Someone had the notion that it would be artistic work to slice away the breasts of the Indian women. One breast was worn as a cap, another was seen stretched across the bow of a saddle."[42]

One detachment of Chivington's troops that did not participate in the atrocities or even in the battle was Company D of the 1st Colorado Cavalry, commanded by Captain Silas S. Soule. Upon arrival at Black Kettle's camp, Soule, who had already voiced his opposition to killing Indians he deemed friendly, had determined that the lodges were occupied mainly by women and children. He implored Chivington not to attack but was ordered back to his post to do his duty as a soldier.

Instead, Soule ordered his men not to fire. He moved his company to the south end of the village, positioned between other troops and the fleeing Cheyenne, where they sat and watched the actions of their comrades.

Soule wrote a letter dated December 14 to Major Ned Wynkoop, in which he summarized the events surrounding the attack. It reads in part:

> I tell you Ned it was hard to see little children on their knees have their brains beat out by men professing to be civilized. One squaw was wounded and a fellow took a hatchet to finish her, she held her arms up to defend her, and he cut one arm off, and held the other with one hand and dashed the hatchet through her brain. One squaw with her two children, were on their knees, begging for their lives of a dozen soldiers, within ten feet of them all firing—when one succeeded in hitting the squaw in the thigh, when she took a knife and cut the throats of both children, and then killed herself. One old squaw hung herself in the lodge—there was not enough room for her to hang and she held up her knees and choked herself to death. Some tried to escape on the Prairie, but most of them were run down by horsemen. White Antelope, War Bonnet and a

number of others had Ears and Privates cut off. Squaws [privates] were cut out for trophies. You would think it impossible for white men to butcher and mutilate human beings as they did there, but every word I have told you is the truth, which they do not deny.[43]

Chivington, who later preferred charges against Soule, called his former friend "a coward and a deserter in time of battle, [an officer] who abandoned his leadership post, disobeyed lawful orders of his superiors, refused to fight when the battle got underway, and—in fact—threw down his weapon and ran from the scene of the battle."[44]

Soule's testimony against Chivington at the congressional hearings would be perhaps the most damning evidence heard.

Another officer who apparently did not take part in the fighting was Lieutenant Joseph A. Cramer. Soule remarked in his letter that he, Soule, had been threatened with being cashiered from the service and added, "I think they will try the same for Cramer for he had shot his mouth off a good deal, and did not shoot his pistol off in the Massacre. Joe has behaved himself first rate during this whole affair."[45]

Cramer also wrote a letter to Wynkoop to offer his observations. It reads, in part,

Bucks, women and children scalped, fingers cut off to get the rings on them, and this as much with officers as men, and one of those officers a Major: and a Lt. Col. cut off Ears, of all he came across, a squaw ripped open and a child taken from her, little children shot, while begging for their lives (and all the indignities shown their bodies that ever was heard of) (women shot while on their knees, with their arms around soldiers begging for their lives.) things that Indians would be ashamed to do. To give you some idea, squaws were known to kill their own children, and then themselves, rather than to have them taken prisoners.

The only lieutenant colonel who was with the command was Lieutenant Colonel Leavitt L. Bowen. The major who was mentioned could have been William F. Wilder, Hal Sayre, Samuel L. Logan, or Scott Anthony.

After listing several chiefs, including Black Kettle, who had been killed, Cramer added, "Black Kettle said when he saw us coming, that he was glad, for it was Major Wynkoop coming to make peace . . . after all the pledges made by Major A[nthony]—to these Indians and then to take the course he did. I think as comments are necessary from me; only I will say he has a face for every man he talks."[46]

There can be no doubt that Chivington, although perhaps not actively participating in the atrocities, was aware of the butchery that took place around him.

The Indian agent Samuel G. Colley later said: "Colonel Chivington did, on the morning of the 29th of November, surprise and attack said camp of friendly Indians and massacre a large number of them, mostly women and children, and did allow the troops of his command to mangle and mutilate them in the most horrible manner."[47]

No evidence exists to indicate that Chivington encouraged his command to satiate their bloodlust with such barbarity, but he certainly could have prevented it. The colonel likely viewed their actions as a reward for this decisive victory that they had handed him.

Meanwhile, Black Kettle and the Cheyennes who manned the rifle pits in the creek bank two miles above the camp refused to yield to the mass of troops that had for hours maintained a steady assailment of rifle fire into their position. At one point, the soldiers were able to move within firing range at the upper end of the pits and killed about thirty people—men, women, and children. This battle of wills, with the Indians vowing to fight to the death, would prove to be a hollow, yet moral, victory for the Cheyennes.[48]

It was about 5 p.m., sundown on this frosty autumn day, when the soldiers finally wearied of their assault on the rifle pits upstream and began to straggle back to Black Kettle's village with their comrades, who were busily looting the lodges.

According to George Bent, after the troops had withdrawn, the surviving Cheyennes, perhaps thirty of the hundred who had initially sought refuge, remained in their pits for some time, afraid that the soldiers would return. "At last we crawled out of the holes, stiff and sore, with the blood frozen on our wounded and half-naked bodies. Slowly and painfully we retreated up the creek, men, women, and children dragging themselves along, the women and children wailing and crying, but not too loudly for they feared the return of the whites."[49]

Black Kettle, however, did not accompany his people as they made their way up the creek bed to seek safety. His thoughts were of Medicine Woman Later. He had witnessed the brutality of the soldiers, the mutilations and the scalping, and could not bear to live with the thought that his wife had been victimized in such a manner. The chief ignored the pleas from his people to join them in their escape and headed alone back toward the place where he had last seen Medicine

Woman Later. He would take his wife's body away and bury her where the soldiers could not find her.

Black Kettle could hear the distant shouts and the commotion as the soldiers looted the lodges and the bodies—taking scalps, cutting off fingers and ears for the jewelry, slicing off pieces of flesh, cutting the long tresses off the women, and collecting Cheyenne personal possessions left in the lodges to save as keepsakes.[50]

He knew that the dead bodies of scores of his people—perhaps more than 150, two-thirds of them women and children—lay strewn about the vicinity of his camp, among them Chiefs White Antelope, Standing Water, War Bonnet, Spotted Crow, Two Thighs, Bear Man, Yellow Shield, Yellow Wolf—as well as the informant One Eye. And the chief was keenly aware that his name would be added to that list, that he would go to live with the spirits, should his presence become known to the soldiers who roamed about searching for someone else to kill.

Chivington would later claim that his men had killed between 400 and 600 Indians that day at Sand Creek. George Bent stated that 137 Indians—28 men and the remainder women and children—had lost their lives. Bent later amended those figures to 53 men and 110 women and children killed. Ed Guerrier, Bent's brother-in-law, set that figure at 148—60 of them men. By contrast, the soldiers lost 10 killed and 38 wounded.[51]

Black Kettle continued moving cautiously ahead, his old, aching legs protesting with each step. He paused now and then in this field of gory, abused corpses, straining in the dim light to recognize that one special person.

At last he found her. Medicine Woman Later was covered with blood and riddled with bullet holes, but she had not been scalped or otherwise mutilated. He lowered himself to the ground beside her and was astonished when a moan escaped from her lips. Her breath was ragged and her heartbeat faint, but, miraculously, Medicine Woman Later was alive.

Black Kettle tenderly lifted his wife onto his back and hastily retraced his route along the creek bed. He carried her through the maze of bodies, past the abandoned rifle pits, until finally overtaking the small group of survivors that was steadily moving away from the soldiers. Several horses had been rounded up, and the chief placed Medicine Woman Later onto the back of one of them.[52]

Black Kettle's band of beaten, wounded Cheyenne then resumed the journey up the creek for perhaps as many as ten miles. The night was bitter cold and a brisk wind raked across the land with a vengeance. When they lacked the endurance to go any farther, they halted in a ravine on the barren plain, without shelter or wood to build a fire.

The men and women who had not been severely wounded immediately set to work trying save the lives of their companions. When the soldiers had attacked, most people were forced to flee their lodges without time to adequately dress and were half-naked. Clothing, buffalo robes, and blankets belonging to the healthy were used to cover the wounded. Prairie grass was painstakingly collected by hand and heaped on top of freezing bodies for warmth. Piles of grass were ignited to make small, quick-burning fires, and the wounded were placed nearby.

Black Kettle believed that others had also escaped from the village and were now wandering about, lost, wounded, and freezing. Throughout the night, his people called out into the darkness to alert any fellow tribe members who may have been within earshot of their location. Several of them straggled in to seek refuge, but the village had dispersed in every direction when the soldiers attacked, and many others were now fending for themselves in various places within the vast expanse of prairie.

The chief at this time had the opportunity to examine Medicine Woman Later's wounds and discovered that his wife had been struck by no less than nine bullets. She told him that the soldiers had shot her again and again as she lay there helpless in the sand. His wife was made as comfortable as possible, but she, as was the case with many others, was in grave condition.[53]

In spite of the valiant efforts to warm and nurse the wounded, the elements were overwhelming and the suffering immeasurable. Black Kettle came to the conclusion that this makeshift camp would not protect them from freezing to death, and by dawn the soldiers would likely take up their trail. He decided that although it was still dark, they must move. Their only hope for survival was to reach the camps of the Dog Soldiers at the headwaters of the Smoky Hill River, some fifty miles away. Carrying the wounded on their backs, others shuffling along as best they could, the most severely wounded on horseback, Black Kettle's desperate people headed in a northeasterly direction across the open plain.

This weary group of Cheyenne moved slowly but steadily throughout the night and into the early morning. Suddenly, appearing from within the glow of the rising sun, they noticed the approach of a large party of horsemen.

To their surprise and relief, it was a rescue party of Cheyennes from the Smoky Hill camps, and they had brought along with them a string of ponies laden with blankets and food. A few men had leaped astride ponies and fled from Black Kettle's village when the soldiers attacked that morning, and they had ridden all day to reach the Smoky Hill. They bravely returned with reinforcements and supplies to save any others who might have also managed to escape.

Black Kettle and his band were fed and mounted and, with renewed hope, reached the camps on the Smoky Hill late that day.[54]

George Bent described the scene that greeted them upon their arrival: "Almost everyone in that camp had friends or relatives in our camp, and when we came in sight of the lodges, everyone left camp and came out to meet us, wailing and mourning in a manner that I have never heard equalled."[55]

That wailing and mourning would soon change into war cries, as the Cheyennes and their allies vowed to avenge this bloody betrayal at Sand Creek.

9

REACTION TO THE MASSACRE

Wʜɪʟᴇ ʙʟᴀᴄᴋ ᴋᴇᴛᴛʟᴇ ᴀɴᴅ ʜɪs ʙᴇʟᴇᴀɢᴜᴇʀᴇᴅ ʙᴀɴᴅ ᴏғ ᴄʜᴇʏᴇɴɴᴇ survivors made their way to safety, Colonel John Chivington, basking in the glory of his victory, ordered that camp for the night be made near the site of the vanquished village. The men straggled back to assemble around the bivouac area and whiled away the time boasting about their heroic deeds and collecting and showing off their gory souvenirs. Captain Silas Soule, who had held his men out of the fight, was detailed as an escort to accompany Major Anthony and the supply train to Fort Lyon. John S. Smith roamed about the field to identify the notable chiefs among the dead. He pointed out one badly mutilated body as that of Black Kettle. This premature report of the demise of the Cheyenne chief was subsequently passed on to the public and government officials.

Chivington, after posting a guard in case the Indians returned in a fighting mood, finally got around to writing his report of the "battle" to General Samuel Curtis:

> In the last ten days my command has marched 300 miles, 100 of which
> the snow was two feet deep. After a march of forty miles last night I, at
> daylight this morning, attacked Cheyenne village of 130 lodges, from
> 900 to 1000 warriors strong; killed chiefs Black Kettle, White Antelope,
> Knock Knee, and Little Robe, and between 400 and 500 other Indians,
> and captured as many ponies and mules. Our loss 9 killed, 38 wounded.
> All did nobly. Think I will catch some more of them eighty miles, on
> Smoky Hill. Found white man's scalp, not more than three days' old, in
> one of the lodges.[1]

Chivington also dispatched a messenger, who carried a letter to the editor of the *Rocky Mountain News*. The colonel stated that he had won a victory in "one of the most bloody Indian battles ever fought on these plains." He added, "I shall leave here, as soon as I can see our wounded safely on the way to the hospital at Fort Lyon, for the villages of the Sioux, which are reported 80 miles from here on the Smoky Hill, and three thousand strong; so look for more fighting."[2]

The following morning the soldiers patrolled the surrounding area and located a few Cheyenne who had either been too badly wounded to escape or had been hiding. These Indians were quickly killed.

Apparently, the bloodletting of the past day had not satiated the desire of the soldiers for killing. Camp talk circulated that Jack Smith, John S. Smith's half-Cheyenne, half-white son, should also be killed, for he was no better than a full-blooded Cheyenne. The younger Smith had been awarded a section of land for his work as an interpreter at the Fort Wise Treaty of 1861.

Word reached Chivington about this contemplated murder. The colonel had it within his power to save the young man, who already had proven valuable in the past as a guide and an interpreter, but he replied, "I have given my instructions; have told my men not to take any prisoners."[3]

John S. Smith was hailed by a soldier from the lodge where he and Jack were staying. Smith later related, "I got up and went out; he took me by the arm and walked towards Colonel Chivington's camp. Said he, 'I am sorry to tell you, but they are going to kill your son Jack.' I knew the feeling towards the whole camp of Indians, and that there was no use to make any resistance. I said, 'I can't help it.' I then walked to where Colonel Chivington was standing by his campfire; when I got within a few feet of him I heard a gun fired, and saw a crowd run to my lodge, and they told me that Jack was dead."[4]

Major Anthony, who was not present, later wrote to his brother that Jack Smith "was taken suddenly ill in the night, and died before morning." Major Hal Sayre related that Smith had accidentally shot himself while looking at a gun.[5]

Actually, about fifteen soldiers approached Smith's lodge, and one stuck a pistol inside and pulled the trigger. The bullet struck Jack Smith in the right side of his chest, killing him instantly.[6]

Later that day, Lieutenant Joe Cramer was ordered by Chivington to command the detail that would burn the lodges and the remnants of Black Kettle's village. Perhaps Chivington intended to implicate the lieutenant in the massacre, inasmuch as Cramer had not participated in the previous day's activities. Cramer, who was keenly aware of the bloodthirsty mood of the soldiers, would not have wanted to invite attention to himself and therefore grudgingly complied with the colonel's order.

This task was zealously carried out by a group of the "Bloody Third-sters." The troops then returned to their blankets and spent another night sleeping near the place where the mutilated bodies of at least 150 slaughtered Cheyenne lay within a short distance of them.

Chivington marched his troops away from the ashes of Black Ket-tle's village on the morning of December 1, but his direction was not north toward the Smoky Hill, where bands of Dog Soldiers and Lakota Sioux were camped, as he had previously indicated. Instead, the colonel, perhaps suffering from a dose of cold feet when considering that he might have to face warriors who were anxious to fight, headed south-ward toward the Arkansas River. He intended to strike a small, less dangerous camp of Arapahoes under Chief Little Raven.

Chivington led his troops fifteen miles down Sand Creek before halting for the night. The dead and the wounded soldiers were sent on their way toward Fort Lyon. Shortly afterward, Major Anthony and Captain Soule returned from the fort with a wagon train loaded with fresh supplies.[7]

The atrocities, however, had not ended at Black Kettle's village. Lieutenant Joe Cramer reported, "One little child 3 months old was thrown in the feed box of a wagon and brought one days march, and there left on the ground to perish."[8]

Another day's ride brought the command to the reported vicinity of the Arapaho camp, but a forty-two-mile all-night march, which crossed into Kansas, proved futile. Chivington arrived at the Arapaho camp to find the inhabitants long gone. He pushed his troopers down the Arkansas River for several days in his quest to locate any Indians to attack but was unable to catch up with his quarry.

By December 7, Chivington had tired of chasing an elusive prey and realized that the Indians were aware of his presence and had no interest in waiting around to greet him. He decided that his command would head toward Fort Lyon, and from there, they would make their triumphant return to Denver.

Chivington rode ahead of his troops and arrived in Denver on December 16. At that time, he wrote a formal report of his actions for headquarters. The colonel characterized the incident as a battle waged against hostile Indians and defended that position by falsely stating that he found "several scalps of white men and women in the Indian lodges; also various articles of clothing belonging to white persons."[9]

On December 17, likely after a lengthy discussion with Chivington, the *Rocky Mountain News* trumpeted the news of the Sand Creek affair:

> Among the brilliant feats of arms in Indian warfare, the recent campaign of our Colorado Volunteers will stand in history with few rivals, and none to exceed it in final results.

Perhaps the only "facts" reported by the *News* editorial were in the part that chronicled the march of the 3rd Cavalry to Sand Creek. The story presented the view that the affair had indeed been a monumental battle against a stubborn, warring enemy. "Although utterly surprised, the savages were not unprepared. . . . defensive works a half-mile long and a similar line of work on the adjacent bluffs," was recorded, as proof that Black Kettle's village was ready to fight. This claim that the Cheyenne had dug fighting positions prior to the arrival of the troops was one of the many falsehoods that became fact for most residents of Colorado.

The newspaper concluded its praise with "A thousand incidents of individual daring and the passing events of the day might be told, but space forbids. We leave the task for eye-witnesses to chronicle. All acquitted themselves well, and Colorado soldiers have again covered themselves with glory."[10]

The troops of the 3rd Regiment, Colorado Volunteer Cavalry, now hailed as the "Bloody Thirdsters," reached Denver on December 22 and triumphantly paraded through the streets—Chivington riding in front, with a live eagle tied to a pole—to the adoration of the local citizenry, particularly the young ladies. The men proudly displayed their souvenirs, showing off earrings and rings—many attached to pieces of flesh—to the throngs along the way, on one occasion waving a hundred scalps to cheering patrons in various theaters. Colonel John Chivington was hailed as a hero for his defeat of the Cheyennes in this "battle" at Sand Creek.[11]

The jubilant soldiers bragged to one and all about their daring exploits, but, it was noted, "no two men give the same version of the big battle, and, of the stories of a score of them, there ain't three alike respecting the minutiae of the great glorious victory."[12]

Within a week, however, an ominous shadow was cast across the community when the *News* reprinted a dispatch from Washington, dated December 20, 1864:

> The affair at Fort Lyon, Colorado in which Colonel Chivington destroyed a large Indian village, and all its inhabitants, is to be made the subject of congressional investigation. Letters received from high officials in Colorado say that the Indians were killed after surrendering, and that a large proportion of them were women and children.[13]

This item "created considerable of a sensation." Many of the participants—most of whom had been mustered out on December 28—expressed their interest in "going for" any "high official" who could be identified. That informant, by the way, was later revealed to be Stephen S. Harding, Chief Justice of Colorado, or perhaps, as some sources have named, the former Colorado judge Benjamin F. Hall.[14]

In the following day's edition, December 30, the *News* mounted a passionate defense of the "Boys of the Third." The newspaper ridiculed the notion of "friendly Indians" and a "surrendered village," calling it "all bosh." The Indians who had been killed, the daily reported, were the "confessed murderers of the Hungate family." Furthermore, "it is unquestioned and undenied that the site of the Sand Creek battle was the rendezvous of the thieving and marauding bands of savages who roamed over this country last summer and fall." Any idea that these were friendly Indians who had surrendered "must have been the happy thought of an exceedingly vivid imagination."

The *News* listed as evidence the many items "found" in the village that surely must have been stolen from individuals and the government, such as "underclothes of women and children, stripped from their murdered victims," and the scalps of white men, women, and children.

The Denver newspaper discouraged any formal investigation but stated that if one was undertaken, "we advise the honorable congressional committee, who may be appointed to conduct it, to get their scalps insured."[15]

Congressional committees would indeed investigate the tragic affair at Sand Creek, but it would not be the scalps of their members that were placed in jeopardy—rather, those of Colonel John M. Chivington, Governor John Evans, and the sadistic, murderous mob that proudly called itself the "Bloody Thirdsters."

Meanwhile, the Cheyenne who had survived the massacre were camped on the head of the Smoky Hill River, at a place they called Bunch of Timber. The wounded had been attended to as best as possible, and, although no record exists, it was likely that some of them died from their injuries along the way and others suffered the same fate at the camp. Black Kettle's wife, Medicine Woman Later, had been severely wounded, but she clung to life during the journey and her condition steadily improved to the point that she was now out of danger. Medicine Woman Later would live, but the scars from the nine bullet holes in her body were a painful reminder of this tragedy that she would carry for the rest of her life.

Black Kettle, who had run a gauntlet of bullets and survived the vicious onslaught at the rifle pits, had escaped unscathed. He did, however, incur the wrath of the tribe members, who blamed him for moving his people to Sand Creek, where they were easy prey for the soldiers. The Dog Soldiers ridiculed him for his belief that peace could be made with the white man, and his status as a Council chief was threatened.

There can be no question that the loss of so many of his band— lifelong friends, those with whom he had vowed as chief to protect— caused Black Kettle's heart to ache as never before. Moreover, the implication by the People that he had somehow violated their trust had deeply affected him. But his conscience was clear, for he knew that it was he who had been betrayed.

Black Kettle would have maintained his dignity during this time of derision toward him. He would not have offered excuses for the decision that had placed his people in a position of vulnerability. Rather, he would have been comfortable with the knowledge that his actions had been honorable and forthright, in accordance with Cheyenne custom, and it was the white man who had violated any trust.

It is reasonable to speculate that Black Kettle spent countless hours mulling over the events that preceded the massacre, searching for any indication of betrayal by the white man that he may have overlooked at the time. Major Wynkoop, the Tall Chief, had surely been sincere, but he had been removed as post commander in favor of Major Anthony. But this major had pledged to abide by Wynkoop's assurances of protection.

Perhaps Black Kettle came to the conclusion that the sign of which he had not been conscious had come from the Big Chief in Denver, Colonel John Chivington. The colonel's statement at the conclusion of the Camp Weld council had been most confusing to the chiefs—its interpretation the subject of lengthy discussions during the return trip to Fort Lyon.

"I am not a big war chief," Chivington had said, "but all the soldiers in this country are at my command. My rule of fighting white men or Indians is, to fight them until they lay down their arms and submit to military authority. You are nearer Major Wynkoop than any one else, and you can go with him when you get ready to do that."

This odd declaration had not been intended as a friendly advisement but had been an ominous warning. Now, the meaning was clear, that peace may have been in the hands of Major Wynkoop, but the one who had replaced him, Major Anthony, was not bound by inherited promises; rather, he was under the command of Colonel Chivington. Wynkoop had made the mistake of trusting what had been said at Camp Weld and had sought to correct that error with a higher authority in Kansas. Had Wynkoop escorted the chiefs to an audience with General Curtis, instead of with Chivington, perhaps the massacre could have been averted. Black Kettle would not have blamed Wynkoop but himself for not perceiving the danger posed by the removal of the Tall Chief.

After a few days, however, the anger and the resentment toward Black Kettle faded away, as the People came to the realization that their chief had not betrayed them but had truly believed that his camp was under the protection of the soldiers at Fort Lyon while they waited for word of peace. He was exonerated of any blame and restored to equal status with the other chiefs.[16]

News of the Sand Creek Massacre spread across Indian Country to the various winter gathering places like a Plains wildfire. And instead of striking fear into the heart of each Indian, this act of treachery by the soldiers served to stir up a cry for vengeance. Cheyenne Dog Soldier messengers carried the war pipe to the camps of every band of the Lakota Sioux and the Northern Arapahoes, most of which were located on the Solomon and the Republican rivers. The chiefs smoked the pipe, formally declaring war on the white man and pledging allegiance with the Cheyenne avengers. Chiefs Spotted Tail and Pawnee Killer, the Sioux war leaders, commenced preparations for this great undertaking.[17]

By January 1, 1865, the beginning of the hoop-and-stick-game moon, a huge village—900 lodges and about 1,500 warriors—had assembled on Cherry Creek to plan a course of action in retaliation for this mass murder by Chivington and his Colorado volunteers. The chiefs waited to hold a formal council until the arrival of several raiding parties that had set out to strike ranches along the South Platte River. These raiders returned with a small number of livestock and goods from several wagon trains—far too little compensation to pacify the People.[18]

The chiefs of the three tribes, along with the headmen of the warrior societies who respectfully sat behind the sacred circle, discussed the subject of revenge for the people and the possessions lost at Sand Creek. In spite of everything that had happened to his people, Black Kettle urged that they seek peace with the white man. War, he told them, would only bring more death and suffering to the Cheyennes. Although his argument for peace was sound, and a handful of chiefs supported him, the majority of the Council Chiefs voted for war.

The chiefs decided that the initial attack would not target wagon trains or isolated ranches. Instead, they would raid the small settlement of Julesburg that was located on the south side of the South Platte River, one mile east of the mouth of Lodgepole Creek, in the northeastern corner of Colorado Territory. This town was the place where the Oregon Trail forded the river, at a point called Upper California Crossing, where many wagon trains of whites had crossed over the years.

Julesburg boasted a stage station, which employed about forty to fifty people and was critical to overland travel. It also had an express and telegraph office, a large store, a restaurant, a granary, a warehouse that contained food and other items, and stables and corrals that were enclosed by a high sod wall. Every building in this settlement had been solidly constructed from cottonwood logs and sod.

Fort Rankin (later Fort Sedgwick), which had been established the previous summer in response to warriors avenging the murder of Starving Bear, was located a mile west of town. This small post was surrounded by a log stockade and encircled by a ditch, with sod packed against the stockade walls to prevent them from being set on fire. Fort Rankin was guarded by one company of the 7th Iowa Cavalry, under the command of Captain Nicholas J. O'Brien.[19]

The town of Julesburg could present a formidable challenge, but, if successfully attacked, the Cheyennes and their allies would make quite a statement in response to Sand Creek.

The Indian war party, which numbered about a thousand Arapahoes, Cheyennes, and Sioux, broke camp on January 5 or 6 and headed in a northwesterly direction toward Julesburg. A group of women accompanied the expedition, leading extra ponies on which to load the plunder they planned to capture by sacking the town.

Not every available warrior, however, rode off with his brethren toward Julesburg. Black Kettle had managed to convince many men from the Southern bands to remain behind, perhaps to ensure the survival of his people should this attack prove disastrous.

The war chiefs were aware that if the soldiers spotted such a large assemblage of warriors, they would never venture out of the stockade, and the prospects of an assault on that fortified position would be suicidal. Therefore, a plan was devised to lure the soldiers outside the post, where they would be easy prey.

Before daybreak on January 7, this immense war party assumed concealed positions around the sand hills south of Julesburg. The Elkhorn Scraper headman, Big Crow, and ten men were chosen to approach Fort Rankin and attempt to coax the soldiers out of the fort and into the hills.

As the sky brightened into day, Big Crow's decoy party, now secreted within a ravine behind sandy banks, noticed a detail of soldiers walking around outside the stockade. The warriors mounted their ponies, rode out of the ravine, and charged the troopers, who dashed inside the fort.

Within moments, Captain O'Brien and perhaps as many as sixty men—including an undetermined number of civilians—thundered out of the fort to chase these brazen Indians. Big Crow and his party of ten pretended that the appearance of the soldiers had taken them by surprise. They wheeled their ponies around and raced toward the sand hills south of the fort, with the troopers in hot pursuit.

The hidden Indians could hear the firing as the Fort Rankin troopers raced toward their concealed position. The warriors quickly painted themselves and their ponies, asked for blessings for their war bonnets and shields, and formed by soldier society into a column behind the sand hills. Within moments, they would burst over the top of the hill and engage the soldiers.

The plan designed by the chiefs was unfolding perfectly—until a group of young men lost patience and bolted from the hiding place to charge the troops. The trap had been sprung prematurely while the troops were still at least a half mile away. Now that the element of surprise had been compromised, the chiefs had no choice but to give the signal for the entire war party to charge. One thousand painted, screaming Cheyenne, Arapaho, and Sioux warriors rose from their positions behind the sand hills and kicked their ponies into a gallop.

Captain Nicholas O'Brien, no doubt shocked by the sight of this superior force, immediately pulled up and ordered his men to retreat. The troopers raced for their lives toward the safety of the fort, with the Indians—Big Crow and his party in the advance—nipping at their heels.

These lead Indians overtook the rear of the column about three hundred yards from the fort. The bugler's horse fell, and Starving Elk touched the downed trooper, thereby counting the first coup of the skirmish. The Cheyenne warrior then dispatched the bugler. Other soldiers were forced to dismount and fight on foot, and those men were quickly overwhelmed and killed.

Captain O'Brien and the rest of his men were surrounded by a number of circling warriors, as they struggled in a running battle to reach the fort. Fortunately for those troops, they managed to outrun the main body of Indians and burst through the gate to safety inside the sturdy walls. O'Brien's detail left fourteen soldiers and four civilians lying dead behind it, during the mad dash back to the security of the post.

By this time, the residents of Julesburg, along with recently arrived stagecoach passengers, had heard the firing and took refuge inside Fort Rankin. The warriors exchanged fire with soldiers manning parapets around the fort but, after a while, decided to turn their attention to the deserted town of Julesburg.

The exultant warriors broke into a warehouse and a store and commenced looting everything in sight—sacks of cornmeal, sugar, bacon, molasses, smoked meats, shelled corn, flour, and other delicacies. They had never before encountered canned goods, however, and had no idea what was inside the containers. Therefore, most of these tins were ignored.

George "Tex" Bent had recuperated from his thigh wound with his mother's people and was healthy enough to participate in this war party. Tex and his brother Charles had painted themselves and dressed in traditional Cheyenne clothing, and now rode with the Dog Soldiers. The Bent brothers visited the stage station, where they discovered a freshly cooked meal that had been recently set out on the tables for the passengers of the incoming stagecoach. The two men, accompanied by a few warriors, sat down and helped themselves to the home cooking.

In another room of the stage station, a group of warriors found a metal box, which was taken outside and smashed open with tomahawks. These men were disappointed to discover that it held only "green paper" and dumped the contents on the ground. This strongbox had been abandoned by a stage passenger in his haste to reach the fort and contained the pay for Colorado troops. One warrior chopped bundles of the bills into thirds with his tomahawk and tossed the pieces of "green scalps" into the air, where they were caught by the wind.

George Bent heard about the strongbox and hurried outside. Most of the money had been scattered across the valley by that time, but he was able to salvage, according to his description, as much as he could comfortably carry.

Less than half of the original sum of money contained in the strongbox would later be recovered around the valley floor.

While the looting was taking place, one group of warriors rode across the frozen river to round up a herd of cattle. This act brought the warriors within range of the howitzers at the fort, but the ensuing fire was not effective and the soldiers decided not to waste their shells.

The Indians plundered the town of Julesburg well into the evening hours. Some of the men prepared to set fire to the buildings, but the chiefs stopped them by saying that they might wish to return at some future date for more supplies.

Finally, the procession of warriors, leading heavily laden pack ponies, returned to the temporary camp in the sand hills. It took them three full days to transport this immense amount of plunder to the main village on Cherry Creek.

The arrival of the raiders was greeted with victory songs and great jubilation. Although the quantity of goods did not come close to payment for the six or seven hundred horses that had been stolen by Chivington's soldiers at Sand Creek, it was a welcome sight to the People and their allies. That night, scalp dances were held, with dancing and drumming and the waving of the soldiers' scalps. The sorrow of the massacre was temporarily set aside, for now it was the white man's turn to mourn his losses.[20]

Several days later, the huge village was moved to White Butte Creek, also known as Frenchman's Fork, a small stream that flowed between the south fork of the Republican and the South Platte Rivers.

The chiefs of the three tribes, flush from the success of the Julesburg raid, retired to their Council Lodge to determine the future actions of the allied avengers. Black Kettle and several other Cheyenne chiefs once again spoke strongly against resuming the war. The Council listened to these pleas for peace but voted to continue the attacks in the north, along the South Platte.[21]

Black Kettle wanted no part of this expansion of the war. He informed the Council that he and most of his people would not accompany the three tribes north to fight the white man. Instead, he would lead eighty families south of the Arkansas River, where they would await another opportunity to make peace. A number of other Council Chiefs chose to accompany Black Kettle—Seven Bulls, Black White Man, Red Moon, and Little Robe—as well as the Bowstring society leader Eagle Head, and another headman, Bull That Hears. This difficult decision by Black Kettle was respected by the Cheyennes, and many people visited the departing Southerners to shake hands and say their good-byes.

In the last days of January 1865, while the Cheyennes, the Arapahoes, and the Sioux planned their war parties, Black Kettle and his destitute, ragged band started their journey south. Their possessions had been lost at Sand Creek, and most were afoot, with little more than buffalo robes wrapped around them, transporting but a few lodges for shelter. The People worried that they might encounter soldiers, many were distressed about leaving loved ones behind, and others wondered if they would die of starvation before reaching their destination.

Black Kettle, however, was a calm and confident leader and gave them hope by professing his great faith that Maheo would provide for them. His prayers and prophesy were answered when buffalo in plentiful numbers were found along the way, and no one went hungry.

Finally, the Cheyennes reached the Arkansas River and crossed to join the village of Little Raven and his Arapahoes. Black Kettle, however, feared that the soldiers might be on their trail and thought it best to move farther south. It was the middle of February when this band of Cheyennes and Arapahoes reached the Cimarron River, twenty miles south of Bluff Creek, and found a large village of Kiowas, Comanches, and Prairie Apaches.[22]

Black Kettle and the Sand Creek survivors were warmly welcomed by the three tribes and were shown friendliness and great sympathy. The host chiefs called the Cheyennes who had lost the most possessions to the center of the village and gave them lodges just as they stood, with beds, kettles, dishes—everything necessary for daily camp life. The Comanches were especially rich in horses, and they presented a horse and a bridle to each of their Cheyenne friends. Other presents, including lodges for everyone, were distributed, as it was the custom among all Indians to give freely to visitors from other tribes.

The Kiowa chief Black Eagle demonstrated his respect for Black Kettle by giving the chief a fine lodge of buffalo skin, with three beds and bedding, riding and pack saddles, bridles, lariats, and all the kettles and dishes.[23]

This outpouring of generosity by the Kiowas, the Comanches, and the Prairie Apaches would be remembered for many winters as a glorious moment in the history of Black Kettle's band of Southern Cheyenne.

Black Kettle had safely guided his people to a familiar land, with familiar people, away from the soldiers and the fighting in the north, where the People could recover from their trauma and poverty and try to rebuild their lives.

In the north, however, the Julesburg attack had been followed by raids on telegraph lines, ranches, stage stations, supply and mail trains, army patrols, and any travelers unlucky enough to be caught out in the open as the allied Indian tribes swept along both branches of the Platte River to wreak havoc on the region. On February 7, Julesburg was struck again. This time, the warriors sacked a couple of supply trains and burned the town to the ground.

By mid-February, at about the time Black Kettle's band reached the Cimarron, a total of about 50 whites had been killed, at least 1,500 head of cattle had been taken, tons of government hay had been burned, and a vast amount of food and supplies had been carted away. At that time, the Council Chiefs apparently believed that they had exacted sufficient revenge for the Sand Creek Massacre, and the village—about 6,000 strong—headed northward toward the vicinity of the Black Hills, hostile Indian country, where the soldiers dared not pursue them.[24]

On January 10, 1865, the U.S. House of Representatives ordered "that the Committee on the Conduct of the War inquire into and report all the facts connected with the late attack of the third regiment of Colorado volunteers, under Colonel Chivington, on a village of the Cheyenne tribe of Indians, near Fort Lyon."[25]

In an effort to ward off this investigation, Brigadier General Samuel Curtis called for a court-martial of Chivington, but by that time the colonel's term of service had expired and he was now a civilian—beyond the reach of military justice.

Major Edward Wynkoop, now restored to commander of Fort Lyon, was ordered by Curtis to make a thorough investigation of events surrounding Sand Creek. Wynkoop, who was personally outraged by the incident, set to work immediately and compiled a report that without exception condemned the actions of Chivington and his men.[26]

On March 13, 1865, the House of Representatives' Committee on the Conduct of the War began its hearing into the attack by the Colorado Volunteers. A parade of witnesses testified—Colonel Jesse Leavenworth, John S. Smith, Captain S. M. Robbins, Dexter Colley, Major Scott Anthony, Samuel Colley, and Governor John Evans.

Colonel John Chivington did not testify in person; rather, he answered written questions submitted by the committee. Chivington presented his case, stating that he was unaware that the Indians were under the protection of the government and that he had found nineteen scalps of white people in the camp, which was never confirmed.

The committee listened to the testimony, then retired to prepare a report of its findings.[27]

Two additional investigations were held. A Joint Special Committee of the two houses of Congress collected testimony from Washington to Forts Larned, Riley, Lyon, and as far away as Santa Fe. This body interviewed eyewitnesses to the massacre and other informed parties, such as Kit Carson, who was regarded as an expert in relations between Indians and whites.[28]

Perhaps the most difficult investigation for Chivington to endure was the February 1865 military commission inquiry. This three-man commission consisted of Lieutenant Colonel Samuel F. Tappan, Captain Edward A. Jacobs, and Captain George H. Stillwell. All were members of the 1st Colorado Cavalry, but none had been at Sand Creek. The hearing, which took place in Denver, featured a great number of officers and men who had been present at the massacre, testifying in the colonel's presence and open to cross-examination.[29]

The sentiment in Denver was decidedly pro-Chivington, with former members of the "Bloody Thirdsters" vocal in their support, as they angrily milled around saloons and street corners, ready to vent their wrath against anyone who spoke against their commander.

The first witness called, Captain Silas S. Soule, was perhaps the most damning in his indictment of Chivington. Soule outlined his protest against marching to Sand Creek and his refusal to fight and weathered a vicious cross-examination by Chivington. Soule's testimony outraged certain segments of society, and threats were made against him. Other witnesses—Major Edward Wynkoop; Lieutenants James Cannon, W. P. Minton, and C. M. Cossitt; Jim Beckwourth; John Prowers; Private David Lauderback—were badgered and berated by Chivington, who challenged their integrity and veracity.

The people of Denver absorbed every word of testimony and were unwavering in their support of Chivington—until the night of April 23, when an incident occurred that would shock that city.

Captain Silas Soule and his bride of less than one month were strolling home from the theater when gunfire erupted ahead. Soule, who as provost marshall was responsible for maintaining order, ran toward the sound. When he reached the corner of Lawrence and F Streets, he was confronted by Charles Squiers, a soldier from the 2nd Colorado, who held a gun. Soule recognized that it was an ambush and drew his own weapon. The two men shot simultaneously. Soule's bullet hit Squiers in the right arm; the bullet fired from Squiers's gun struck Soule in the cheek and lodged in his brain. Soule died instantly, while Squiers disappeared into the darkness.

The following day, Colonel Tappan addressed the hearing room, stating that Soule's death could not be classified as a shooting or even a murder but was an assassination. The clerk recorded that description in the day's proceedings.

Silas Soule had been regarded by the public as a man of high character and integrity. This act, in which every finger pointed toward John Chivington as the instigator, served to turn opinion—even by many of his staunch supporters—against the former colonel. Crowds attended Soule's funeral, as if to show where their loyalties lay. The belief that Chivington was somehow involved in the assassination was bolstered when he—a leading citizen and a former preacher—was conspicuously absent at the funeral. Neither did Chivington publicly condemn the crime or offer his condolences to Soule's family.[30]

In July, Charles Squiers, Soule's assassin, was captured in New Mexico. He was arrested by Lieutenant James Cannon and escorted to Denver to await a military court-martial. On July 14, Lieutenant Cannon was found dead under mysterious circumstances in his hotel room at the Tremont House. It was speculated that Cannon, who had testified against Chivington, had been poisoned—murdered. Squiers later escaped custody and was said to have fled to California.[31]

The hearings continued, with Chivington calling witnesses who testified on his behalf—Lieutenants Clark Dunn and Harry Richmond; captains T. G. Cree, Presley Talbot, and Jay J. Johnson; and several others—as he attempted to establish that Black Kettle's village was hostile. He hammered three points home—that rifle pits had been prepared, that white scalps had been found in the village, and that Captain Soule, John S. Smith, and Samuel Colley had conspired with the Cheyennes in order to profit from the war. Little was mentioned by Chivington's witnesses about the atrocities that had been committed against Cheyenne men, women, and children.

On May 30, 1865, this military commission stood adjourned. The commission was powerless to draw conclusions or make recommendations and existed solely as a fact-finding body.

No formal action or punishment could be taken against John Chivington as a result of any of these probes. The former colonel professed until the day he died that Sand Creek had been an honorable victory. And, to this day as then, Chivington has many supporters who embrace his statement: "I stand by Sand Creek."

The government investigative committees, however, disagreed with public sentiment. The Senate and House members found it "difficult to believe that beings in the form of men, and disgracing the uniform of the United States soldiers and officers, could commit or countenance the commission of such acts of cruelty and barbarity as are detailed in the testimony." They accused Chivington and Evans of inciting the war and of illegally authorizing citizens to kill Indians at random and confiscate their belongings.

The harshest criticism was reserved for Chivington: "As to Colonel Chivington your committee can hardly find fitting terms to describe his conduct. Wearing the uniform of the United States, which should be the emblem of justice and humanity; holding the important position of commander of a military district, and therefore having the honor of the government to that extent in his keeping, he deliberately planned and executed a foul and dastardly massacre which would have disgraced the veriest savage among those who were the victims of his cruelty."[32]

Samuel Colley was removed as an Indian agent and returned with his wife to Beloit, Wisconsin, where he served as a county sheriff for nearly fifteen years before retiring to his farm. Dexter Colley also returned briefly to Wisconsin, then moved on to Dodge City, Kansas, where he was the co-owner of the Long Branch Saloon. He served as a deputy sheriff and was elected as president of the city council. He later became a railroad conductor and eventually disappeared from the pages of recorded history.

Major Scott Anthony resigned his commission and returned to his real estate business. Lieutenant Colonel George Shoup became the governor of Idaho. Major Jacob Downing became a millionaire as a Colorado businessman. John S. Smith continued to serve as a guide and an interpreter for the army on the Plains. Major Edward Wynkoop, one of the most hated men in Colorado for his sympathy for the Indians, was appointed chief of cavalry for the District of the Upper Arkansas.

The massacre cost John Evans his federal appointment as governor—and his political future. Evans, however, secured federal land grants and county bonds, which he used to develop Colorado's railroads. He created a railroad empire and was a wealthy man when he died on July 2, 1897.

John Milton Chivington was considered a hero by many Coloradans—including the newspaper publisher William Byers—but, perhaps to escape the scene of his crimes, he decided to move his family to Nebraska. He invested his life savings in a freight business, which faired poorly due to frequent Indian attacks. His wife and his son drowned when one of his wagons sank in the North Platte River.

At that point, Chivington sold his business and drifted to California, then back to his childhood home in Warren County, Ohio. In 1873, he married a widow, bought a newspaper, and in 1883 was the Republican candidate for the state legislature. His race for office was cut short when he was forced to withdraw after his opponent brought up the subject of Sand Creek as an example of Chivington's fitness. He departed Ohio for Denver, where he worked as a deputy sheriff.

John Chivington died of cancer in Denver on October 4, 1894. His funeral was attended by hundreds of people—the former governor Evans, former Colorado volunteers, the former major Scott Anthony, who served as a pallbearer—some of whom had traveled great distances to honor his memory. He was laid to rest with the words of his old friend, the Methodist minister Robert McIntyre: "When Colorado lifts aloft the scroll of honor, the name of Colonel John M. Chivington will be emblazoned near the top."

During the course of the Chivington hearings, the allied Indians made their presence known by resuming raids along the primary travel routes across the Plains. The army was unable to effectively prevent or punish the perpetrators, and the governors of western states and territories called on Washington for assistance.

The future of Black Kettle and his Cheyennes, whether there would be peace or war, now rested in the hands of the federal government, where the army reigned supreme.

Colorado Superintendency Indian Affairs.

Denver, June 27th, 1864.

To the Friendly Indians of the Plains:

AGENTS, INTERPRETERS, and TRADERS, will inform the friendly Indians of the Plains that some members of their tribes have gone to war with the white people. They steal stock and run it off hoping to escape detection and punishment. In some instances they have attacked and killed soldiers and murdered peaceable citizens. For this the Great Father is angry, and will certainly hunt them out and punish them. But he does not want to injure those who remain friendly to the whites. He desires to protect and take care of them. For this purpose I direct that all friendly Indians keep away from those who are at war, and go to places of safety.

Friendly Arapahoes and Cheyennes, belonging on the Arkansas River, will go to Major COLLEY, U. S. Indian Agent at Fort Lyon, who will give them provisions and show them a place of safety.

Friendly Kiowas and Camanches will go to Fort Larned, where they will be cared for in the same way.

Friendly Sioux will go to their Agent at Fort Laramie for directions.

Friendly Arapahoes and Cheyennes of the Upper Platte, will go to Camp Collins on the Cache-la-Poudre where they will be assigned a place of safety, and provisions will be given them.

The object of this is to prevent friendly Indians from being killed through mistake. None but those who intend to be friendly with the whites must come to these places. The families of those who have gone to war with the whites must be kept away from among the friendly Indians.

The war on hostile Indians will be continued until they are all effectually subdued.

JOHN EVANS,
Governor of Colorado, and Superintendent of Indian Affairs.

Proclamation by Governor Evans to "Friendly Indians of the Plains"

Cheyenne Village Aug. 29th/64

Maj. Colley.

Sir

We received a letter from Bent. wishing us to make peace We held a consel in regard to it all came to the conclusion to make peace with you providing you make peace with the Kiowas, Commenches Arrapahoes Apaches and Siouxs.

We are going to send a messenger to the Kiowas and to the other nations about our going to make with you.

We heard that you some prisoners in Denver. We have seven prisoners of you which we are willing to give providing you give up yours. there was another yet out of Arrapahoes. they been out some time and expect now soon.

When we held this counsel there were few Arrapahoes and Siouxs present. we want true news from you. in return, that is a letter

Black Kittle &

other Chiefs

Brought to Maj Lyon Sunday Sept 4th 1864 by One Eye

Letter dictated by Black Kettle requesting a peace council in response to the proclamation by Evans

Banks along Sand Creek where Black Kettle and his companions held off the Colorado cavalrymen on November 29, 1864

George Armstrong Custer during the winter campaign of 1868

Site of Black Kettle's village on the Washita River, 1868, looking north

Location along the Washita River where it is said that Black Kettle was killed

The Black Kettle Museum, Cheyenne, Oklahoma

Original painting
of Black Kettle by
award-winning
artist Lynn Cahill

10

COUNCIL ON THE
LITTLE ARKANSAS

THE PROSPECT OF A LASTING PEACE BETWEEN BLACK KETTLE'S Cheyennes and the white man diminished with every attack by the Indians who regarded Sand Creek as a declaration of war. The army was accustomed to negotiating from a position of power, and the means to this end was to respond to force with force. The guilty parties, or those assumed to be guilty, must be vanquished before there could be any consideration of initiating a peace process.

General Ulysses S. Grant had become concerned that troops needed in the East were engaged in this losing cause on the frontier and blamed the ineptitude of the officers in charge. To remedy the problem, Grant appointed Major General John Pope to the post of commander of the new Division of the Missouri, which would be responsible for all operations in the plains region.[1]

Pope immediately went to work planning an aggressive campaign that called for three columns to march under orders to rid the Plains of hostile Indians and secure the roads leading to the mines in Montana.[2]

There was one individual in Colorado, however, who opposed military action and believed that peace was attainable without any more bloodshed. Jesse H. Leavenworth, a former colonel in Chivington's 2nd Regiment, embarked on a one-man crusade to convince the government to hold talks with the Plains tribes.

Jesse Leavenworth had been born in 1807 in Danville, Vermont. He was the son of Colonel Henry Leavenworth, the man who in 1827 established the fort in Kansas that bears his name. Jesse graduated from the U.S. Military Academy at West Point in 1830 and two years later fought against the Sac Indians in the Black Hawk War. Leavenworth resigned his commission in 1836, moved to Chicago, and spent twenty-two years as a civil engineer. In 1860, after two years working as a lumber merchant in Wisconsin, he emigrated to Colorado. Leavenworth was appointed a colonel in the Colorado volunteers, and, while the 1st Regiment was stationed in New Mexico, he was assigned the task of recruiting the new 2nd Regiment.[3]

Leavenworth was the post commander at Fort Larned in 1863, providing security for the Santa Fe Trail, when he became involved in an incident that demonstrated the heavy-handed authority of Colonel John Chivington. Colonel Samuel Tappan, a former correspondent for the *New York Tribune* and one of the founders of Lawrence, Kansas— as well as second in command at the La Glorieta battle—had assumed command of Fort Lyon. Both Leavenworth and Tappan were annoyed that Chivington was holding so many soldiers in Denver when they were undermanned on the eastern Plains. Leavenworth, who had more duties than men to carry them out, requested assistance from Tappan's garrison. Chivington denied this request, but Tappan went ahead on his own and dispatched a detachment of troops to reinforce Leavenworth. Chivington responded by removing Tappan from Fort Lyon and exiling him to out-of-the-way Fort Garland. Ironically, Tappan, over Chivington's objections, had served on the commission investigating the colonel's actions at Sand Creek.[4]

No doubt Chivington had been waiting for an opportunity to punish Jesse Leavenworth as well. When recruiting the 2nd Regiment, Leavenworth had the dubious task of appointing the officers. Some of the men who believed that they were slighted in either rank or assignment fostered hard feelings toward the colonel. In August 1863, Leavenworth authorized W. D. McLane to establish an artillery company to support the 2nd Regiment. At the time that this company was mustered in, the order was issued relegating the men to infantry service, not artillery, and they balked at this lowly assignment. An appeal by disgruntled officers was made through military channels to Washington, and as a result, in October, Leavenworth and three of his officers were abruptly dishonorably discharged from the service. A later review of the facts in the matter, however, led the judge advocate to change Leavenworth's discharge to honorable. Regardless, Leavenworth's career with the Colorado volunteers was over.[5]

In early 1864, when Evans and Chivington had embarked on their military offensive designed to provoke the Cheyennes into waging war, Leavenworth prophetically wrote to the commissioner of Indian affairs, stating that if "Colonel Chivington was not stopped in his course of sending Lieutenant Eayre after these Indians we should get into a general war on the frontier." His warnings were not heeded, and the Sand Creek Massacre was the culmination of this treachery by the governor and his military henchman.[6]

In late 1864, Jesse Leavenworth replaced Samuel Colley as the Indian agent for the Upper Arkansas tribes, which included the Cheyennes. He immediately set to work making amends for the Sand Creek Massacre by trying to educate the government to the fact that a peace treaty, not war, was the only way in which to bring an end to hostilities. The former colonel did take time out from his duties to testify against Chivington at the congressional hearings on Sand Creek, although Leavenworth had no firsthand knowledge of what had occurred that day.[7]

Leavenworth's first order of business as an Indian agent, beginning in early January 1865, was to write a series of letters from his headquarters at Fort Larned to Indian Commissioner William P. Dole in Washington. The agent stated that nearly every one of the chiefs of the Cheyennes and the Arapahoes who had desired peace with the white man and was acting as a mediator had been "cruelly murdered" at Sand Creek. (Leavenworth likely did not know at this time that Black Kettle had survived the massacre.) Leavenworth implored Cole to do everything within his power to curtail the operations of the army. He wrote that if the soldiers would hold off on committing "outrages on these Indians, I can give peace to the frontier at once (and) . . . save millions to the government."[8]

The Indian agent's requests for restraint by the army had no effect on the field commanders, other than perhaps minor concessions. Major General Grenville M. Dodge wrote, "I do not consider such fights as Chivington's to be of any benefit in quelling Indian disturbances or of any credit to our service." Therefore, his subordinates were ordered to capture, rather than kill, women and children.[9]

Secretary of War Edwin M. Stanton, when informed about Leavenworth's efforts, echoed the army's sentiments by saying that "the military have no authority to treat with the Indians. Their duty is to make them keep the peace by punishing them for hostilities."[10]

Leavenworth not only appealed to the army to hold back on an offensive but was compelled to pacify the Indians as well. In early 1865, Confederates in Arkansas had approached the various tribes to urge them to accompany Rebel soldiers in an attack along the Kansas border. Leavenworth sent out runners to each camp with a plea that they refrain from raiding and not join the Confederates and with a promise that he would arrange for a council that would lead to lasting peace. Black Kettle and his fellow Council Chiefs apparently respected the agent's words and refused—for the time being, at least—to negotiate with the Confederates.[11]

Colonel James H. Ford was one of the more outspoken field commanders calling for a major offensive against the Indians. Leavenworth appealed to Ford for patience and received the reply: "One good thrashing will gain peace that will last forever." This sentiment was echoed by Ford's superior, General Dodge, who held to the opinion that the frontier would be well served if the Indians were subjected to a show of force. By March, eight hundred to a thousand cavalrymen were poised to march against the Cheyennes and their presumed allies.

Jesse Leavenworth came to the realization that if he were to be successful in his endeavor, he must impress the highest authorities of the importance of curbing the army and initiating peace talks. He decided to travel to Washington in an effort to rally support. Leavenworth, accompanied by his ally Senator James R. Doolittle of Washington, presented his case to the army chief of staff, Major General Henry W. Halleck. The general, however, refused to place restraints on the troops or initiate a peace treaty.[12]

Leavenworth worked tirelessly throughout the early months of 1865, badgering, pleading, and reinforcing his position, until finally he was aided by a historic moment in time, one that the country had been looking forward to for four long and bloody years.

On the afternoon of April 9, 1865, Generals Ulysses S. Grant and Robert E. Lee met at the home of Wilmer McClean in Appomattox, Virginia, and signed a surrender that ended the Civil War.

This action was a welcome relief to a nation weary of war and desiring peace. But this conclusion of hostilities in the East would provide only a brief respite from bloodshed for the postwar U.S. Army.

Pope's ambitious campaign, intended to strike several fronts in Indian Country, was now stalled by volunteer units that were mustering out and the wait for regular troops to replace them. Another problem for the army was a peace movement that had been initiated after the Sand Creek Massacre.

Government policy with respect to the "Indian problem" had become the subject of fierce contention between two diverse factions. The Indian Bureau combined with eastern humanitarian groups to encourage a policy of tolerance, generosity, and fair treatment for the Indian, which they believed would convince the Indians to respond in kind. Westerners were of like mind with the army and ridiculed this notion, which they deemed idealistic and impractical. They were of the opinion that the only way to deal with the Indian was by a show of military strength—first punishment for their actions and then supervision on reservations.

Both sides, however, did agree that all Plains Indians should be removed from the pathway of westward expansion between the Platte and the Arkansas rivers and resettled onto reservations north of Nebraska and south of Kansas.[13]

The army commanders on the Plains sensed an indecisiveness in Washington with respect to campaigning against the Indians, and they also recognized that Leavenworth's plan for peace might have merit. These commanders became hesitant to mount an offensive of any consequence without the full support of their superiors.[14]

In late April, however, a war party—identified as Cheyennes and Sioux—raided a Mexican wagon train along the Santa Fe Trail, east of Fort Larned, killing and scalping four men. Soon after, another war party struck Cow Creek Station on that trail and ran off all the stock.

These incidents convinced Secretary of War Stanton to loosen restraints on the troops, and he also informed his western commanders that Jesse Leavenworth was not authorized to initiate any peace treaty with these hostiles. Preparations commenced immediately for a campaign against the Indians. It certainly appeared that Leavenworth's efforts had gone for naught, that blood would once again be spilled onto the Plains.[15]

Before these troops could take to the field, however, President Andrew Johnson personally intervened in this conflict on the side of peace. He ordered that Senator James Doolittle's congressional committee was authorized "to make peace, if you can, with [the] hostile Indians." This treaty would be subject to presidential approval. The army would now wait in garrison while Doolittle and Leavenworth made arrangements with the tribes for a council.[16]

During May, the time when the horses got fat, Black Kettle's Southern Cheyennes, along with the Southern Arapahoes, the Kiowas, the Comanches, and the Prairie Apaches, gathered on the Washita River, near Fort Cobb. The chiefs and the headmen of these tribes held a council in this great village and discussed the prospects for peace with the white man. Black Kettle spoke forcefully for ending hostilities and was heartily supported by the older Cheyenne chiefs, as well as by many chiefs of the other tribes.

There were, however, a number of Southerners, especially the younger men, who refused to forgive and forget Sand Creek. These warriors resumed raiding—running off horses and mules from Fort Dodge on June 8; attacking four wagon trains at Cow Creek on June 9; harassing an army patrol; and killing and scalping two soldiers carrying dispatches on June 11. These incidents were followed by a series of other acts that continued throughout June and into the first part of July.[17]

By now, Senator Doolittle and his commission members had taken refuge at Bent's Old Fort and were monitoring the violence that was occurring all around them. General Dodge requested permission to take to the field and retaliate for these raids, but Doolittle held the soldiers back, fearing that any military action would compromise his attempt to make peace. Jesse Leavenworth made efforts through traders to contact the various tribes to inform them of this new peace entreaty.

During the middle of July, Dodge took matters into his own hands and ordered his new commander, Major General John B. Sanborn, to lead a detachment of troops on a mission to hunt down the marauders and punish them.

While Sanborn readied his troops, Senator Doolittle traveled to New Mexico Territory to meet with Kit Carson and William Bent. Both men professed that they could make peace with the Upper Arkansas Agency tribes. Bent insisted that he would guarantee peace "with his head." Doolittle dispatched letters to Washington, requesting that the army be ordered to hold off while Carson and Bent tried to convince the Indians to talk peace.[18]

At that time, four Kiowa men, with their wives, arrived at Leavenworth's headquarters at the mouth of the Little Arkansas River—perhaps in response to the agent's messengers. These men claimed to have been designated as spokesmen for all of the Upper Arkansas tribes. They professed that the Cheyennes, the Arapahoes, the Kiowas, the Comanches, and the Prairie Apaches wanted peace and promised to cease raiding along the Santa Fe Trail while details of a treaty council could be worked out. These Kiowa men were soon joined by their head chief, Dohasan, and seventy-five Kiowas and Prairie Apaches. By August 15, every tribe was represented at Leavenworth's headquarters—except Black Kettle's Cheyennes and Little Raven's Arapahoes. Leavenworth was informed that after what had happened at Sand

Creek, the Cheyennes were leery about showing themselves. The agent told the visiting chiefs to let the Cheyennes know that the army would not harm anyone while the peace process was taking place.

Regardless of assurances, Black Kettle and Little Raven did not appear with the others but, apparently, were waiting to see if the white man was truly serious about talking peace.[19]

This initial meeting between the informal commission and the tribal chiefs was not a peace council—rather, a truce. The chiefs signed a statement promising that there would be no attacks by their tribes against settlements or travelers. It was also agreed that they would assemble on October 4, at Bluff Creek, a tributary of the Salt Fork of the Arkansas River forty miles south of the Little Arkansas, to discuss and sign a treaty of lasting peace.

On August 18, the day that Dohasan and the other chiefs signed the truce document on behalf of their bands, Black Kettle and a handful of Southern chiefs, with assurances of safety and the demonstration of sincerity by the white man, made their presence known at the council. The appearance of Black Kettle may have caused quite a stir among the officials, inasmuch as he had been listed as killed at Sand Creek and this was his first contact with the white man since that time.

At the insistence of Black Kettle, another truce document was drawn up, which identified the reason—namely, the Sand Creek Massacre—that their young men had taken to the warpath:

> We, the undersigned, chiefs and headmen of the bands of Arapahoe and Cheyenne Indians, now south of the Arkansas River, having been forced, in self-protection, to fight the United States troops under the command of Colonel J. M. Chivington, at Sand Creek, Colorado Territory, and having, through the interposition of a kind providence, escaped our intended massacre, and having heard from our friend Colonel J. H. Leavenworth, through his runners and agents, that we could in safety visit him at the mouth of the Little Arkansas river, have come to him to ask that he will use his influence to restore kindness between our bands, and if possible between our whole tribes and the government of the United States.

Black Kettle was satisfied that this declaration portrayed and justified the true reasons for any raiding, and he promised to attend the formal council at Bluff Creek in October. He was the first to sign the truce document for the People, followed by chiefs Little Robe, Black White Man, and Seven Bulls.[20]

The Cheyenne chiefs kept their promises, and there were no further raids by the young men during the two-month period preceding the council.

In early October, Black Kettle and his Southerners were camped at Bluff Creek awaiting the commission members when they were informed by messengers that the site of the council had been moved to the mouth of the Little Arkansas River. On October 11, Black Kettle and his people—eighty lodges—arrived at the treaty grounds, which were located near present-day Wichita, Kansas.[21]

Black Kettle was greeted by an old friend, Major Edward "Ned" Wynkoop, the Tall Chief. Wynkoop approached the chief's camp with caution, for he feared that he would be blamed for the disaster at Sand Creek. The Tall Chief, however, was warmly welcomed and was told by Black Kettle that not for one moment had the Cheyennes doubted Wynkoop's good faith. The relieved major said, "Through their extraordinary natural intelligence they had seemed to comprehend the whole state of affairs."[22]

The following morning, October 12, the council was called to order. The commission members were Major General John B. Sanborn, who had been appointed as president; Major General William S. Harney; Judge James Steele, who represented the Bureau of Indian Affairs; Thomas Murphy of the General Superintendency; the Indian agent Jesse Leavenworth; Kit Carson; and William Bent. Mrs. Margaret Wilmarth, the remarried widow of the former Indian agent Thomas Fitzpatrick, interpreted for the Arapahoes. John S. Smith once again served as an interpreter for the Cheyennes.

Black Kettle was the only chief of the People who was recorded as being present. It was likely that other chiefs also attended—including Little Robe, Black White Man, and Seven Bulls. The Arapahoes, the Cloud People, were represented by Chiefs Little Raven, Spotted Wolf, Storm, and Big Mouth.[23]

The council opened with the pipe being passed and smoked. General Sanborn then rose to speak, his words calm and conciliatory. He told the chiefs that the president was aware of the massacre at Sand Creek and admitted that the Cheyennes and the Arapahoes had been "forced to make war." Now, the president wanted to offer reparation for that bad treatment. The government was "willing to give to the chiefs in their own right three hundred and twenty acres of land as his own forever, and to each of the children and squaws, who lost husbands or parents, we are willing to give one hundred and sixty acres of land, as their own, to keep as long as they live."

This unusual offer likely surprised and perhaps somewhat offended Black Kettle and the other chiefs. Grandmother Earth was not meant to be broken up and given away to individuals; rather, her body provided life for all the People. Black Kettle politely rejected Sanborn's offer, saying that there were but eighty lodges of Cheyennes present at the council, and the remainder, as many as four hundred lodges, were north of the Platte River. He was not about to cause trouble within the tribe by accepting or ceding parcels of land without agreement by the rest of the People.[24]

Sanborn went on to state that the government believed that the Indians should be located south of the Arkansas River or north of the North Platte River, which would keep them away from the primary white travel routes. The Cheyennes and the Arapahoes should settle south of the Arkansas, if that was acceptable. He then said, "We are disposed to acknowledge Black Kettle as chief of the Cheyenne nation, and will support and protect him in everything he does for the nation. We have understood that some of his people were dissatisfied with his actions before the affair at Sand Creek, but upon investigation we are satisfied that he did right, and we would protect him in all that he has done, and that it was the fault of our bad white officers."[25]

Sanborn concluded by urging the chiefs to be friends and allies of the government, that peace under any conditions was better than war, and that they would be supported and sustained at all times.

The Arapaho Little Raven was the first chief to speak, and he reiterated Black Kettle's hesitancy to agree to a treaty when most of the Cheyennes and the Arapahoes were not present. Sanborn replied that these missing people would have five months in which to accept the terms.

Little Raven told Sanborn that it would be difficult to leave their traditional country, that "our friends are buried here," and wondered if there was not some way that they could remain in the Arkansas River valley. He suggested that it might be best to wait until next spring, when all the tribes would gather, before finalizing this treaty.

Sanborn sympathized but said that with respect to moving, "Events over which you have no control have made it necessary to do so."

Little Raven was not appeased by Sanborn's response and ended his remarks by stating that ever since Fitzpatrick had left as agent, Little Raven's people had been cheated by their agents.[26]

Black Kettle was the next speaker. He rose and, one by one, shook the hands of the commission members. The chief then said,

> The Great Father above hears us, and the Great Father at Washington will hear what we say. Is it true that you came here from Washington, and is it true what you say here to-day? The Big Chief he give his words to me to come and meet here, and I take hold and retain what he says. I believe all to be true, and think it is all true. Their young white men, when I meet them on the plains, I give them my horse and my moccasins, and I am glad to-day to think that the Great Father has sent good men to take pity on us.
>
> Your young soldiers I don't think they listen to you. You bring presents, and when I come to get them I am afraid they will strike me before I get away. When I come in to receive presents I take them up crying. Although wrongs have been done to me, I live in hopes. I have not got two hearts. These young men, (Cheyennes), when I call them into the lodge and talk with them, they listen to me and mind what I say. Now we are again together to make peace. My shame (mortification) is as big as the earth, although I will do what my friends advise me to do. I once thought that I was the only man that persevered to be the friend of the white man, but since they have come and cleaned out (robbed) our lodges, horses, and everything else, it is hard for me to believe white men any more.[27]

Black Kettle paused and requested that his wife, Medicine Woman Later, be brought in. He pointed out to the commissioners the wounds that she had received at Sand Creek. He told them about how his wife had lain helplessly on the ground while soldiers fired bullet after bullet into her body. The commissioners counted nine scars on Medicine Woman Later that had been caused by bullet holes. General Harney was so impressed with Black Kettle that he presented the chief with a fine bay horse.[28]

After his wife had been escorted out, Black Kettle resumed his speech.

> Here we are, altogether, Arapahoes and Cheyennes, but few of us, we are one people. As soon as you arrived you started runners after us and the Arapahoes, with words that I took hold of immediately on hearing them. From what I can see around me, I feel confident that our Great Father has taken pity on me, and I feel that it is the truth all that has been told me to-day. All my friends—the Indians that are holding back—they are afraid to come in; are afraid they will be betrayed as I have been. I am

not afraid of white men, but come and take you by the hand, and am glad to have an opportunity of so doing. These lands that you propose to give us I know nothing about. There is but a handful here now of the Cheyenne nation, and I would rather defer making any permanent treaty until the others come. We are living friendly now.

There are a great many white men. Possibly you may be looking for some one with a strong heart. Possibly you may be intending to do something for me better than I know of.

Inasmuch as my Great Father has sent you here to take us by the hand, why is it that we are prevented from crossing the Arkansas? If we give you our hands in peace, we give them also to those of the plains. We want the privilege of crossing the Arkansas to kill buffalo. I have but few men here, but what I say to them they listen, and they will abide by their promise whatever it may be. All these young soldiers are taking us by the hand, and I hope it will come back good times as formerly. It is very hard to have one-half of our nation absent at this time; we wish to get through at once. My friends, I want you to understand that I have sent up north for my people, and I want the road open for them to get here. I hope that which you have said will be just as you have told me, and I am glad to hear such good counsel from you. When my friends get down from the north I think it will be the best time to talk about lands. There are so few here it would not look right to make a treaty for the whole nation, and so many absent. I hope you will use your influence with the troops to open a road for my men to get here. You may mark out the lands you propose giving us, but I know nothing about them; it is a new country to me.

I have been in great hopes that I may see my children that were taken prisoners last fall, and when I get here I do not see them. I feel disappointed. My young men here, and friends, when we meet in council and come to the conclusion, it is the truth, we do not vary from it.

This lady's husband (Mrs. Wilmarth, formerly Fitzpatrick) Major Fitzpatrick, when he was our agent and brought us presents he did not take them into forts and houses, but would drive his wagons into our villages and empty them there. Every one would help themselves and feel glad. He has gone ahead of us, and he told us that when he was gone we would have trouble, and it has proved true. We are sorry. But since the death of Major Fitzpatrick we have had many agents. I don't know as we have been wronged, but it looks so. The amount of goods has diminished; it don't look right. Has known Colonel Leavenworth for some time; he has treated me well; whether it will continue or not I do not know. He has got a strong heart, and has done us a great deal of good. Now that times are so uncertain in this country I would like to have my old friend Colonel Bent with me.

There may be wrongs done, but we want to show who does these wrongs before you censure us. I feel that the Great Father has taken pity on us, and that ever since we have met Colonel Leavenworth's words have been true, and nothing done since that time but what is true.

I heard that some chiefs were sent here to see us. We have brought our women and children, and we want to see if you are going to have pity on us.

This is all by Black Kettle.[29]

Black Kettle's speech indicated his desire for peace and his respect for the white man's army. He referred to some Cheyenne children who had been taken prisoner during the 1864 war and was disappointed that they had not been returned. Jesse Leavenworth explained that he had promised to deliver the children, who were said to have been in Denver, but these children had not been found in that city. Leavenworth vowed not to rest until he located them.

The council adjourned until the following morning. At that time, William Bent addressed the chiefs, saying that "this is the best opportunity you will ever have to make so favorable a treaty as will be now offered to you by them." The words of Bent, a friend and a tribe member by marriage, carried considerable weight with Black Kettle, who had sought advice from the trader on several occasions over the years.[30]

Judge James Steele, who represented the Bureau of Indian Affairs, described the land promised to the Cheyennes and the Arapahoes in glowing terms and painted an appealing picture of peace and friendship.[31]

Little Raven spoke once more. He shrewdly pointed out that the lands above the North Platte River had already been given to the Lakota Sioux, and those lands to the south were Kiowa and Comanche country. The Arapaho chief, however, agreed to accept the lands that the commissioners had indicated, if arrangements could be made to free them from any other claim.[32]

Black Kettle rose to speak. His voice was filled with sorrow as he lamented the fact that they must give up the land of his ancestors. He said that he would, however, abide by the treaty provisions if it would mean peace between the two races.

Friends, I have never seen you before. My forefathers used to live all over this country. I have seen one that is here, (General Harney.) I don't know how small I was. The general must have a great and strong heart. Our forefathers, when alive, lived all over this country; they did not know about doing wrong; since that they have died, and gone I don't know where. We have lost our way. Major Fitzpatrick was a good man; he came to us, and we had just such meetings as this. Major Fitzpatrick was our agent; he brought us our goods annually; he did not drive to forts and houses to unload them, but drove to our villages and threw them out, and our women were glad. Major Fitzpatrick said: "My children, when I am dead and gone, you will get into trouble with the whites."

Our Great Father sent you here with his words to us, and we take hold of them. Although the troops have struck us, we throw it all behind and are glad to meet you in peace and friendship. What you have come here for, and what the President has sent you for, I don't object to, but say yes to it.

I will live around here, as I have sent up for the balance to come down. I expect to live in the old reservation until they come down. I don't feel right over here, or at home, where there are so many tribes of Indians. These thoroughfares, I may live about them, but I shall not be the first one to interrupt them. The white people can go wherever they please and they will not be disturbed by us, and I want you to let them know. In broad daylight we talk, and talk the truth; we want nothing bad, and expect nothing but truth to be derived from it. We are different nations, but it seems as if we were but one people, whites and all. I feel highly gratified that we have met once more in peace. The Big Chief in Washington has sent you here. Again I take you by the hand, and I feel happy. These people that are with us are glad to think that we have peace once more, and can sleep soundly, and that we can live.

What is proposed now by this commission I do not object to nor any part of it, but I want the privilege of roaming around until it is necessary for me to accept the proposed reservation.

The Great Father will know, from time to time, how we are living, and how we are progressing, and when we are poor and need something to eat, the Great Father will know how to relieve us. Now the path that you mark out is a good one. The roads are open, and we consider that we are living as in the olden time when we were one people together for fear of other troubles. Other nations may commit wrongs that we may be blamed for, and to prevent this we want Colonel Bent and Major Wynkoop to live with us.[33]

The following afternoon, October 14, 1865, each article of this new treaty was read to the Cheyenne and the Arapaho chiefs.

The Cheyenne-Arapaho reservation was not specifically plotted but was intended to begin at the mouth of the Cimarron River on the Arkansas River, upstream to a place opposite Buffalo Creek, then north

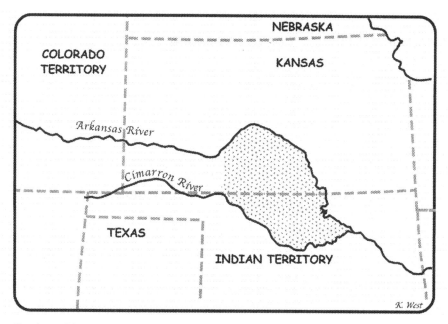

Southern Cheyenne–Arapaho Territory, Little Arkansas Treaty of 1865

to the Arkansas, and down that river to the confluence of the Cimarron and the Arkansas rivers. Entitlement to all other land was ceded to the government.

The two tribes would not inhabit this reservation until the government had settled any claims to this land by other Indians, but they could freely roam, as long as they did not venture within ten miles of any road, fort, or town, unless authorized to do so. When the land was finally occupied, the Cheyennes and the Arapahoes would not be permitted to leave the confines of that boundary—even for hunting—without permission from their agent or another authorized party. The government would be allowed to build forts or roads across this reservation.

The Cheyennes would receive a $40 per capita payment when they moved onto the new reservation and $20 per capita until that time, for a period of forty years. Each Cheyenne who signed the treaty was entitled to 320 acres of land, and the Sand Creek survivors would receive 160 acres. Also, the chiefs requested that certain other people, including the four children of William Bent, Thomas Fitzpatrick's widow, and John S. Smith's children—thirty-one people in all, most of mixed blood—be granted a section of land.

One article to which Black Kettle and the other chiefs raised objections, which authorized the U.S. Senate to make amendments without consulting the tribes, was stricken.

Black Kettle was the first Cheyenne to make his mark on the treaty and was designated by the title "head chief." Three other Council Chiefs, Seven Bulls, Little Robe, and Black White Man, also signed, as did the soldier society headmen Eagle Head and Bull That Hears.

Signing for the Arapahoes was Little Raven, as "head chief," then Storm, Big Mouth, and Spotted Wolf.[34]

The document called the Treaty of the Little Arkansas had been signed—but by only four of the forty-four Cheyenne chiefs who sat in the sacred circle of Council Chiefs. It was now the task of Black Kettle and the others to persuade the remaining forty chiefs of the wisdom of agreeing to this treaty, an endeavor that would prove difficult, inasmuch as their traditional home, the prime lands between the Arkansas and the Platte rivers, had been signed away—as had the lands of the Northern bands in the Smoky Hill country.

Black Kettle went into camp for the winter on Bluff Creek below Fort Dodge, and, true to his word, his people remained peaceful. The influence of the chiefs was bolstered in part by the presence of William Bent, who had settled in the Cheyenne camp to trade—obliging a request that Black Kettle had made at the Little Arkansas council.[35]

The Dog Soldiers, however, were outraged when they discovered that a new stage line had been established in the Smoky Hill country. The Butterfield Stage route ran from the Missouri River to Denver—directly through prime Cheyenne buffalo hunting range. Young warriors protested this intrusion by running off stage line stock but were thwarted in their attempts to attack the stage stations. Each station had been dug deep into the ground, with only a sod roof rising several feet above the surface. Portholes from which those inside could fire without fear of being hit dotted the walls. The Dog Soldiers, frustrated in their efforts to destroy the stations, turned their attention to striking travelers and wagon trains on the Smoky Hill Road.[36]

After the first of the year, 1866, Dr. I. C. Taylor was appointed as the new Indian agent for the Cheyennes and the Arapahoes. He would be assisted by an old friend of Black Kettle's. Edward Wynkoop had resigned from the cavalry and been assigned to special duty with the Interior Department, "to bring about a union of the Cheyenne and

Arapahoes Indians" and to cooperate with General Dodge to assure the safety of the Overland routes.[37]

In late February, the Tall Chief, accompanied by the new agent and four companies of cavalry, pulled a wagonload of annuity goods into Black Kettle's village. Wynkoop had requested that the chiefs who had not been present at the Little Arkansas council meet with him and discuss the terms of the treaty. The Dog Soldier chief Tangle Hair and the war chief Medicine Arrows listened to Wynkoop explain the benefits of accepting the treaty. At first they objected, but eventually, due to the influence of Black Kettle, who vouched for the trustworthiness of the Tall Chief, the chiefs signed the treaty papers.

Wynkoop also managed to gain the release of a sixteen-year-old white girl named Mary Fletcher, who had been captured from a wagon train the previous summer. The girl was turned over to John S. Smith for safekeeping, and she later reported that she had been treated by the Indians with nothing but kindness.[38]

In early March 1866, four hundred Dog Soldiers massed within striking distance of the Butterfield Overland route and were poised for a massive attack, when Little Robe rode into their camp. The chief brought word of the peace treaty that Tangle Hair and Medicine Arrows had signed and urged the other Dog Soldier chiefs to meet with Wynkoop and learn about this new peace initiative.

On April 4, 1866, Bull Bear, Tall Bull, and White Horse all made their marks on the treaty and promised that they would accept the provisions, as outlined in the Little Arkansas.[39]

The Dog Soldiers, the militant, warring faction of the Cheyenne, surprisingly, had finally agreed to make peace with the white man, which would require them to relinquish their beloved Smoky Hill country, where buffalo were still plentiful. It can be assumed that these chiefs had no intention of vacating their land and either were misled, misunderstood the boundaries, or were motivated to sign by the promise of presents.

That spring, George Bent married Magpie, Black Kettle's niece and, as was the custom, went to live in the chief's lodge. Black Kettle presented Bent with a wedding gift—the fine bay horse that General Harney had given the chief on the Little Arkansas.

Bent also stated, "Black Kettle had two wives, one of whom was a captive Ponca woman. He had no children. He was very fond of my wife and her brother, Blue Horse, and treated them as his own children. These were happy days for us. Black Kettle was a fine man and highly respected by all who knew him."[40]

This is the only known mention about Black Kettle taking a wife in addition to Medicine Woman Later. Cheyenne men practiced polygamy, but the second wife was normally related to the first, perhaps a younger sister, which strengthened the circle of family relations. It has also been noted that if the second wife was not related to the first, the first wife would likely be insulted and leave the lodge. Medicine Woman Later, as evidenced by later events, did not leave Black Kettle. It could be speculated that she had been incapacitated in some manner from her wounds at Sand Creek, and this Ponca woman had been brought into the household to work and thereby hold together the extended family structure.[41]

Throughout the spring and the summer, the Dog Soldiers remained in the Smoky Hill country—land that they vowed to protect at any cost from the white man. The young warriors obeyed the chiefs, however, and there were no raids against stage stations, settlements, or travelers.

On July 21, Black Kettle led his people to Fort Zarah, where Agent Taylor distributed a portion of the annuity goods. The chief received permission from the agent to hunt buffalo near the Smoky Hill River and notified Taylor that the annual Sun Dance would be held in that location. Black Kettle also promised that he would speak to the Dog Soldier chiefs and try to convince them to relinquish right of way to the Smoky Hill country.[42]

While ratification of the Little Arkansas Treaty was delayed in the U.S. Senate, which also held up promised annuities, Black Kettle carried through with his promise to speak to the Dog Soldier chiefs. Bull Bear, Tall Bull, and the others were adamant; they still refused to give up their traditional territory.

Perhaps Black Kettle reminded them that they had made their marks on the treaty document, which was an agreement to observe the conditions. If so, the chiefs likely told Black Kettle, with all due respect, that the word of the white man was worthless, as evidenced by the betrayal at Sand Creek, and therefore promises made to white men had little validity. In addition, the Great Spirit had given the Smoky Hill country to the People, and it was meant to be their home, regardless of claims made by the white man.

Black Kettle likely could not argue with such reasoning and departed his meeting with the Dog Soldiers aware that if this concession was not eventually made, there would be no alternative but war with the white man.

In August 1866, Black Kettle led a delegation of chiefs to a council with Ned Wynkoop at Fort Ellsworth. Other notable Cheyenne attendees were Council Chiefs Old Little Wolf and Big Head, as well as Roman Nose, who was neither a chief nor the head of a soldier society. Roman Nose, however, was known as a brave and fierce warrior and was allowed to sit at the council to listen and, if asked, respond to questions from the chiefs.

Conspicuously missing from this gathering were the Dog Men chiefs Bull Bear, Tall Bull, White Horse, and Tangle Hair, who remained upset over the proposed fate of the Smoky Hill country. The Dog Soldiers were represented by several older men—Setting Bear, the Man That Shot the Ree, and Gentle Horse, Black Kettle's brother, who was also known as Little Black Kettle.

The pipe was passed around and smoked, then the chiefs aired their grievances to Wynkoop. They were concerned because the annuities had been delayed and asked if the government had forgotten about them. The young men were angry about this broken promise. The chiefs complained that this situation had made it difficult for them to keep the warriors under control. The issue of leaving the Smoky Hill country remained quite controversial, and they hoped that the government would take pity on them and live up to its word in every aspect of the treaty provisions. Wynkoop assured them that the government would fulfill its obligations.

Black Kettle and the other chiefs reiterated their pledge of continued friendship with the white man, then made an unusual statement. According to Wynkoop, the chiefs said that if any of their young warriors committed a crime against whites, the chiefs would take away his possessions, "or, if necessary for an example, kill him." This was an odd promise for the Cheyennes to put forth, if it was indeed made, inasmuch as killing one of their own would stain the Sacred Arrows and place the future of the entire tribe in jeopardy.[43]

The chiefs were asked by Wynkoop how they desired their annuity funds to be disbursed. It was decided that this money should be used to purchase six hundred horses to replace those that had been confiscated at Sand Creek. Wynkoop told them that the horses and the annuity goods would be in their hands by the end of September.

Black Kettle raised another issue, one that he had also presented to the commissioners at the Little Arkansas council. The chief made an emotional plea for the return of the two children who had been captured at Sand Creek and, contrary to the promise of Jesse Leavenworth, had as yet not been turned over to the Cheyennes. In fact, one of these children remained in Denver; the other had been placed on exhibit in a traveling sideshow, now in parts unknown. Wynkoop told them that he would personally look into the matter.[44]

On that sad note, the council concluded. Although the talks with Wynkoop had been amiable, Roman Nose remained greatly disturbed about the impending ratification of the treaty that would take away the land where the Dog Soldiers lived.

Roman Nose was an Elkhorn Scraper but had the heart of a Dog Man and was a fearless warrior who was confident about his abilities in battle, particularly against the white man. Much of his strength was derived from his war bonnet, which was said to have the power to repel enemy bullets.[45]

Roman Nose had no intention of allowing the white man to steal traditional Cheyenne lands and decided to take matters into his own hands. In late August, accompanied by Spotted Horse and a group of warriors, he visited stage stations along the Smoky Hill Road and informed the employees that they had fifteen days to vacate the area, or the Cheyennes would drive them out by force.

Scout Will Comstock was sent around to the villages to confirm this threat and was told that as soon as the annual Sun Dance had concluded, the Dog Soldiers would take to the warpath and rid the Smoky Hill Road of whites.

The Dog Soldier chiefs, however, managed to convince the hot-tempered young men—including the impulsive Roman Nose—to avoid the whites on the Smoky Hill Road. Only one incident occurred, when on September 19 a war party led by Spotted Horse ran off a cavalry horse herd at Fort Wallace, the westernmost post in Kansas.[46]

Hostilities had decreased for the time being, but the resentment of the Dog Soldiers toward the white man did not subside; rather, it grew in intensity. The Smoky Hill country would soon become the scene of further bloodshed, which would be answered by force from the government.

11

TREATY AT MEDICINE LODGE

In october, the u.s. senate approved the little arkansas Treaty but added an amendment that specified that the Cheyennes and the Arapahoes could not occupy any part of Kansas. This would effectively remove the Dog Soldiers from all of their traditional territory.

Black Kettle and the other chiefs, however, had objected at the treaty council to the provision that the Senate could add amendments at will. Therefore, the Bureau of Indian Affairs appointed W. R. Irwin and Charles Bogy as special agents, with the responsibility of convincing the chiefs to approve this new provision. The outlook for a positive result for the government was enhanced when William Bent was awarded the contract to buy and deliver the annuity goods to Fort Zarah for the mid-October council with the chiefs.[1]

The Fort Zarah council convened on October 16, 1866. Black Kettle, Little Robe, and a handful of Southern chiefs were present, but Bull Bear, Tall Bull, and the other Dog Soldiers chiefs and headmen chose not to attend. The influence of those missing chiefs was soon revealed, however. Black Kettle, Little Robe, and the other peace chiefs notified the government representatives—including Ned Wynkoop, who by now had been appointed as agent to the Cheyennes, the Arapahoes, and the Prairie Apaches—that they had changed their minds. They now repudiated their earlier approval of the treaty amendments and would not under any circumstances relinquish the Smoky Hill and the Republican river country.

It was evident that the soldier societies had gained great power within the tribe by their popular position with respect to tribal lands and had in some manner convinced or coerced the peace chiefs into echoing their sentiments. Whatever the means, the end result was that

Black Kettle and the Southerners refused to sign the proposed Treaty of the Little Arkansas.

To make matters worse, whisky peddlers were selling their wares to the warriors. Charles Bent was one of the best customers and in a drunken state had urged the Dog Soldiers to never give up their lands. Charles also threatened to kill his father and his brother George, who had left the Dog Men when he had married and went to live with the peace chief Black Kettle's band. William Bent attempted to have his rogue son Charles arrested, but this was prevented by the warriors. With the treaty doomed and upset by his son's behavior, William Bent sold the annuity goods to David A. Butterfield and disgustedly departed Fort Zarah.[2]

Meanwhile, the Dog Soldiers punctuated their determination to protect their home country with a demonstration of violence. Bull Bear led a war party to Chalk Creek on the Smoky Hill Road, killed two station employees, and burned the building to the ground.

Word of this incident reached Fort Zarah and convinced Wynkoop and the other officials that they must maintain positive relations with Black Kettle and the other peace chiefs. Otherwise, the entire Cheyenne tribe would follow the example of the Dog Men and take to the warpath. Black Kettle was wined and dined, until finally he and his fellow peace chiefs agreed to discuss the terms of the treaty once again in November. Perhaps the main reason that Black Kettle and the others agreed to this future meeting, knowing that it would be unpopular with the militant faction of the tribe, was that the special agents had promised to purchase $14,000 worth of gifts that would welcome the chiefs at the November council. The display of wealth from a rich nation could work wonders on those of an impoverished nation—in spite of the fact that the impoverished nation had been placed in that position by the power and the treachery of the rich nation.[3]

On November 9, while Black Kettle was slowly moving his village north toward Fort Zarah from their camp forty miles below the Arkansas, a drunken young Dog Soldier named Fox Tail was making threats about killing a white man. Fox Tail was angry at the whites because of the treaty that would steal Cheyenne land. He had visited William Bent at a small Cheyenne camp and made his intentions known. Bent disregarded the young warrior, dismissing the boasts as drunken talk. Fox Tail then moved on to another lodge and was told by the occupant to forget such an absurd notion. The young warrior departed that lodge, mounted his pony, and voiced another threat. At that moment, a Mexican herder employed by William Bent had the misfortune of passing by as he worked Bent's stock. Fox Tail trotted up to this Mexican and shot him in the head, killing him instantly. The drunken warrior then rode off toward the north, where the Dog Soldiers were assembling. The entire camp, believing that soldiers would be coming to avenge this killing, packed up and hastened to join the main village in the south.[4]

On November 13, Black Kettle met with Indian Agent Ned Wynkoop and Special Agent Charles Bogy in the scheduled council at Fort Zarah. Wynkoop asked the chief about depredations that had occurred in the north and demanded that the warrior Fox Tail be handed over to face punishment for the murder of Bent's Mexican herder. The agent reminded Black Kettle that he was obligated by treaty to deliver anyone who had committed a crime against whites.

Black Kettle responded,

> The questions you have asked us regarding the killing of two men at Chalk Bluffs and running off stock from Fort Wallace I know nothing about, having never heard of it before. The Sioux have been stealing our horses and have stolen horses around this place and have probably killed the men and stolen the stock you spoke of. Mr. Smith, your interpreter, was with us nearly all last summer,—(Mr. Smith stated that he had never heard of these depredations before, except some floating rumors around here) and he knows we're not guilty. I have heard from some of the last Indians that came in, that the Sioux had taken seven horses from the Smoky Hill and that the Dog-soldiers had taken these from them and were bringing them in. The Sioux have stolen horses from the Cheyennes and the Dog soldiers have recovered them. White Horse, a Cheyenne, went with a party of his men and took seven horses from the Sioux and returned them to the whites, four more horses are still in possession of the Sioux belonging to the whites. Ever since we crossed here in the summer to go north, Smith has been with us and has been trying to get us to come back. At Fort Ellsworth you promised us to be back in six weeks. We came here and waited until we were tired and then went south. I told Col. Bent and Mr. Smith that I was mad and not to send for me.
>
> Notwithstanding the promises made to me had not been fulfilled when we heard that commissioners were here and had sent for us, Chiefs and soldiers got on their horses and came to hear what you had to say. It is very hard for us to move so often, and we are without proper clothing. Yet we have come again to see you as you requested. We do not approve of the killing of the white man (Mexican) by one of our foolish young

men. We have come here to arrange it in some way. What is right is all we want. The reason why we moved from this place as soon as we did was to get away from trouble. By remaining here we are liable to get into trouble. If all had left when I did the murder would not have occurred. Ever since we made peace last fall at mouth Little Arkansas river we have been promised that when our goods came out, wherever we were or wherever we were directed to go there we were to receive our goods. We did not leave here angry or object to receiving our goods, but left through necessity, hoping that you would have these goods issued to us in our villages according to your promises. The distance is too far for us to come in for our goods. I have never refused to obey your calls and have always come when sent for, but it is hard for us to obey your request to come back without villages to receive our goods at this time. You are here again as a Chief sent here to represent the Great Chief at Washington. Your talk is all good and we are going to listen to you. Will it be true, or as heretofore not come out as you represent it? We will leave once again. There may be some jumping around yet, but we will trust you. Our women and children at this season are not in condition to come here, and if you can take our goods where we camped, it would be highly helpful.[5]

Black Kettle blamed the Sioux for inciting hostilities in the north and stated a desire to straighten out the situation regarding Fox Tail. The chief also sternly reminded the council that the government had not fulfilled the promises made in the Little Arkansas Treaty. Black Kettle did, however, conclude by pledging his hope for continued peace, in spite of minor difficulties between them.

Also, Black Kettle and the others once again told Wynkoop how disappointed they were that the two captive children had not been returned to the Cheyennes, as promised. And they argued that if Fox Tail had been killed by the Mexican, the Mexican likely would not have been punished. In effect—if the white man was not going to keep promises made to the Cheyennes, why should the Cheyennes keep promises made to the white man?

Wynkoop responded by warning the chiefs that if Fox Tail was permitted to escape punishment for his deed, it would be a sign to other Cheyennes that they could get away with murder. This could spell disaster for the entire Cheyenne tribe.

This council was attended only by the Southern peace chiefs, the Dog Soldiers having gone north to defend their lands in the Republican and the Smoky Hill river country. Therefore, without the intimidation of the Dog Soldiers and with the enticement of treaty goods,

Black Kettle and the other chiefs finally agreed to make their marks on the amended treaty. They had, for the good of their bands, effectively signed away—at least, in the minds of the government—the part of Grandmother Earth that was dear to the Dog Soldiers.

The Dog Men, however, had no intention of moving from their territory. They were content to roam their land and, unlike Black Kettle and his impoverished band, were not dependent upon other tribes or the whites for food, shelter, and clothing. The northern lands were still home to abundant herds of buffalo, which provided nearly every basic daily need. And they would remain at peace with the white man, as had been promised at the Horse Creek Treaty, unless provoked. In that case, they vowed to protect the north country from the whites until the last drop of their blood had been shed.[6]

During the spring of 1867, the Dog Men reacted to the pressure of the white invasion. Accompanied by warriors from other Plains tribes, they could be found roaming western Kansas, incessantly menacing homesteaders, settlements, and workers on the Kansas Pacific Railway. Officials appealed to the government for relief from these raiders. The government decided that force would be required to convince the Indians to live peaceably or suffer the consequences.

In late March, more than 1,400 soldiers under the command of Major General Winfield Scott Hancock—including eight companies of the 7th Cavalry, led by Lieutenant Colonel George Armstrong Custer—were sent into the field to demonstrate the might of the U.S. Army and punish these marauders for their crimes.

This three-month expedition became a series of miscalculations and breakdowns of military discipline and ended in miserable failure. Hancock, the Civil War hero, sought a scapegoat to blame for his own ineptitude. George Armstrong Custer stood a court-martial, accused of various offenses that fell into the category of "conduct to the prejudice of good order and military discipline." Custer was found guilty and sentenced to a one-year suspension from duty.[7]

One despicable event occurred during this expedition, however, that infuriated every Plains tribe.

On April 12, Hancock met at Fort Larned with the Dog Soldier chiefs Tall Bull, White Horse, Bull Bear, Little Robe, and White Head and the Lakota chief Pawnee Killer and made it clear that they must cease hostilities. The general then told them that he wanted to resume talks at the combined Cheyenne-Lakota village, about three hundred lodges, twenty-one miles up the Pawnee Fork—or Red Arm Creek, as the Cheyennes called it. The chiefs repeatedly requested that he remain distant from their village, but their protests fell on deaf ears. Hancock formed his troops and marched upstream toward the village.

At about the halfway point, a party of Cheyenne Dog Soldiers, painted for war, rode out to block the approach of Hancock's column. The general responded by ordering his men into battle formation.

Edward "Ned" Wynkoop rode out between the two forces and convinced the chiefs that a battle should be avoided. Hancock said that he would camp 300 yards from the village and promised that his men would not enter it or molest the inhabitants. The chiefs, assured by Wynkoop's assertions that Hancock could be trusted, grudgingly agreed to meet the general for further talks after he had camped.

That pledge by Hancock and Wynkoop evidently held little credence with the Cheyenne. While this parley was taking place, the women and the children were fleeing the village.

When Hancock heard about this, he believed that he had been somehow tricked. In a council with the chiefs, he demanded that the women and the children be brought back. Instead, the chiefs and the warriors, unsure of Hancock's intentions, also took flight.

Hancock ordered Custer to surround and search the village. It was discovered that the lodges had been abandoned in such haste that the inhabitants had left behind most of their personal possessions, including at least a thousand valuable buffalo robes.

To Hancock's way of thinking, this insulting action was a declaration of war. He ordered Custer and the 7th Cavalry to pursue the fleeing Cheyennes and Lakotas. Custer chased the Indians for thirty-five miles, but, inasmuch as they had split into numerous small groups, he was unable to overtake any of them.

Meanwhile, Hancock was contemplating whether to employ Civil War standards of warfare and destroy the village. The soldiers, against orders, were already ransacking the lodges and looting for souvenirs.

On the morning of April 19, General Hancock, against the pleas of Ned Wynkoop and other officials, ordered that the village and its contents be burned to the ground. The Cheyenne-Sioux village—three hundred lodges—was put to the torch, destroying every lodge and possession that had not already been stolen by the plundering soldiers.

Angry warriors retaliated for this outrage by terrorizing the Smoky Hill, Platte, and Arkansas areas for the remainder of the summer. Hancock's rash act also opened an already gaping wound between the mil-

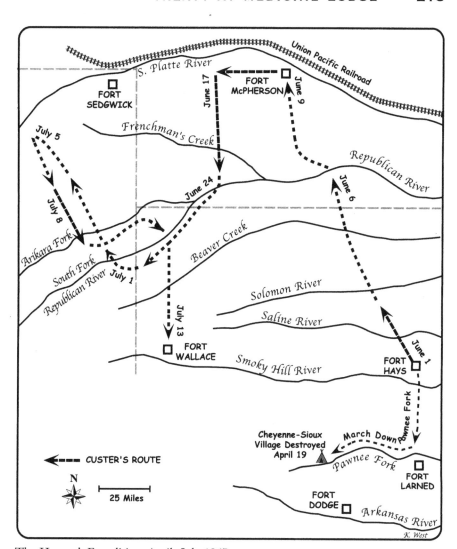

The Hancock Expedition, April–July 1867

itary and the Indian Department, with respect to the proper course of action to contend with the "Indian problem"—by treaty or by force.[8]

Black Kettle's village had been located on the Cimarron River, south of the Arkansas, during Hancock's expedition. The chief had made every effort to restrain his warriors, but some of them chose to wage war on the white man to avenge the burning of the village on Pawnee Fork. One war party of seventy-five warriors from Black Kettle's band swept along the Arkansas but, other than striking terror into the white inhabitants, caused little damage.

During this time, Black Kettle offered to meet Hancock at Fort Larned to talk peace. The general, for reasons unknown, was unable to visit the fort. He did, however, send word to Black Kettle that if the chief would move his band to some military installation, the government would provide for them until Hancock was available for a parley.

Black Kettle had heard such promises before and decided that it would be best to remove his band from the area; he moved farther south to the North Fork of the Red River.[9]

Ironically, the only Cheyennes killed during the course of this expedition were six members of Black Kettle's band, who had been visiting the Pawnee Fork village. These warriors had fled on foot, with intentions of returning home, when Hancock's troops approached. Two troops of cavalry happened upon the six men near Anthony's Stage Ranch on the Santa Fe Trail, west of Dodge City, and killed them.[10]

In early June, a Mexican named Sylvester (or Salvatore) appeared at Black Kettle's village with a letter written in English. Inasmuch as no one in the camp was proficient in that language, Black Kettle asked the man to stay until George "Tex" Bent had returned. Bent was presently a member of a war party led by Lame Bull that was out pillaging and plundering west of Fort Larned. These Cheyenne raiders had destroyed two wagon trains and stolen the contents and had also managed to gather up a fair-sized horse and mule herd.

Several days later, Bent rode into camp with his companions and read the letter that Sylvester had delivered. Jesse Leavenworth, the agent for the Kiowas and the Comanches, had written to request that the chiefs of the various tribes meet with him at the mouth of the Arkansas River to discuss a new peace proposal. Black Kettle was agreeable to this parley with Leavenworth and immediately made plans for the visit. He dispatched the old Crier to pass the news around the circle of lodges that the village would be moving in the morning.

There was a moderate degree of apprehension on the part of Black Kettle and the other chiefs, however. And not due to the prospects of another peace entreaty that might prove disappointing and divisive but on account of a recent incident that had the potential to place the People in harm's way. Earlier, a war party from Black Kettle's village had killed a member of the Wichita tribe in a dispute over stolen horses. The main Wichita village was camped near Leavenworth's headquarters. Black Kettle worried that they might be attacked should they venture into Wichita country. Sylvester told Black Kettle that Buffalo

Goad, the Wichita head chief, had assured him that the Cheyennes would not be molested if they came to talk peace. Black Kettle, although skeptical, was anxious to end hostilities and was willing to risk his life for this cause.[11]

The following day Black Kettle led his People to Lake Creek. When camp had been made, he prepared to ride off to meet Leavenworth. He was aware that his route would take him through the territories of several enemy tribes, culminating with the Wichitas. After some discussion, the other chiefs regarded this trip as too dangerous an undertaking and chose to remain behind in the village. Therefore, Black Kettle, accompanied only by his wife, his cousin Lone Bear, Lame Man and his wife, the Mexican Sylvester, and George Bent, who would serve as an interpreter, started out for the mouth of the Arkansas River.[12]

Black Kettle and his small party moved steadily toward their destination for several days, at times riding for hours within the comforting presence of great herds of buffalo.

Eventually, they happened upon a group of Osages, traditional enemies, who were out hunting. The Cheyennes boldly rode up to one of the chiefs, who was skinning a buffalo, and introduced themselves. Surprisingly, the Osage leader cordially greeted them and invited Black Kettle and his people back to his wigwam to share a meal. That evening, Black Kettle became the subject of fascination for those in the village, many of whom visited their chief's lodge to gawk at this notable Cheyenne.

The next day, Black Kettle encountered other adversaries, the Sacs (Sauks) and the Foxes, but once again was welcomed into their camp and honored with a feast.[13]

This friendly and respectful treatment by known enemies was totally unexpected. It was now evident that Black Kettle, the man who had suffered so much at Sand Creek yet remained resolute in his quest for peace, was not only well-known but held in high esteem by those who had been his enemies. Most tribes had come to the conclusion that peace with the white man was the only manner in which to survive and perhaps regarded this Cheyenne chief as the Plains prophet who long ago had the foresight to embrace this uncertain, perilous pathway.

When finally the Wichita village came into view in the distance, Black Kettle dispatched Sylvester to inform Jesse Leavenworth that his party was approaching. They crossed the swollen Arkansas River and noticed an older Wichita man and woman, both crying, who were sitting apart from the circle. It was their son who had been killed by the Cheyenne war party.

Also waiting on the other side of the river was a welcoming committee headed by Jesse Leavenworth, which included the Wichita chief Buffalo Goad, all of whom shook hands with the Cheyennes. Black Kettle and his party were escorted to the home of the trader William "Dutch Bill" Griffenstein and his Cheyenne wife, who was known as "Cheyenne Jennie," where they were made comfortable.[14]

The next day, Agent Leavenworth told Black Kettle and several Comanche chiefs that a number of prominent men, including Major General William S. Harney and Nathaniel G. Taylor, the commissioner of Indian affairs, wanted to meet with all the Plains tribes in a council that would result in lasting peace. As an enticement to attend, Black Kettle and the others were promised that many wagonloads of food and presents would await them when they arrived to talk peace. The chiefs responded favorably to the agent's words. Leavenworth asked that they select a site for the council somewhere near Fort Larned, so that this great quantity of goods could be easily delivered. It was tentatively decided that a location along Medicine Lodge Creek would be a convenient place for everyone concerned.[15]

George Bent was engaged to remain behind and would be sent out to notify the various camps of the date and the place of the meeting as soon as authorities in Washington informed Leavenworth. This could be regarded as an odd arrangement, inasmuch as Bent had taken a major risk even by accompanying Black Kettle to the parley. He and his brother Charles had been the subject of numerous articles in newspapers and magazines that had chronicled, and at times exaggerated, their Dog Soldier exploits, and the two renegades had become quite notorious across the country. Apparently, authorities were willing to overlook Bent's participation in Cheyenne war parties, due to his ability to freely roam throughout Indian country on their behalf.[16]

Black Kettle returned home but was unable to immediately announce to most of the other chiefs the news of the impending peace council. The Cheyenne bands had scattered across the Plains for the summer buffalo hunt, while others remained with the Dog Soldiers in raiding around the Smoky Hill country. Black Kettle did exert his influence and authority to eventually convince most war parties from the Southern people to cease their actions against the whites and return to his camp.[17]

It was late August, the time when the cherries are ripe, when George Bent, accompanied by Cheyenne Jennie Griffenstein, was dispatched with instructions from Jesse Leavenworth and began visiting camps with the particulars of the council.[18]

By this time, Stone Forehead, the Keeper of the Arrows, had sent word to every Cheyenne band that at the end of the summer, the Sacred Arrows would be renewed on Beaver Creek, just below where Wolf Creek runs into it, south of the Arkansas River. Black Kettle and the Southern bands were the first to arrive for this sacred ceremony and waited for their Northern brethren. The trip from the north required passing through territory occupied by whites—forts, settlements, roads, and army patrols—and these potentially dangerous obstacles hindered expeditious movement.[19]

When every band had settled on Beaver Creek in anticipation of the renewal ceremonies, Black Kettle told the Council Chiefs about his meeting with Jesse Leavenworth and the prospect of a new treaty. Many Southern chiefs—Black White Man, Little Robe, Little Wolf, and Seven Bulls—readily agreed to this new council. The Dog Soldier chiefs and headmen, however, angrily voiced their opposition to the proposal. Bull Bear, Black Shin, Tall Bull, White Horse, and Stone Forehead vowed to never give up their country. The Dog Men did not fear the soldiers and bragged about their recent victories. In fact, they envisioned the day when the white man would be driven from the Smoky Hill.

Black Kettle was openly ridiculed and taunted and was called a coward for his willingness to talk peace with the white man. Other Cheyenne chiefs who favored peace also became the targets of tribal wrath, as did the leaders of the Arapahoes and the Prairie Apaches who wanted peace.[20]

In spite of this abuse and intimidation, Black Kettle was not deterred in his desire to make peace with the white man and, speaking from the heart, encouraged his peers to reconsider their position against this new treaty. Perhaps he argued, as he had on countless previous occasions, and rightly so, that the future welfare of the entire tribe was at stake. His logic was not well received by the Dog Soldier chiefs or the warriors, for the chiefs' hatred of the white man was as

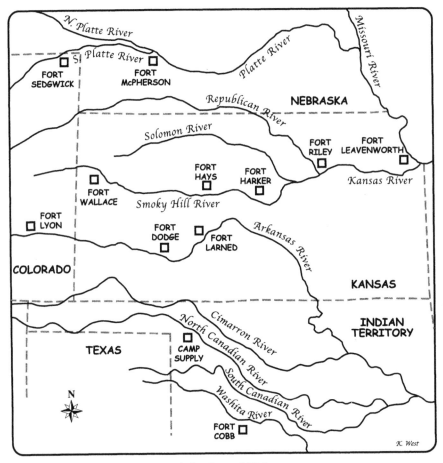

Military forts on the Southern and the Central Plains

strong as their love for their territory, and the young warriors were impetuous and near-sighted and regarded themselves as invincible.

George Bent, after visiting Little Raven's Arapahoes, arrived at the Cheyenne camp. Black Kettle summoned all the chiefs to Council and escorted Bent into the Sacred Arrow Lodge, which stood at the center of the village. The Sacred Arrows would bear witness to the reading of the letter from Leavenworth and would bless them in subsequent deliberations.[21]

Tex Bent read and interpreted the letter, relaying the information that the peace council soon would be held on Medicine Lodge Creek. When Tex finished, his brother Charles, who had come south with the Dog Men, also read the letter to the chiefs.[22]

The Council Chiefs discussed and debated the merits of this new entreaty for some time, without reaching a favorable decision. They did, however, agree to move the village closer to Medicine Lodge Creek—but not too close, for they had not as yet renewed the Sacred Arrows and did not wish to be near any other tribe during this holy ceremony.[23]

Although no other chief had responded that he would go to Medicine Lodge Creek for the treaty council, Black Kettle was determined to attend—even if he was the only representative of his tribe. He departed the village with his family, accompanying Tex Bent, who was carrying the news to the Kiowas and the Comanches. The Arapahoes and the Prairie Apaches had already moved to the treaty grounds, and Bent received the promise from the Kiowas and the Comanches that they would follow.

At this point, Black Kettle asked Bent to escort his family to the Arapaho village. Threats had been made by the Dog Soldiers against the lives of Black Kettle and his relatives, and Black Kettle wanted to keep his family members clear of other Southerners to ensure their safety.[24]

This was the beginning of an extremely critical period for Black Kettle in his relations with the Dog Soldiers. Heightened emotions had created a tension that, if not tactfully handled, could escalate into violence. Other peace chiefs may have been intimidated by the Dog Men, but Black Kettle had fought many battles and would have viewed this test of wills as merely one more. He remained resolute in his belief that the People must end hostilities and make peace. And, to accomplish that end, he was willing to lay down his life.

Black Kettle, along with chiefs from the Kiowas, the Comanches, the Arapahoes, and the Prairie Apaches, formed a party of sixty or seventy people—mostly Arapahoes, and only eight of them Cheyenne—and traveled together some seventy miles to Fort Larned. Inasmuch as Superintendent Thomas Murphy had not as yet arrived, they were greeted by Major Meredith W. Kidd of the 10th Cavalry, who commanded the post. Black Kettle, perhaps reminded of the army's past treatment of his people or simply worried about his family, was less than cordial when meeting this soldier chief. In the major's words, Black Kettle was "sullen and morose and reluctantly" shook hands.[25]

On September 8, 1867, Superintendent Murphy and agent Ned Wynkoop met with Black Kettle, Little Raven, and the Prairie Apache chief Poor Bear. These officials were informed by Black Kettle that although only one raiding party remained out, people in the main body of Cheyennes were angry with the white man and opposed to a treaty. His Southerners, however, were anxious to make peace.

The chiefs also reiterated their wishes that the talks be held on Medicine Lodge Creek, which was a safe distance between the military forts and the Indian villages, in addition to having plentiful resources to sustain many people. After this meeting, Thomas Murphy wrote that the warriors had been provoked into revenging attacks upon their villages, but "if they [the Cheyennes] will agree to be friendly, I would trust them much more than any of the other tribes."[26]

On September 17, the three chiefs, with about forty warriors, escorted Murphy and Wynkoop to the council grounds on Medicine Lodge Creek. The warriors formed a guard to protect the white officials and the long, lumbering wagon train that carried loads of treaty goods.

Three days and 60 miles later, they arrived at the appointed place, a wide, level natural basin on the north side of the stream, to find that about 1,400 Arapahoes and Prairie Apaches were already camped there. The Kiowas and the Comanches had not as yet arrived. Black Kettle's Southern Cheyenne village, on the south side of the stream, was composed of about 25 lodges, perhaps 150 people, most of them either Black Kettle's family or loyal followers.[27]

Little Raven's Arapahoes formed a circle around the wagon train, with warriors standing guard at all times. Other wagons hauled provisions from Fort Larned to the council grounds almost daily, delivering such treats as coffee, flour, sugar, and dried fruits. A herd of cattle was driven out and became the favorite of the Kiowas and the Comanches when those tribes arrived. Black Kettle and his people also dined on their chosen meat, buffalo, which was plentiful in the area.

Eventually, some five thousand Indians had raised their lodges in the vicinity of the Council grounds on Medicine Lodge Creek. An observer later noted that the women in Black Kettle's camp were the most attractive, always wearing their best dresses adorned with polished elk teeth or other ornaments.[28]

Meanwhile, the main Cheyenne Dog Soldier village remained three days' ride away on the Cimarron River. On September 20, late on the night that Black Kettle and the others had arrived, six Cheyenne wolves from this village visited Superintendent Thomas Murphy's camp for a parley. It was agreed that Ed Guerrier would return with them, carrying a letter of invitation from the superintendent to the Dog Soldier chiefs. "These Cheyennes," Murphy later told the commissioners, "being fooled by whites so often and many of them but recently from war are very timid, and are determined to understand well who they will be expected to meet before they come."[29]

The dissident Cheyenne chiefs—Stone Forehead, Tall Bull, Bull Bear, White Horse, Tangle Hair, and the others—sat in the holy presence of the Sacred Arrows and listened to what Ed Guerrier had to say. It was decided that Roman Nose and Gray Beard, accompanied by eight Dog Soldier warriors, would return with Guerrier and personally speak with Thomas Murphy.

Three days later, these warriors rode into Black Kettle's camp just as the chief sat down to supper with Little Raven, Ned Wynkoop, and Murphy. The superintendent was delighted to see them and expressed his intentions by saying that he himself would take the tribe "by the hand & make a good road for our peace and happiness." Murphy went on to describe the goods that he was prepared to give to the Cheyennes.

Gray Beard, although impressed by Murphy's words and that the superintendent was not surrounded by soldiers, was skeptical. He had heard the white man's promises before and replied, "A dog will eat provisions. The provisions you bring us make us sick. We can live on buffalo, but the main articles we do not see: powder, lead, and caps. When you bring us these we will believe you are sincere." He also told Murphy that the reason the Cheyennes were so angry and kept fighting was to avenge the village that Hancock had destroyed.

Murphy assured them that the village had not been burned on orders from Washington, a statement that the warriors accepted as truth. The superintendent asked that they return to their village with an invitation to the other chiefs. Gray Beard and Roman Nose promised to do that and told Murphy that "where [Stone Forehead] goes all of us follow." At this time of renewal, apparently, Stone Forehead, the Keeper of the Arrows, had emerged as the leader of the militant faction.[30]

There is no record to indicate whether Black Kettle was present for this conversation, but he must have been elated that the Dog Soldier chiefs had not completely turned their backs on peace. Perhaps Black Kettle, by attending the council in spite of threats against himself and his family, had encouraged the chiefs to consider that his constant pleas for peace might truly be the proper course for the good of the entire tribe.

At mid-morning on October 16, 1867, the procession of 165 wagons carrying the peace commissioners and other dignitaries, baggage, and loads of presents for the Indians approached the council grounds from Fort Larned. The 600 total people, which included numerous camp followers, were escorted by 500 troopers from the 7th Cavalry, riding in pairs, supported by a battery of two gatling guns and commanded by Major Joel Ellicott.

The members of this peace commission who had endured the grueling three-day ride from the fort were Senator John B. Henderson of Missouri; Nathaniel G. Taylor, the commissioner of Indian affairs; Colonel Samuel F. Tappan; Major General John B. Sanborn; Major General William S. Harney, Major General Alfred H. Terry; and Brigadier General C. C. Augar, commander of the Department of the Platte, who had replaced General William T. Sherman. Sherman had been removed from the commission by General U.S. Grant, after Sherman made statements in the press indicating that he was not particularly inclined to make peace with the Indians.

Dignitaries in the entourage included Governor Samuel J. Crawford of Kansas; his lieutenant governor J. P. Root; the Kansas senator Edmund G. Ross; and Henry M. Stanley, who would later gain fame as the discoverer of the lost Livingstone in Africa. Stanley was one of eleven newspapermen who would observe the council proceedings.[31]

When the caravan came into view, Black Kettle mounted his horse and rode out at the head of a delegation of chiefs to welcome the commissioners. He embraced Generals Harney and Sanborn as old friends and shook hands with everyone else. Black Kettle also warned them that warriors from the Dog Soldier village on the Cimarron were not to be trusted and explained the situation, emphasizing that the wagon train should be protected at all times. He also told them that if the other Cheyenne chiefs were to appear at the council, it would only be after the Sacred Arrows were renewed, which would be at least eight days.

This news predictably caused an uneasiness among the new arrivals. Harney established the commission camp about a half-mile away from the villages and ordered that the wagons be circled, with the tents and the campfires safely inside.[32]

The following morning, a preliminary council was held. Black Kettle, his face brightly painted for this important occasion, and wearing a tall dragoon's hat instead of a headdress, sat in the front row. His clothing was richly decorated with quills and beads and designs in sacred Cheyenne colors, and a blue blanket trailed along behind him. All the other chiefs, also painted, wore their feathered war bonnets and were dressed in full regalia—breastplates, rings, and arm bands, with several displaying medals. Seated behind these 25 chiefs and head-men were as many as 475 warriors from the various tribes. Each tribe was represented, except for the Comanches, whose chief, Ten Bears, perhaps intended his absence as a show of independence.[33]

After the pipe had been passed and smoked, Commissioner of Indian Affairs Nathaniel Taylor opened the talks. He distributed twenty suits of clothing to each tribe and promised that many more presents would be given away once the terms of peace had been agreed upon. At this point, Ten Bears made his entrance in time to hear Taylor de-clare that the commissioners desired that a peace treaty be made with each of them. He would prefer that they accomplish this all together on one day, but, if this was not possible, he would accommodate each tribe individually.[34]

Black Kettle sat in silence while, one after another, the chiefs of the various tribes told Taylor when they would be ready to talk. Dur-ing the course of the discussion, the Kiowa chief Black Eagle changed his mind several times, which angered Ten Bears, who taunted the Kiowa by saying, "What I say is law for the Comanches, but it takes half a dozen to speak for the Kiowas."

Finally, Black Kettle had heard enough of this bickering and rose to his feet. "We were once friends with the whites," he said, "but you [the Kiowas and the Comanches] nudged us out of the way by your intrigues, and now when we are in council you keep nudging each other. Why don't you talk, and go straight, and let all be well? I am pleased with all that has been said."

Little Raven echoed Black Kettle's sentiments, appealing to them "to behave themselves and be good."

Black Kettle explained that the Cheyennes were offering the Sacred Arrow ceremonies, which would cause a delay, but said that he was willing to meet the commissioners again in four days.

The council adjourned for the day.[35]

Black Kettle remained behind and issued a warning to the com-missioners. He calmly told them that when any of the people camped on the Cimarron finally decided to come in, it would be wise to have plenty of food available, for they would be hungry. In his own way, Black Kettle was telling them that if there was any chance of winning over the hearts and the minds of these militant chiefs, proper etiquette must be followed. The chiefs would expect to be fed and then smoke the pipe with those who were asking them to make peace.[36]

At dusk that night, fifty well-armed Dog Soldiers, their faces painted, loudly singing society songs, thundered across Medicine Lodge Creek on their ponies into the camp of the commissioners. General Harney stepped out to greet the warriors, who were led by Chiefs Tall Bull and White Head (Gray Head). Harney and these chiefs had established a cordial relationship some nine summers before, when the general was chasing the Lakota Sioux up on the North Platte. While the warriors remained mounted, keeping a wary eye on the soldiers, the chiefs entered the general's tent to talk. Harney, with either George Bent or John S. Smith serving as an interpreter, told his guests that he intended to hold an inquiry into Hancock's actions of the previous summer and invited the chiefs to attend. After some time, the chiefs exited the tent, and White Head mentioned that they were hungry. Harney said that rations had been provided for them across the stream in Black Kettle's camp. The chiefs and their warriors happily raced off to eat and rest.[37]

The primary mission of the peace commissioners was to negotiate treaties with the Plains tribes, but they had also been charged with the duty of determining the causes for the recent warfare. While they waited for the various chiefs to decide on a date for the grand council, Nathaniel Taylor convened the commission to hear testimony pertaining to Hancock's campaign. Tall Bull and White Head had accepted Harney's invitation and sat with the general as the proceedings got under way.

The witness who interested the two Cheyennes the most was Edward "Ned" Wynkoop, whom the Dog Soldiers blamed for the burning of their village. Several days earlier, Wynkoop had narrowly escaped when Roman Nose rode into the camp and threatened the agent's life. Wynkoop explained his version of events from Sand Creek to the present, concluding that the current warfare had been the result of Hancock's impulsive burning of the village. White Head was also asked to speak and told the commissioners how difficult it was to convince his people that soldiers could be trustworthy when the Cheyennes had suffered so much at their hands.

After hearing Wynkoop's testimony, the two chiefs were impressed enough to absolve him of any blame. As an expression of friendship, they warmly shook hands with their agent.[38]

White Head and Tall Bull then rode over to Black Kettle's village. Tall Bull, speaking on behalf of the chiefs on the Cimarron, told Black Kettle that he was expected to visit the main village and explain exactly what the Cheyennes would gain if they agreed to this new treaty. If the chief failed to do that, the Dog Men would kill every pony that he owned.[39]

The grand council convened on October 19 inside a great arbor constructed of brush and limbs on the north bank of Medicine Lodge Creek, surrounded by a grove of cottonwoods and elms. The Cheyenne chiefs from the main village refused to attend, and the tribe was represented only by Black Kettle and White Head, neither of whom had the authority to speak for any band but their own. George and Charles Bent sat behind the two chiefs, ready to interpret.

Black Kettle remained silent throughout. White Head, however, rose to state that neither he nor Black Kettle would have anything to say until the other chiefs decided to come in, but they would listen to what the others said.[40]

The commission turned its attention to the Kiowas and the Comanches. For two days, they listened to each chief make a speech, declaring his particular views about past relationships and future needs. Finally, Senator John Henderson outlined the terms of the treaty, and the chiefs of the two tribes agreed to sign it.[41]

On the morning of October 21, the Kiowa and the Comanche chiefs made their marks on a new treaty. The tribes would relinquish over 60,000 square miles of their traditional homeland and move onto a 48,000-square-mile reservation in the southwestern corner of Indian Territory—present-day Oklahoma. They would receive $30,000 worth of houses, barns, schools, and other buildings that they had already said they did not want. The tribes could, however, retain the right to hunt buffalo off their reservation on any lands south of the Arkansas River. Once the treaty had been signed, the Kiowas and the Comanches hurried away toward their villages to await the next morning, the time when their annuity goods would be distributed.[42]

That night, dark clouds swirled overhead and a raging thunderstorm pounded the treaty grounds. Black Kettle was resting inside his lodge when Chiefs Little Robe and Gray Beard and the Bowstring headman Eagle Head suddenly appeared out of the darkness and beckoned him to follow them to the commissioners' camp.

The drenched and dripping Cheyennes were greeted by General Harney and Commissioner Nathaniel Taylor, with John S. Smith on hand to interpret. Inasmuch as the Cheyennes had not spoken to Black Kettle earlier, they excused themselves to a corner of the wind-battered tent to confer, while the other commissioners and a number of correspondents straggled inside.

As the four Cheyennes spoke in hushed tones, it was apparent that Black Kettle had become extremely nervous. He had already placed himself in a precarious position by being an outspoken peacemaker and lived under a constant threat to his family and personal property. Also, he had not been attending the renewal of the Sacred Arrows, the holiest ceremony in Cheyenne culture, which some may have regarded as an insult. It is not known what transpired in this conversation, but Black Kettle's reaction indicated to even the whites across the tent that the chief was visibly upset by what he was hearing. These observers noted that the chief had undoubtedly placed himself in grave danger from enemies within his tribe by standing firm with his determination to make peace.[43]

Finally, Little Robe addressed the commissioners. He explained that the chiefs on the Cimarron had been delayed by the Sacred Arrow Renewal ceremonies, and that it might be four or five sleeps before they could arrive for a council. The commission was anxious to finish its business with the Southern tribes and move north. Taylor suggested that they cut the time to three days. Little Robe, however, told him that no one could leave the camp until the ceremonies had concluded.[44]

Black Kettle spoke and explained how important the renewal ceremony was for his tribe, and that it had been delayed due to certain difficulties and had to be started over. He requested four more days for its completion, emphasizing how eager he was for the trouble along the Smoky Hill to end and a lasting peace be made. He encouraged the commission to understand. He then said, "I give you my word (that) I will not ask you to stay here six or seven or eight days. When I look to my left I see you, and that you intend to do right; and when I look to my right I see my men, and know that they intend to do right. I want you both to touch and shake hands."[45]

The commissioners engaged in a heated argument over whether or not to wait this additional four days. Senator Henderson exclaimed, "Bah! This Medicine is all humbug." To which General Augur replied,

"Oh, no, it ain't, it is life and death with them. It is their religion, and they observe all the ceremonies a great deal better than whites theirs." Henderson remarked, "It must be. I never knew a white man that would not put aside religion for business."

Nathaniel Taylor made the decision: "Tell them that they must send a runner to their villages: that we can wait four days, and that is all."[46]

Black Kettle and his companions assured the commissioners that the ceremonies would be concluded by that time, and they looked forward to talking peace. The four Cheyennes then slipped out of the tent and into the miserable night.

The whereabouts of Black Kettle for the next several days cannot be accurately documented, other than the night of October 26 when he convinced the commissioners to wait two extra days, until Monday, October 28. The medicine-making ceremonies, he told them, would require this additional time.[47]

It can be concluded, however, that Black Kettle was splitting his time between his camp at Medicine Lodge Creek and the Dog Soldier village on the Cimarron. Perhaps he participated in the Sacred Arrow ceremonies, while holding talks with the Dog Soldier chiefs, urging them to meet with the commissioners. There can be no doubt that the chief, at great personal risk, was acting out the role of principal peacemaker, both within his tribe and with the commissioners, during this critical period.

At about 10 a.m. on Sunday, October 27, the commissioners' camp was informed that a large body of Cheyennes was headed their way. This news created a near-panic in the Arapaho, the Kiowa, and the Comanche camps, which aroused the commission camp as well. Major Joel Elliott alerted his 7th Cavalry troops and ordered the gatling guns manned. No one—white or red—was certain about whether the Cheyennes had come to make peace or wage war.

Henry M. Stanley described what happened next:

"The Cheyennes are coming," shouts a gaddling gaberlunzje of the camp, and we hastily rush out to view the approach of the dusky caballeros. Simultaneously with that movement their voices are heard breaking out into a chant, and away to the right of the timber is seen a column of the long-expected Cheyennes on the double trot. At the same moment Black Kettle is seen making his way towards us on a full gallop, his horse covered with foam. The Commissioners meet him, and the head chief informs them that all his tribe are approaching.[48]

As Black Kettle returned to the formation, a correspondent for the *New York Tribune* observed,

> Five columns of a hundred men each, forty paces apart, dressed in all their gorgeous finery. Crimson blankets about their loins, tall, comb-like headdresses of eagle feathers, variegated shirts, brass chains, sleigh bells, white, red and blue bead-worked moccasins, gleaming tomahawks, made up the personnel of a scene never to be forgotten.
>
> Their chief, Mo-ko-va-ot-o, or Black Kettle, mounted upon a wiry horse, sprang forward, dressed in a dingy shirt and dingier blanket, his long black hair floating behind him like a bashaw's tail, and waved his hands. In most admirable order they moved by the left flank by divisions; another wave and they marched obliquely across the Neo-contogwa—up to within 50 yards of Commission Camp, where they halted, but still continued their lively exhilarating chant until the commission appeared in full dress and halted within a few paces of the line.[49]

Black Kettle had assumed the role of military maestro and orchestrated a masterpiece of spectacle and pageantry. The chief rode triumphantly at the head of this magnificent, colorful exhibition of chiefs, headmen, and warriors—five hundred men in all—as it advanced toward the awestruck onlookers in the commissioners' camp.

This must have been a most satisfying moment for Black Kettle, perhaps punctuated by relief. He had traversed a perilous obstacle course and had successfully convinced the entire tribe to talk peace. While other peace chiefs had been silenced by the Dog Soldiers, this one chief out of forty-four, with his prestige and perhaps his life hanging in the balance, had not wavered in his belief that a treaty to end hostilities was the only option. It can only be imagined what abuse he may have endured in the Dog Soldier camp to bring about this result.

The next morning, the commissioners convened the council with the Cheyennes and the Arapahoes. Chiefs Black Kettle, Tall Bull, White Horse, Tangle Hair, and Old Little Wolf sat in the front of their delegation, forming a half circle, with the other chiefs and headmen behind them.

Senator John Henderson opened the talks by professing the government's desire for peace. He apologized for the mistake General Hancock had made by burning their village. The senator told them that they must relinquish their land between the Arkansas and the South Platte and settle on a reservation in western Indian Territory. The Cheyennes would receive various annuities—including arms and

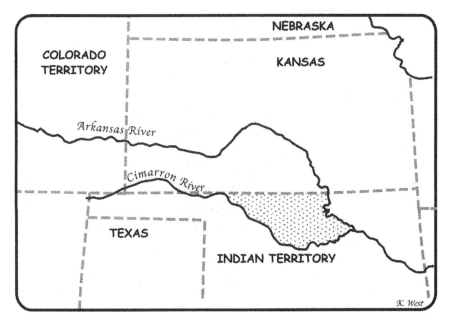

Southern Cheyenne–Arapaho territory, Medicine Lodge Treaty of 1867

ammunition—for a period of thirty years, similar to the treaty the Kiowas and the Comanches had signed.

There was only one issue that concerned the Dog Soldiers, however. They vowed to never give up their beloved Smoky Hill country, which would be required by this treaty. Buffalo Chief made it clear that this provision was unacceptable.[50]

That response perplexed the commissioners, who were hoping for a quick signing. Senator Henderson decided to take matters into his own hands. He called aside the chiefs, away from the rest of the commissioners, along with George Bent and John S. Smith to interpret. Henderson told them that they would not have to immediately go to this reservation, and that they could hunt buffalo between the Arkansas and the south fork of the Platte as long as buffalo remained in that area. This statement pleased the chiefs, who were certain that the buffalo would never disappear from their homeland. They agreed to sign the treaty.[51]

The commissioners were aware that the Dog Soldiers were the key element to this treaty and asked Bull Bear to sign first. He initially declined but finally, with Henderson's words of flattery, made his mark and declared, "We will hold that country between the Arkansas and the Platte together. We will not give it up yet, as long as the buffalo and elk are roaming through the country."[52]

The second chief to sign was Black Kettle, whom the government recognized as the head chief of the Cheyenne nation.

The Cheyenne chiefs who made their marks on this document were Bull Bear, Black Kettle, Little Bear, Spotted Elk, Buffalo Chief, Lean Face, Little Rock, Curly Hair, Tall Bull, White Horse, Little Robe, Old Whirlwind, Heap of Birds, and White Head. Those who refused to sign included Black Shin, Gray Beard, Old Little Wolf, Seven Bulls, Crow Chief, Black White Man, and Sand Hill.

Conspicuously missing at the council was Stone Forehead, the Keeper of the Sacred Arrows. In fact, the Sacred Arrows had not been present to witness and bless this treaty, as they had sixteen years earlier at Horse Creek. The absence of the Sacred Arrows could be interpreted to mean that the treaty was not valid in the eyes of the Cheyennes.[53]

It was not only the Cheyennes who would question the validity of the treaty. Several witnesses, including Henry M. Stanley and Major Joel Elliott, later charged that the treaty was a mockery, that the Cheyennes had not been read the provisions and had no idea what they were signing.[54]

In effect, the government had once again tricked the Cheyennes into agreeing to a treaty by making promises that it had no intention of honoring.

12

BLOOD ALONG THE WASHITA

The winter of 1867–1868 proved to be relatively quiet for Black Kettle and the Cheyennes. The chief had led his followers into a camp in the vicinity of Fort Dodge to wait out the cold months. Buffalo were plentiful and in prime condition during this time of year, and the men were able to provide food for their families and hides for use at home or to trade for other necessities.

The Cheyennes, however, could not fully take advantage of this excellent opportunity to hunt. The arms and the ammunition that the commissioners had promised them at the Medicine Lodge council had not been issued, which caused ill feelings toward the government within the tribe, particularly among the young men.[1]

The Cheyennes were not the only ones who were out hunting buffalo. White settlers had invaded the valleys of the Republican, the Saline, the Smoky Hill, and the Solomon rivers, where the last of the great bison herds roamed, and were soon followed by the hide hunters. These white hunters quickly discovered that this shaggy beast was easy prey. When one animal fell, the others simply continued grazing. And, unlike the Cheyenne, who utilized every part of the animal, these white hide hunters skinned off the hides and cut out the tongues, leaving the meat to rot on the prairie. And the railroads, which had brought the hunters, made it convenient to ship large quantities of hides to eastern tanners. The Cheyennes could only watch with mounting anger and resentment as these buffalo killers went about their business with no regard for how many were slaughtered and with no respect for this animal that the People held sacred.[2]

In March 1868, Major General Philip H. Sheridan, commander of the Military Department of the Missouri, made a tour of the Plains forts. He had initially refused to council with the Southern tribes, but

Black Kettle and the chiefs tracked him down at Fort Dodge and he finally agreed to talk. Sheridan was told that the government had not kept its promises, and the tribes were suffering—women and children were starving. Sheridan was unsympathetic and argued that the Cheyennes were not in as bad a shape as they claimed.

After the council, Agent Ned Wynkoop asked the general if he could issue rifles and ammunition to the Cheyennes and the Arapahoes. Sheridan answered, "Yes, and if your Indians go on the warpath my soldiers will kill them." Council Chief Stone Calf heard that remark and responded, "Let your soldiers wear long hair so that we will have some honor in scalping them when we kill them."

Sheridan smiled coldly and informed the chief that soldiers were not permitted to wear long hair due to lice, and therefore he could not accommodate the request. Also, no provisions or firearms would be distributed.[3]

Finally, in April 1868—six months after the Medicine Lodge Treaty had been signed—Agent Wynkoop managed to issue several wagon-loads of food but not the rifles and the ammunition that had been promised.[4]

Black Kettle understood that the prevailing sentiment among the tribe was that this treaty was falling apart, that the Dog Soldiers would never accept the new reservation, and this eventually would lead to violence. The chief, however, had an idea that could, if successful, re-move the People from the white pathway of progress. He instructed George Bent to initiate peace talks with the Utes, the Black People, the enemy tribe that years earlier had captured Black Kettle's wife. Black Kettle was willing to forget the past and attempt to make amends with the Utes. This would open the way for the Cheyennes and the Arapahoes to move farther west, into the mountainous Ute territory, which had not as yet been invaded by white settlements. Apparently, the Utes were not about to let bygones be bygones and allow their former enemies into their homeland. This peace entreaty by Black Kettle was rejected.[5]

Additional annuity goods were distributed in mid-July at Fort Larned, but, to the ire of the Cheyennes, once again firearms were missing. The Dog Soldiers had been skirmishing with the Kaws, which the government cited as the reason that guns and ammunition had been withheld. The Cheyennes protested, to no avail, that the Kaws had provoked them to fight. Black Kettle addressed Agent Ned Wynkoop, telling him that the whites had been firing on their people, yet they had not retaliated. His people, he argued, had done nothing to warrant such punishment. Black Kettle added, "Our white brothers are pulling away from us the hand they gave us at Medicine Lodge; but we will try to hold on to it. We hope the Great White Father will take pity on us and let us have guns and ammunition he promised us so we can go hunt buffalo to keep our families from going hungry."[6]

On August 9, Black Kettle and the other chiefs were summoned to Fort Larned by Agent Ned Wynkoop. Indian Commissioner Nathaniel Taylor had determined that the failure of the government to live up to its terms of the Medicine Lodge Treaty could result in hostilities. He authorized Wynkoop to issue arms and ammunition to the tribes, in the hope that it would preserve peace. The Cheyennes received about 80 rifles, 160 revolvers, 12 kegs of powder, $1\frac{1}{2}$ kegs of lead, and 15,000 caps. This was less than expected but at least served as a gesture of goodwill.[7]

Black Kettle, with about 150 followers, subsequently reported to Fort Hays, professing friendship, and notified the army that the people in his village were heading north to hunt with their new firearms. His appearance was reported in the newspaper:

> A band of Cheyennes under command of Black Kettle, a noted chief, was in town on Thursday. They had a white child with them, which they claimed to be a half-breed, the offspring of an officer at Dodge and a squaw of the tribe. Some think there is no Indian blood in the child, but that it was stolen from Texas by Kiowas or Comanches and sold to the Cheyennes. Anyhow, if it belongs to any of our shoulder-strapped friends at Larned, they shouldn't be ashamed of it. Cheyenne stock is good stock.[8]

Along the way, Black Kettle encountered a large war party of Lakota Sioux, Northern Arapaho, and Dog Soldiers that was planning to attack the Pawnee, the hated Wolf People. A handful of Black Kettle's young men decided to accompany this war party. Instead of raiding the Pawnee, however, these Indians—about two hundred in number—bolstered by whisky, began terrorizing white settlers in the vicinity of the Saline and the Solomon river valleys. The warriors swept through the countryside, killing at least a dozen men, capturing some women and children, stealing livestock, and burning buildings.[9]

In August, Chief Little Rock, a member of Black Kettle's band, visited Fort Larned and identified the Cheyenne who had been guilty of the raids on white settlers—including the few from Black Kettle's village who had joined the war party that initially was formed to fight the Pawnee. The military, in its infinite wisdom, viewed this as evidence that Black Kettle was personally guilty of taking up arms against the whites by encouraging his young men to fight.[10]

In truth, Black Kettle and the other chiefs had been unable to restrain every young Southern warrior from raiding but did manage to keep the majority of them at home.

The attacks by small war parties continued throughout the summer and into the fall and compelled the governors of Kansas and Colorado to demand protection from the U.S. Army.[11]

These wanton acts, committed with government-issued rifles, had played into the hands of Generals William T. Sherman and Philip H. Sheridan, both of whom advocated using force against the Plains tribes. Sheridan was said to have first made the statement "The only good Indian is a dead Indian," although this was a common phrase at the time. The two military commanders were directed to take whatever measures were necessary to force the hostiles onto reservations and punish those responsible for the atrocities.

Rarely could these nomadic Indians be caught in the summer, but a winter campaign would find them vulnerable. Sherman and Sheridan intended to invade Indian Territory and not only kill every Indian they deemed hostile but also destroy property—lodges, food stores, and pony herds—thereby breaking the will of the Indians and discouraging them from waging war. This tactic, known as "Total War," had been introduced by General William Harney at Ash Creek in 1855 and had struck fear into the hearts of the Plains tribes for many years thereafter.[12]

Sheridan's first move was to send an elite force of scouts under the command of Major George A. "Sandy" Forsyth to patrol the railroad up the Smoky Hill Road. On September 17, Forsyth and his fifty-one men were attacked by nearly nine hundred Sioux, Arapahoes, and Cheyennes, led by the war chiefs Pawnee Killer and Roman Nose. Forsyth and his men were pinned down by this war party on a tiny island in the Republican River for nine days until rescued by the 10th Cavalry, the Buffalo Soldiers, in what would be called the Battle of Beecher Island.[13]

On the first day of this siege, the noted Cheyenne warrior Roman Nose was killed, shot through the spine. He had fully expected to die that day, believing that the medicine had been removed from his war bonnet the previous night. Either a woman had touched the headdress, or he had eaten with metal utensils, both of which were considered an omen of death.[14]

Black Kettle, meanwhile, heeding a warning from John S. Smith to avoid Forts Larned and Cobb for the time being, decided to move his people back into Indian Territory. Sheridan later claimed that he had invited Black Kettle to parley at Fort Larned, but, if true, that probably brought back memories to the chief of Sand Creek. The offer, if actually made, was ignored. By late October, Black Kettle had returned to Indian Territory, just north of the Antelope Hills, hunting buffalo with the Kiowas and the Comanches.

Sheridan next dispatched Colonel Alfred Sully and his 3rd Infantry, bolstered by eight companies of the 7th Cavalry under Major Joel Elliott, to hunt down the Cheyennes who had been raiding south of the Arkansas River. Sully's actions were timid, and, much to the disgust of Sheridan, the colonel returned empty-handed after only one week in the field.

Sheridan, however, was well acquainted with an officer who had the tenacity to implement his strategy of total war. Twenty-eight-year-old Lieutenant Colonel George Armstrong Custer, the Civil War hero who had been serving a one-year suspension from duty, was summoned from his home in Monroe, Michigan, to assume field command of the 7th Cavalry.[15]

In early November, Black Kettle and the other Council Chiefs ordered that the village be moved from the Canadian River southeast to the Washita River—or the Lodge Pole River, as the Cheyennes called this waterway in western Indian Territory. This area, where they would spend the cold winter months, would be home to one of the largest gatherings ever on the southern Plains, with Cheyennes, Arapahoes, Kiowas, Comanches, and Prairie Apaches all represented—altogether, some six thousand people.

The spot chosen for these camps in the Washita River valley was an ideal location to sustain such a huge number of people. It afforded every necessity—high ridges to the south that offered protection from the wind, an abundance of winter grass available for the horse herds, thick stands of timber and brush for fuel and lodgepoles dotting the bottom lands, and fresh running water nearby. The area was also teeming with wildlife—vast herds of buffalo, deer, antelope, and game birds.

Black Kettle placed his camp far south of a sharp horseshoe in the river, in a sheltered pocket, quite a distance downstream and somewhat

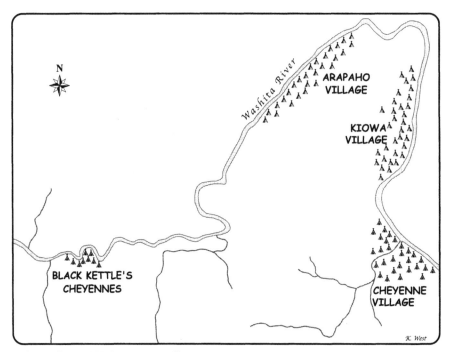

Indian villages, Washita River valley, winter, 1868

isolated from the other villages. The river was shallow at this particular location, which provided a natural ford to reach a horse trail that led to the main villages. The chief's personal lodge was raised beneath a towering cottonwood tree at the western edge of the camp. Only one lodge was located farther west, and a few others stood in close proximity to the chief's. In all, Black Kettle's followers inhabited forty-seven lodges in this area, with two lodges of Lakota Sioux and two of Southern Arapahoes camping with them.

The fall buffalo hunt had been greatly successful, as evidenced by the strips of curing meat that hung from every lodgepole and the piles of hides waiting to be dressed and fashioned into robes or articles of clothing. All the natural elements were in place for these tribes to anticipate a winter of comfort and security in the quiet, sheltered valley of the Washita.[16]

The human element was another story. Comfort and security would be dependent upon the whims of the army. It was hoped by the residents of the Washita valley that the fighting, if there was any, would remain to the north, and that the army would finally conclude that a winter campaign was impractical.

On November 12, however, Colonel Alfred Sully and his five infantry companies, accompanied by Lieutenant Colonel George Armstrong Custer and eleven companies of the 7th Cavalry, departed Cavalry Creek and marched in a southerly direction. The destination of this column was a supply depot intended to support Sheridan's winter campaign, appropriately named Camp Supply, which recently had been established at the point where the Wolf and the Beaver creeks met to form the North Canadian River.

Along the way, Custer's scouts happened upon the fresh trail of a presumed Indian war party, estimated at seventy-five warriors. Custer was anxious to follow this trail, but Sully refused permission. The colonel told Custer that they must wait until the 19th Kansas Volunteer Cavalry had arrived from Topeka to reinforce them before engaging the enemy. Custer was furious with the decision, but his hands were tied. Sully was in command, and the 7th Cavalry remained with the column the entire way to Camp Supply.[17]

While Sully's infantry and Custer's cavalry bivouacked at Camp Supply, Black Kettle received word from Dutch Bill Griffenstein that the trader's wife, Cheyenne Jennie, had died the previous month. Griffenstein asked the chief to come to Fort Cobb and retrieve Jennie's possessions for distribution among the tribe, which was the custom of the People.[18]

Black Kettle and Little Robe, along with the Arapahoes Big Mouth and Spotted Wolf, traveled the seventy to eighty miles from their Washita River camp to Fort Cobb. Upon arrival, Dutch Bill handed over Jennie's belongings. The trader then suggested that Black Kettle meet the new district agent, Colonel William B. Hazen, and talk about making peace. The chief heartily welcomed this opportunity and was introduced to Colonel Hazen.

Hazen, a thirty-eight-year-old West Pointer and a Civil War veteran, had assumed command at Fort Cobb less than three weeks earlier. He had been greeted by at least seven hundred Comanches and over a thousand Indians from other tribes—Anadarkoes, Caddoes, Kichais, Wacoes, and Wichitas—all waiting to be issued subsistence. Hazen, who reported directly to General William T. Sherman, had been allocated $50,000 for the welfare of the Indians in his district and quickly discovered that he needed more than twice that amount to adequately care for his charges. He also had the unenviable task of helping the army sort out which tribes were friendly or hostile, but he was not authorized to negotiate treaties.[19]

On November 20, Black Kettle and his three companions were escorted into an audience with Hazen. Black Kettle was asked to speak first and said,

> I always feel well while I am among these Indians, the Caddoes, Wichitas, Keechies (Kichais) etc., as I know they are all my friends; and I do not feel afraid to go among the white men, because I feel them to be my friends also. The Cheyennes, when south of the Arkansas, did not wish to return to the north side, because they feared trouble there, but were continually told they had better go there, as they would be rewarded for so doing. The Cheyennes do not fight at all this side of the Arkansas; they do not trouble Texas, but north of the Arkansas they are almost always at war. When lately north of the Arkansas, some young Cheyennes were fired upon and then the fight began. I have always done my best to keep my young men quiet, but some will not listen and since the fighting began, I have not been able to keep them all at home. But we all want peace, and I would be glad to move all my people down this way. I could then keep them all quietly near camp. My camp is now on the Washita, 40 miles east of Antelope Hills, and I have there about 180 lodges. I speak only for my own people. I cannot speak for nor control the Cheyennes north of the Arkansas.[20]

Big Mouth spoke briefly, professing his peaceful intentions and blaming the soldiers for following his people wherever they went. He asked Hazen to notify the Great Father and "tell him to have this fighting stopped; that we want no more of it."

Hazen believed that Black Kettle truly wanted peace, but the idea of moving the Cheyennes and the Arapahoes closer to Fort Cobb and promising them protection, as the chief had requested, troubled him. His orders from General Sherman had directed: "I want you to go to Fort Cobb, and to make provisions for all the Indians who come there to keep out of the war . . . to afford the peaceful Indians every possible protection, support, and encouragement, whilst the troops proceed against all outside of the Reservations, as hostile . . . their safety now is in rendezvousing at Fort Cobb."[21]

It would seem clear from Sherman's orders that Hazen should have been permitted to offer sanctuary to Black Kettle's people. There was one factor, however, that fueled his indecision. General Phil Sheridan had declared that the Cheyennes and the Arapahoes were hostile, and his forces were at present marching against those tribes. If Hazen were to invite the Cheyennes and the Arapahoes to camp near Fort Cobb, with the understanding that they were under army protection, it had the potential to result in another Sand Creek Massacre. He was not sure that he wanted to assume such responsibility without Sheridan's knowledge and approval.

Finally, Colonel William Hazen had made up his mind, and said,

I am sent here as a peace chief. All here is to be peace, but north of the Arkansas is General Sheridan, the great war chief, and I do not control him, and he has all the soldiers who are fighting the Arapahoes and Cheyennes. Therefore you must go back to your country, and if the soldiers come to fight you must remember they are not from me, but from that great war chief, and with him you must make peace. I am glad to see you, and glad to hear that you want peace and not war. I cannot stop the war, but will send your "talk" to the "Great Father," and if he gives me orders to treat you like the friendly Indians I will send out to you to come in; but you must not come in again unless I send for you, and you must keep well out beyond the friendly Kiowas and Comanches. I am satisfied that you want peace, that it has not been you but your bad men who have made the war, and I will do all I can for you to bring peace: then I will go with you and your Agent on to your reservation, and care for you here. I hope you understand how and why it is that I cannot make peace with you.[22]

Black Kettle, perhaps reliving in his mind the events that preceded Sand Creek, told Colonel Hazen that he understood. He was likely quite disappointed that an opportunity to move his people to a safe haven had once again been dashed by the actions of the militant faction of his tribe. And now, as had been the case at Sand Creek, the Southern Cheyennes were at the mercy of troops in the field.

Black Kettle did, however, demonstrate his loyalty and commitment to the People. Hazen decided to offer the chief personal sanctuary and told Black Kettle that he and his extended family could move to Fort Cobb, where they would be provided for and protected. The offer must have been quite tempting—to set up his lodges in a place where safety for himself and his loved ones awaited, away from the threat of the soldiers.

Black Kettle, to his credit, declined Hazen's invitation, stating that he spoke not just for himself but for all the Cheyennes. Until all Cheyennes could move to safety at the fort, he would remain with them as an advocate for peace.

Although he had risked his life time and again in the name of peace and no doubt deserved sanctuary as a reward for his efforts, Black Kettle was not about to abandon the People when his work had not as yet been completed. He could not direct his young men and influence the Dog Men along the pathway to peace if he was not among them. This act of self-sacrifice was another example of the dedication and the love that he had for his tribe. Black Kettle had without question proven once more that he was the embodiment of those admirable traits expected of a Council Chief; to be anything less, he would have regarded as a betrayal.

Hazen also informed Black Kettle and the others that he would be unable to issue them any provisions. The trader Dutch Bill Griffen-stein, however, generously dipped into his own stores to provide them with various delicacies—coffee, sugar, crackers, and tobacco.

The return trip to the villages on the Washita proved treacherous for Black Kettle and his companions, when they encountered a raging blizzard. An icy north wind carried great amounts of snow that piled deeper and deeper as they struggled to traverse the difficult terrain. It would be six days of enduring this miserable weather before they could enjoy the warmth of their home lodges.[23]

Meanwhile, Black Kettle and his Cheyennes lost a good friend when Agent Ned Wynkoop abruptly resigned his position. Wynkoop, while visiting the East, had been ordered to assemble the Cheyennes and the Araphoes at Fort Cobb. Then he learned that troops were in the field and planned to sweep through the vicinity of the Washita River and Fort Cobb and kill the Indians deemed hostile. Wynkoop recognized all the elements of another Sand Creek Massacre. He wrote, "I most certainly refuse to again be the instrument of the murder of innocent women and children. . . . All left me under the circumstances is now to respectfully tender my resignation."[24]

On November 21, General Sheridan arrived at Camp Supply. He was greeted by Lieutenant Colonel Custer, who complained to his Civil War mentor about Sully's passivity on the march. Sheridan, hav-ing earlier witnessed Sully's sorry Indian fighting prowess, quickly resolved the tug-of-war over command by sending Sully back to Fort Harker. George Armstrong Custer was now free to pursue the Indians whom the army deemed hostile. Two days later, Custer and his 7th Cavalry—eight hundred men—were in the saddle riding south toward the valley of the Washita River to search for their elusive prey.

Custer's orders from General Sheridan read in part: "To proceed south in the direction of Antelope Hills, thence towards the Washita River, the supposed winter seat of the hostile tribes; to destroy their villages and ponies; to kill or hang all warriors, and bring back all women and children."[25]

Custer and Black Kettle were not the only ones traveling through the inclement conditions. At the same time, a war party of Cheyennes—mostly Dog Soldiers but also some young men from Black Kettle's camp—was returning home from raiding whites along the Smoky Hill River. By November 24, this group of warriors had arrived at the South Canadian River, where the warriors broke up into two parties in order to reach their respective camps by the shortest route. One group, led by Bear Shield, moved south by way of Antelope Hills. The other, with Crow Neck as a member, continued down the South Canadian and headed for Black Kettle's village.[26]

Bear Shield's party camped for the night five or six miles below Antelope Hills. On the following morning as the warriors prepared to resume their journey, they could hear the sound of distant firing upriver. They dismissed it as the other party shooting buffalo and returned that night to the main Cheyenne village upstream without mentioning the incident.

Crow Neck's party had not encountered any buffalo and eventually reached the Washita some fifteen miles above Black Kettle's camp. At this point, however, Crow Neck's pony was worn out, and he decided to leave it there for the night. The next morning the warrior returned to retrieve his pony and observed a number of dark objects coming over a hill far off to the north. Upon returning to camp, Crow Neck confided in a friend about what he had seen and wondered if it had been soldiers. His friend speculated that it had probably been nothing but a herd of buffalo, which were plentiful in the area. Crow Neck was hesitant to tell anyone else, fearing that word would reach the ears of Black Kettle that the warrior had been out raiding along the Smoky Hill.[27]

Later that day, November 26, near the Antelope Hills, a Kiowa war party, which had been out raiding against the Utes, noticed a wide trail tramped into the snow that headed south toward the Washita River. The Kiowas, who were heading toward their camp upstream, visited Black Kettle's village on the way home and told everyone about what they had seen, commenting that it might be soldiers. Black Kettle's people did not take this warning seriously and ridiculed the Greasy Wood warriors for their foolishness. The soldiers, who fought in the cold only if necessary, would not be out tramping wide trails in the foot-deep snow during such wintry weather.[28]

These people, however, had underestimated the resoluteness of George Armstrong Custer. The 7th Cavalry field commander had pushed his troops through the bitter cold and the deep, drifted snow for nearly three days in a southeasterly direction up Wolf Creek. Scouting parties combed the area for any sign that Indians were in the vicinity.

On November 25, after this difficult trek had failed to produce results, Custer decided to change direction and turn due south, toward the Antelope Hills. At this point, he ordered his second in command, Major Joel Elliott, to command a scouting detachment. Elliott and three companies of cavalrymen, accompanied by a handful of Osage scouts, would sweep up the valley of the South Canadian River looking for sign, while the main force continued in the direction of the Antelope Hills.

The next morning, November 26, Elliott and his men had covered about twelve miles up the South Canadian, when his scouts discovered a fresh trail. This trail was less than twenty-four hours old and had been made by a war party of undetermined size.

The trail that had been left in the deep snow could have been made by the Cheyennes who were returning from the raids on the Smoky Hill or possibly by the Kiowa war party.

Major Elliott dispatched a scout to inform Custer, then cautiously followed this southeasterly trail.

Upon receiving word that a fresh trail had been struck, Custer immediately prepared for battle. The men were ordered to leave behind everything, including warm but cumbersome overcoats, that could not be carried on themselves or their saddles. They would have a hundred rounds of ammunition apiece, a minimal amount of coffee and hardtack, and a little forage for their horses. Custer also abandoned his wagon train, detailing eighty soldiers to remain behind as guards.

By that evening, Custer and his command had rendezvoused with Elliott's detachment on a small tributary of the Washita River. The men were given one hour to rest, then were back in the saddle, riding four abreast, with Custer and his scouts about a half-mile in the advance.

Eventually, the Osage scouts noticed the faint, glowing embers of a campfire in the distance. Custer and his scouts stealthily moved forward and, straining to see through the darkness, observed a large herd of animals down in the valley, near the Washita River. At first, the scouts believed that it might be a herd of buffalo. Then, in the chilly, still air, they distinctly heard barking dogs, the tinkling of a bell, and finally, the cry of a baby. There could be no doubt now that the animals were not buffalo but horses, and the fire had been built by herders to keep warm. And, combined with the other noises, it was a positive indication that an Indian village was located nearby. The trail of the returning Cheyennes or Kiowas had likely led Custer and his cavalrymen to the doorstep of Black Kettle's village.

Lieutenant Colonel Custer and his scouts slipped away into the freezing night. Custer returned to his waiting troops and sounded officer's call to detail his plan of attack.[29]

Black Kettle, Little Robe, and the others, their ponies exhausted, their bodies beaten after battling the elements for six days, arrived home that night. It must have been quite a relief for the chief to enter his snug, warm lodge and finally relax. He was not a young man anymore, perhaps approaching seventy years of age, and this arduous journey had probably sapped most of his strength.

Black Kettle invited a relative, Big Man, and his son Magpie (not to be confused with George Bent's wife of the same name) to share a meal with him in his lodge. The chief told them about his trip to Fort Cobb, that the district agent had warned that soldiers were in the field on a campaign to punish the Cheyennes for the actions of the young warriors who had been raiding up north. After some discussion, the men dismissed any thought that the soldiers would brave such bitter cold and foot-deep snow to attempt an attack in the immediate future. With that in mind, Black Kettle decided that when the weather cleared, he would lead a delegation to talk peace with the soldier chief. Perhaps the tribe would then be allowed to move to Fort Cobb, away from the threat of the troops.

During the course of this conversation, Black Kettle was nagged by doubt. He decided to assemble the leading men of his band that night and inform them of this potentially dangerous situation.

Later, these leaders, including Chief Little Rock, gathered inside Black Kettle's lodge for the council. Medicine Woman Later, Black Kettle's wife, served them coffee sweetened with sugar, along with the crackers that Dutch Bill Griffenstein had provided at Fort Cobb. Black Kettle passed around the pipe as he related the details of his meeting with Colonel Hazen. Soldiers were at that moment searching for Indians they deemed hostile, he said, and counseled that the young men should be kept close to home. Any hunting party was bound to be attacked on sight and would perhaps place the village in the line of fire. Furthermore, the district agent had refused to permit them to move to the fort until they made peace with General Sheridan, the soldier war chief.

Black Kettle and his circle of companions talked and smoked well into the night. It was decided that the next day—which would be two days short of the fourth anniversary of the Sand Creek Massacre—the village would be moved downstream, where it would be closer to other villages and therefore more secure. And, in order to demonstrate their peaceful intentions, they would send runners out to locate the soldiers and, when found, ask them to meet in a council to discuss the current trouble that had been caused by just a handful of impulsive young warriors, not by the entire tribe. Black Kettle was confident that he could arrange a truce or perhaps a lasting peace, if given the opportunity to speak with the soldier chief.

By the time the council had ended, the clouds had drifted away and the moon shone brightly. This could have been interpreted as a good sign, but the seriousness of Black Kettle's message evoked an apprehensive mood among the People.[30]

One of those who was deeply affected by Black Kettle's words was Medicine Woman Later. Upon hearing that soldiers might be in the vicinity, she was reminded of the nine bullets that had penetrated her body at Sand Creek. Her worry turned to anger, and she stood outside the chief's lodge, saying to anyone close enough to hear, "I don't like this delay; we should have moved long ago. The agent sent word for us to leave at once. It seems that we are crazy and deaf, and cannot hear."[31]

The reason why Black Kettle chose not to move his village without delay cannot be determined. It can be speculated that the prospect of moving all their belongings and lodges miles upstream in the dead of night, with strong winds and drifting snow to hinder progress, would not have been very appealing to a man who hours before had returned from a grueling six-day journey. In practical terms, Black Kettle would have been exhausted and wanted nothing more than to crawl inside his blankets and sleep.

In addition, the consensus of the men had been that the soldiers, who were accustomed to comforts, would wait until more favorable conditions before mounting an attack, if indeed one was planned.

This consensus was probably true of the average soldier and of most commanders—but not of this particular commander. Lieutenant Colonel George Armstrong Custer was undeterred by fatigue, weather conditions, or any other obstacle in his pathway to carrying out a mission. After having futilely chased Indians around the Plains on the Hancock Expedition a year earlier, he understood the importance of the element of surprise. Where other commanders, such as Colonel Sully, might have faltered, Custer would rise to the occasion and push himself and his troops against whatever the odds in an effort to achieve success.

The valley of the Washita became shrouded in dense fog during that cold night. By pre-dawn, November 27, however, the fog had dissipated, and the sky began to clear and brighten.

Some people in Black Kettle's village rose early, anxious to pack their belongings for the move downstream. Black Kettle, who had spent a restless night as he wrestled in his mind with the potential threat to his people, was one of these early risers. No sooner had the chief stepped from his lodge, when he noticed a woman running toward camp along the pony trail across the river. She had been visiting the herd to bring in the family mounts in preparation for the move and had come face-to-face with a frightening sight.

"Soldiers!" she cried. "Soldiers! Soldiers!"

Black Kettle called for her to spread the alarm throughout the camp. He ducked inside his lodge and emerged with his rifle in hand. He raised the weapon into the air and fired off a shot to awaken those who were sleeping and alert the camp to danger.

The village became the scene of mass panic and confusion, as men, women, and children dashed in every direction. Many of the women, not knowing which direction to run or where to seek refuge, simply huddled with their children inside their lodges. Men who had weapons raced toward the nearby timber or ravines in an effort to establish a defensive position and fight off the attackers.

The sound of a bugle that signaled the charge echoed through the still air, and hundreds of heavy cavalry horses crashed through the brush as the troops swept toward Black Kettle's peaceful village on the Washita River.[32]

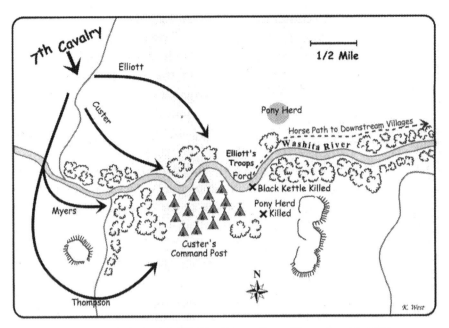

Custer's attack on Black Kettle's Washita River village, November 27, 1868

Custer had separated his command into four detachments, a strategy that he had employed with great success in the Civil War. This
four-pronged assault was designed to surround the camp and assure
that no one could easily escape.[33]

Black Kettle always kept a good horse picketed outside his lodge
in case it was needed in a hurry, and today was no exception. Medicine
Woman Later untied this mount and led it to her husband. The chief
stood in front of his lodge, as he had at Sand Creek, his heart sad,
helplessly watching as soldiers came to slaughter his people.

Perhaps he cursed himself for not sending out wolves the night
before to scout for sign, so that they might have had advance warning
and time to escape. But it was too late now to contemplate what he
might have done wrong. The soldiers were bearing down on the village, and within moments it would be the scene of carnage and destruction. A lifetime of working for peace, at great personal risk, was about
to be trampled under the might of the 7th Cavalry.

Black Kettle's initial instinct may have been to fight, but he had
never fired a weapon at a white man in the past and was not about to
break that vow. Perhaps it crossed his mind to rush forward and
attempt to reason with these soldiers, to explain that they were mak-

ing a terrible mistake, that this was a peaceful village. But he undoubtedly remembered what had happened to his friend White Antelope under similar circumstances at Sand Creek. He had no other choice but to flee.

Black Kettle mounted his horse and pulled Medicine Woman Later up behind him. His only chance to escape was to reach the ford in the river before the soldiers did, so that he could ride up the north side to the safety of the downstream villages. Black Kettle kicked his heels into the pony's ribs and raced toward the Washita.

The crossing to which Black Kettle headed was in the area of responsibility of Major Joel Elliott's command. Elliott and Black Kettle had met the previous year at the Medicine Lodge Treaty grounds. It was Elliott who had written in his report one of the more critical assessments of that treaty, stating that he did not believe that the Cheyenne chiefs understood what they had signed away. By this time, it is likely that Elliott himself had already led a detachment of troopers downriver in an attempt to catch warriors who were fleeing in that direction. His troopers, however, had maintained their position and approached the ford at the same instant as Black Kettle.

Black Kettle and Medicine Woman Later were greeted at the crossing by a volley of bullets from the rifles of Elliott's men. One slug slammed into the chief's stomach, but he managed to remain astride the pony and yank his reins to the right as he continued riding toward the river. Another bullet struck Black Kettle in the middle of his back. He slumped, then slid from his horse and toppled into the icy water of the Washita. The great peacemaker of the Cheyennes was dead even before he landed in the water—the first one of his people killed that day.

Medicine Woman Later remained seated on the pony as the terrified animal bolted through the water. Finally, another volley of bullets struck her, and she joined her husband, lying dead in the shallow ford.

The soldiers resumed their advance toward the objective of the village and rode over the bodies of Black Kettle and his wife, covering them with mud in haste to reach the other side of the river.[34]

Custer's troops gained control of the village within ten minutes of the initial charge but continued exchanging fire with the warriors, and even young boys and women, who fell back to the trees, fired from behind logs, fought from within the overhanging walls of the riverbank, or gathered in a protected ravine. Custer set up his headquarters on a knoll south of the village where he could observe the fighting and could issue orders accordingly.

Ironically, one of the Cheyennes killed was Chief Little Rock, the informant who several months earlier had pointed the finger toward Black Kettle when he stated that some of the young men from this chief's village had been out raiding.

Many Cheyenne people, most of them scantily clad after having been roused from their beds, attempted to escape by wading through the icy waters of the Washita. These people stayed close to the edges, where ice had formed, to conceal themselves in the foliage as they made their way toward the downstream villages. Soldiers hunted them down and killed those whom they could find.

A few others managed to find safety in the hills beyond the village, where the grass was high enough to hide them. One woman, perhaps reminded of the atrocities at Sand Creek, slit the throat of her child, then killed herself. Some women and children hid in the nearby brush, but many were flushed out and shot at as they ran toward the river.

The soldiers who fired on these women and children were under the command of Captain Edward Myers. The overzealous Myers, contrary to explicit orders issued by Custer not to shoot but to capture all noncombatants, was observed firing at women and children. Custer immediately dispatched the scout Ben Clark to order Myers to cease firing and to capture those people.[35]

Many women had remained with their children inside their lodges and could hear the terrifying sounds that emanated from the village— the war cries and the death chants, the bugle commands, the soldiers yelling and calling out orders, the screams and the weeping of women and children.

Custer ordered that the women and children, as well as others who had been captured, be rounded up and placed inside lodges at the center of the camp for safekeeping. Many of the Cheyennes misunderstood the soldiers' intentions and, fearing that they were about to be killed, broke away toward the river. The Osage scouts raced after them with switches cut from nearby trees and whipped them back to the lodges. They eventually gathered fifty-three captives—women, girls, and children, several of whom were bleeding from wounds.[36]

The cavalrymen spent the remainder of the morning attempting to eliminate nearby pockets of resistance. By that time, however, swarms of warriors from the downstream villages began massing to fire at the troopers from the surrounding bluffs. Custer formed his men into a defensive position and ordered that Black Kettle's village be destroyed.

The cavalrymen killed the pony herd, estimated at 875 head, and everything else within the camp was either confiscated or put to the torch. The loss to the Cheyennes included 51 lodges and, reportedly, 1,100 buffalo robes, 470 blankets, 210 axes, 140 hatchets, 75 spears, 47 rifles, 35 revolvers, 90 bullet molds, 535 pounds of powder, 35 bows and quivers, 4,000 arrows, 12 sacred shields, 300 pounds of tobacco, large quantities of dried meat and food stores, and countless items of clothing. The survivors of Black Kettle's village would once again be destitute and at the mercy of others to face the cold winter months ahead.[37]

Meanwhile, as dusk approached, additional warriors arrived to surround the remnants of Black Kettle's village. Perhaps as many as 1,500 men now rimmed the hills, which placed Custer in a precarious position. Custer's men had greatly outnumbered Black Kettle's warriors on the charge into the village, but that advantage was now with the warriors.

Custer realized that he must withdraw without delay. He mounted his troops and, in a bold tactical move, ordered the band to play "Ain't I Glad to Get Out of the Wilderness," an old Civil War tune, while marching down the valley toward the downstream villages. The surprised warriors immediately abandoned their positions on the bluffs and hurried away to defend their families against this apparent attack. Custer, however, used the growing darkness as his ally by countermarching his column and escaping to safety with the supply train before the warriors could regroup and form a pursuit.[38]

Rarely, if ever, have casualties from an engagement on the frontier been accurately reported. Army officers tended to exaggerate the numbers of their enemy killed to embellish the significance of their victories or minimize their own losses. Witnesses on both sides regularly related contradictory estimates of casualties, which may or may not have been due to personal prejudices, hearsay, failing memory in old age, or simply lack of knowledge. The attack on Black Kettle's village was no exception to this rule.

The number of army losses—Major Joel Elliott, Captain Louis Hamilton, and nineteen enlisted men killed, as well as three officers and eleven enlisted men wounded—can be confirmed as correct.[39]

A sampling of eyewitnesses and other interested parties, however, provides a wide disparity in casualty totals for Black Kettle's people.

George Armstrong Custer initially reported the number of Cheyenne dead at 103, claiming that an exact body count had been taken on the field. Custer did confess that "in the excitement of the fight, as well as in self-defence, it so happened that some of the squaws and a few children were killed or wounded." One month later, Custer amended that total and wrote that "the Indians admit a loss of 140 killed, besides a heavy loss of wounded. This, with the Indian prisoners we have in our possession, makes the entire loss of the Indian in killed, wounded, and missing not far from 300."[40]

If Custer's last figure is to be believed, it would mean that every person in Black Kettle's village had been killed, wounded, or captured, which was not the case.

Scout Ben Clark said, "I estimate the Cheyenne loss at seventy-five warriors and fully as many women and children killed."[41]

Captain Henry Alcord, who had recorded the minutes of Black Kettle's meeting with Colonel Hazen at Fort Cobb on November 20, wrote that "The Indians lost five chiefs and distinguished braves, Black Kettle among them, and about 75 of their ordinary fighting men were killed."[42]

Scout James S. Morrison, who had once worked for Major Ned Wynkoop, wrote that "the other scouts all agree in stating that the official reports of the fight were very much exaggerated, that there was not over twenty Bucks killed, and the rest, about forty, were women and children."[43]

The Cheyenne chief Little Robe, along with 26 others, met with Indian Commissioner Vincent Colyer at Camp Wichita, Indian Territory, in April 1869. At that time, the chief confirmed that 13 men, 16 women, and 9 children had been killed. This number had also been given by the Kiowa chief Black Eagle to Colonel William Hazen at Fort Cobb several days after the battle.[44]

George Bent, who was not present, later wrote that 11 Cheyenne warriors, 2 Arapaho warriors, 12 women, and 6 children were killed.[45]

The captive women told an interpreter upon arrival at Camp Supply that 13 Cheyennes, including Chiefs Black Kettle and Little Rock, 2 Sioux, and an Arapaho had been killed.[46]

The figure supplied by Custer, 103 killed, which is the accepted number, has been placed on historical markers at Washita. The lower number mentioned by the Cheyennes, who should have known who among their village was missing, could certainly have been much closer to the truth. If so, this would mean that the element of surprise and the overwhelming fire superiority of the soldiers did not translate into comparable casualties. It would appear that the soldiers, who greatly outnumbered the Cheyennes, lost half the number killed as did their adversary. This premise, however, was of little consequence to the Cheyennes, who had endured yet another defeat and another destroyed village at the hands of the army.

The facts surrounding Black Kettle's death were disputed when a young Osage warrior named Trotter boasted that he had engaged the Cheyenne chief in hand-to-hand combat during the attack. Trotter claimed to have killed Black Kettle, then lifted the chief's scalp, which the Osage man waved during Custer's triumphant return to Camp Supply several days later. More than likely, Trotter's story was made up. It was not unusual for warriors to take credit for the death of a famous person.[47]

Based on the evidence, Black Kettle had been killed by Elliott's troopers at the Washita, as described previously.

One day after the fight, Magpie, Big Man's son, accompanied by several women, located Black Kettle's body in the river, with only his face above water. The chief had not been scalped. Magpie and the women dragged the body along the pony trail for some distance to the top of a sandy knoll. Magpie departed, while the women discussed whether they should bury the chief here or farther away from the river on higher ground.

Another story recounts how Black Kettle's body had been found several days after the attack and by that time had been partially de-voured by wolves. The remains were said to have been "buried" in the forks of a tree.

On July 13, 1934, workmen were excavating for a bridge when they discovered a skeleton under five feet of dirt at the western edge of the battlefield site, near the place that Magpie said that he had left Black Kettle's body. The ornaments—beads, arrow points, hunting knives, conchas, and other items—found with the body were tenta-tively identified as those worn by Black Kettle.[48]

These remains were displayed at the newspaper office and later the museum in the nearby town of Cheyenne. In 1968, after protests by the Cheyennes, the remains were buried on the north side of the museum next to the flagpole. Later, the noted forensic anthropologist

Clyde Snow examined these remains, and concluded that the skeleton was that of a twenty-year-old woman.[49]

Therefore, it would be safe to assume that somewhere within this site along the Washita River rests the remains of Black Kettle, who had been killed by the very people with whom he so valiantly strived to make peace.

13

LEGACY

CUSTER'S ATTACK ON BLACK KETTLE'S WASHITA RIVER VILLAGE WAS considered a great victory in the estimation of the military establishment. Eastern humanitarians, however, called the action a massacre. Newspaper editorials and a deluge of letters criticized the army and condemned Custer—comparing him to Chivington—for the killing of women and children. The military establishment fought back against these accusations that the engagement on the Washita River had been a massacre and that Black Kettle was an innocent victim.

General Phil Sheridan, who would refer to Black Kettle as "a worn out and worthless old cipher," stepped forward as the principal spokesman in defense of the army's actions. He presented his case to the public to justify the attack that "wiped out old Black Kettle and his murderers and rapers of helpless women."[1]

The Battle of the Washita, Sheridan admitted, was a one-sided affair but not a massacre. He refuted comparisons of Custer to Chivington and the battle to the Sand Creek Massacre. Custer had not been a loose cannon, as had been the case with Chivington; rather, he had been under strict orders to spare noncombatants. In fact, Custer had personally stopped one of his units from firing upon women and children. As to charges that the village was not hostile, Sheridan pointed out that Black Kettle's warriors recently had been fighting the soldiers and were out raiding, and were tracked to that location. Furthermore, Black Kettle had not been offered protection by the army but had been told by Colonel William Hazen at Fort Cobb that he must make peace with Sheridan or face the consequences.

Sheridan supported his charges by offering as evidence his word that he had personally observed certain items, such as photographs,

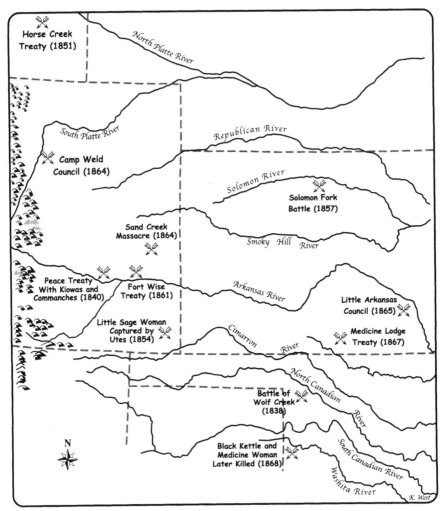

Major events in the life of Black Kettle

clothing, and bedding allegedly stolen from the homes of people massacred on the Solomon and the Saline rivers, in the remains of Black Kettle's vanquished village.[2]

General William T. Sherman dismissed any criticism of the army's role, when he wrote, "This you know is a free country, and people have the lawful right to misrepresent as much as they please—and to print them—but the great mass of our people cannot be humbugged into the belief that Black Kettle's camp was friendly with its captive women and children, its herds of stolen horses and its stolen mail, arms, powder, etc.—trophies of war."[3]

Although the claims of such evidence found in the village were later questioned, the *New York Times* sided with the army and on December 22, 1868, wrote,

> The truth is, that Gen. Custer, in defeating and killing Black Kettle, put an end to one of the most troublesome and dangerous characters on the Plains. Black Kettle was one of the most active chiefs in stirring up the tribes to war. . . . From the beginning of the war in 1864, this Black Kettle, of the Cheyennes, aided by [Satanta], of the Kiowas, and Little Raven, of the Arapahoes, has been always most active in mischief, and it was a fortunate stroke which ended his career and put the others to flight.[4]

Generals Sherman and Sheridan referred to those who defended the Indian position as members of the "Indian Ring," a conspiracy of men who sought to profit from the controversy, identified by the *New York Times* as "a crew of sharks, sharpers, runners, traders, sutlers, swindlers, and Indian agents." This group, according to Sherman, included Commissioner of Indian Affairs Nathaniel Taylor, the peace commissioner Samuel Tappan, and the former Indian agent Edward Wynkoop.[5]

The men whom Sherman and Sheridan accused of being members of a "ring," oddly enough, were those who were well acquainted with Black Kettle and, unlike the two generals or the press, had established a personal relationship with the chief. They had witnessed the courageous efforts that Black Kettle made over the years in the name of peace.

Superintendent of Indian Affairs Thomas Murphy wrote that "I cannot but feel that the innocent parties have been made to suffer for the crimes of others." Black Kettle was "one of the truest friends the whites have ever had among the Indians."[6]

An outraged Edward W. Wynkoop wrote to Taylor on January 26, 1869,

> I am perfectly satisfied that the position of Black Kettle and his immediate relatives at the time of the attack upon their village was not a hostile one. I know that Black Kettle had proceeded to a point at which he was killed with the understanding that it was the locality where all those Indians who were friendly disposed should assemble. . . . In regard to the charge that Black Kettle engaged in depredations committed on the Saline River during the summer of 1868. I know that same to be utterly false as Black Kettle at the time was camped near my Agency on the Pawnee Fork. . . . There have been Indians deserving of punishment but

unfortunately they have not been those who received at the hands of the troops at the "Battle of the Washita."

Black Kettle's village at the time of the attack upon it was situated upwards of one hundred and fifty miles from any traveled road in the heart of the Indian Country.[7]

Wynkoop returned to his native Pennsylvania and established an iron-making business. When that endeavor failed in 1874, Wynkoop headed back out West to participate in the Black Hills gold rush. He later drifted to New Mexico, where he became the adjutant general of that territory and then the warden of the penitentiary. He died of kidney disease in Santa Fe on September 11, 1891.[8]

The peace commission member Major General William S. Harney opposed the army's position and wrote, "I know Black Kettle was as good a friend of the U.S. as I am."[9]

Another peace commission member, Samuel F. Tappan, demanded an "immediate and unconditional abandonment of the present war policy," believing that the present policy would lead to the slaughter of more innocent people such as Black Kettle.[10]

The protests in the East, however, did not deter Sheridan from completing his campaign to rid the southern Plains of Indians whom he deemed hostile.

In early December, Sheridan and Custer returned to the Washita. Downstream from Black Kettle's camp, they found the bodies of two white captives, Clara Blinn and her young son, in an abandoned village reportedly belonging to the Kiowa chief Satanta. Sheridan and his 700-man force followed a trail for 75 miles until they located Satanta and a large band of Kiowas. Sheridan seized the chief and threatened to hang him if his tribe did not submit to the reservation. Most of the Kiowas grudgingly complied to save their chief.

In January 1869, Custer swept through the Wichita Mountains and convinced an Arapaho village of sixty-five lodges under Chief Little Raven to surrender.

The last stand for the Cheyennes came on July 11, 1869, when the 5th Cavalry under Major Eugene Carr defeated Tall Bull's Dog Soldiers at Summit Springs—killing fifty-two, including Chief Tall Bull.

Carr's smashing victory effectively disorganized the Cheyenne and their allies and brought an end to their cohesiveness and their ability to mount a unified resistance. The Cheyennes had little choice but to straggle onto a designated reservation at Fort Cobb.

The goal of Sheridan's winter campaign of 1868–1869 had now been accomplished—the southern Plains between the Platte and the Arkansas rivers had been cleared of all Indians.[11]

Understandably, the Cheyennes to this day regard Custer's attack on the Washita as a massacre of innocent people. Historians over the years have remained divided in their opinions. It can be stated, however, that the army was in no mood to make peace at that time with Black Kettle. Otherwise, Colonel Hazen, who later lied and said that Black Kettle told him that many of his men were on the warpath, would have been permitted to welcome the Cheyennes at Fort Cobb. Sheridan wanted to punish some Indians—any Indians—for the depredations that had occurred in Kansas.

Black Kettle became a handy target when, without his knowledge, several of his warriors participated in the raids and possibly left their trail home in the snow. To the military's way of reasoning, this implicated Black Kettle by virtue of his position as chief of the band. It could, however, certainly be argued that it had been the Kiowas whom Custer tracked to the village and not the few Cheyennes who had been raiding.

Regardless, what the military did not understand was that Black Kettle as a chief did not have dictatorial powers over his people. He had no official means with which to enforce tribal law, such as arrest and incarceration, and could not, other than through his personal influence, prevent anyone from leaving his camp or returning home.[12]

The fact that the two factions of the tribe—Northern and Southern—had never completely severed ties with each other was also a detriment to Black Kettle's peace efforts. The government had recognized them by treaty in 1851 as separate but, when convenient, blamed the entire Cheyenne tribe for depredations that were committed mainly by the more militant Northerners.

Therefore, scholars agree that Black Kettle was a sincere advocate for peace who was a victim of the misdeeds of a small number of warriors from his band who had accompanied the Northerners on raids into Kansas, and he paid for that association with his life.

That may be true, when considering only the specifics of this particular engagement on the Washita, but the reasons for the demise of Black Kettle go far deeper than merely the events preceding Custer's attack on that frosty November morning.

Black Kettle, as was the case with every Native American, was the victim of broken promises, unscrupulous politicians, aggressive military commanders, and, at the root of it all, progress—manifest destiny—the influx of settlers into the primitive paradise that had provided for the native peoples throughout the centuries.

Native Americans were spiritually attached to the land and viewed their pristine wilderness homeland with the idea of removing only those natural resources necessary to sustain a comfortable life. Everything around them was connected—the earth, the sky, the sun, the moon, the animals, the plant life, and man—and these elements together made their world whole. They considered the bounty from the land as sacred, a gift from the Great Spirit, meant to be shared for the benefit of the entire tribe. They relished the unbridled freedom found in roaming the high prairies beyond the reaches of known civilization, stopping or moving wherever and whenever it pleased them.

The European American regarded that same land by calculating the revenue that could be derived by altering or destroying its natural state—plowing, chopping timber, grazing animals, building towns—for in this world, man was superior to nature. This race, which arrived to claim the frontier as its own, tended to regard resources with a covetousness designed to acquire possessions and thereby individual wealth. Its members preferred a structured existence, one of permanent settlements, with stakes driven into the ground to designate private ownership.

Neither race endeavored to learn and respect the beliefs, the traditions, or the inherent behavior of the other, which engendered distrust and fear. Therefore, it was inevitable that the two contrary cultures would eventually clash—no matter what the efforts were on either side to bring about peace. And the more populous, the more powerful, would impose its will on the weaker, the less populous, and would prevail in war or peace.

The fate of Black Kettle, or that of Sitting Bull or Crazy Horse or Geronimo, was sealed from the moment that first emigrant wagon train rumbled across the Plains.

But while most chiefs declared war to defend their homeland, Black Kettle was the exception; he embraced an unpopular position with his steadfast belief that the only way to save his people from misery and even extinction was to make peace.

Perhaps the only clue that Black Kettle ever provided to explain his extraordinary determination to bring about peace between the Cheyennes and the white man can be found in a phrase:

"Coming through the fire."

This phrase was spoken twice by Black Kettle.

The first instance was in reference to Major Edward Wynkoop, when, in September 1864, the chief addressed his skeptical peers in the Council Lodge. The major, accompanied only by a small detachment of troops, had bravely entered hostile Cheyenne territory in response to Black Kettle's letter agreeing to the peace proposal issued by Governor John Evans. "It was like *coming through the fire*," Black Kettle had said, "for a white man to follow and believe in the words of one of our race, whom they have always branded as unworthy of confidence or belief."[13]

At the Camp Weld council, Black Kettle told Governor Evans that "We have come with our eyes shut, following his [Wynkoop's] handful of men, like *coming through the fire*. All we ask is that we may have peace with the whites."[14]

This phrase, "coming through the fire," cannot be regarded as merely a physical act, such as Wynkoop or Black Kettle entering enemy soil in the name of peace, for the words are far more significant and symbolic.

Mari Sandoz, in her classic *Cheyenne Autumn*, wrote that "a vision in a warring time had made a peace man of Black Kettle."[15]

Although no other documentation exists to confirm this statement, it would stand to reason that Black Kettle believed that he was a messenger, a prophet, empowered by a higher authority. The words "coming through the fire" portray powerful mystical qualities that transcend into the spiritual world.

Time and again, Black Kettle braved physical dangers, even from within his tribe, to promote his belief that peace was the only option. This awakening, which motivated him to consider peace with an enemy who had invaded his country and introduced such tragic consequences—disease, starvation, poverty, and countless deaths—could not have been based solely on mortal or human perception or intelligence.

Black Kettle had come through the fire of hatred and resentment of the white man, had risen above prevailing prejudices, to embrace an unpopular crusade in partnership with some supernatural force, and he followed a vision of peace for the good of his people.

The question remains: Was Black Kettle successful in his quest for peace?

If value is placed on human life, both white and red, then Black Kettle's efforts must be regarded as highly successful. Although he lost a great number of his people at Sand Creek and Washita—through no fault of his own—throughout the years he was instrumental in saving countless lives.

On numerous occasions he restrained his young warriors from taking to the warpath, which prevented attacks on settlers, wagon trains, travelers, and soldiers, thereby sparing the lives of many whites and also many of his own people, due to retaliation by the army. His constant voice for peace in the Council Lodge was also influential in this same manner—whether it discouraged all-out war or minimized the number of raids undertaken by the more aggressive Dog Soldiers. In addition, the respect shown to him throughout the years by numerous white government officials and army officers offered hope for a negotiated peace and at times stopped soldiers from taking to the field.

Another contribution that has been overlooked, although Black Kettle was not directly responsible, was the result of the Sand Creek Massacre. The fact that he was known as a peacemaker initiated the investigations that prevented unsavory characters, such as Governor John Evans and Colonel John Chivington, from politically profiting from their treachery in the war that they had provoked for personal gain. Had Black Kettle not been widely known as an outspoken proponent for peace, Sand Creek would have been regarded as a major military victory and likely resulted in additional attacks and the bloodletting of innocent people who were an obstacle in the pathway of progress.

The locations where the most important events in Black Kettle's life took place have been preserved by the U.S. government.

On November 12, 1996, the Washita Battlefield National Historical Site was established to recognize the Battle of the Washita as a nationally significant event in frontier history and as a symbol of the struggles of the Plains tribes. This three-hundred-acre park, maintained by the National Park Service, is located near Cheyenne, Oklahoma, in Roger Mills County. Somewhere within the boundaries of this site rests the body of Black Kettle, buried several days after the attack but never found.

An excellent place to begin a tour of that battlefield is the Black Kettle Museum in Cheyenne, which features exhibits about the Cheyennes and the battle and provides background information about events leading up to and surrounding the conflict.

Also nearby is the Black Kettle National Grasslands, a 31,300-acre preserve, managed by the U.S. Forest Service, which was established on June 30, 1960. This recreation area offers camping, picnicking, fishing, hiking trails, and wildlife viewing.

The Sand Creek Massacre National Historic Site in eastern Colorado was authorized by Public Law 106-465 on November 7, 2000. This National Park Service site, which at the time of this writing was in development stages, will recognize the significance of this tragic event and its importance to the descendents of the massacre victims.

Most important, the memory and the spirit of Black Kettle live on in the hearts and the minds of the Cheyenne People, as a reminder of their tragic history but also as a symbol of hope for harmony between the races.

It is only fitting that a man who had "come through the fire," a man who understood Black Kettle as perhaps no other white had, present the final eulogy of this great Cheyenne chief.

Appearing before the U.S. Indian Commission in Washington on December 23, 1864, Edward "Ned" Wynkoop said of Black Kettle,

> His innate dignity and lofty bearing, combined with his sagacity and intelligence, had that moral effect which placed him in the position as a potentate. The whole force of his nature was concentrated in the one idea of how best to act for the good of his race; he knew the power of the white man, and was aware that thence might spring most of the evils that could befall his people, and consequently the whole of his powers were directed toward conciliating the whites, and his utmost endeavors used to preserve peace and friendship between his race and their oppressors.[16]

NOTES

1. EARLY LIFE

1. The classic work about the Great Plains is Walter P. Webb's *The Great Plains* (Boston: Gin and Company, 1931), 10–47.

2. George Bird Grinnell, *The Cheyenne Indians: Their History and Ways of Life*, 2 vols. (New Haven: Yale University Press, 1923), 1:63, 224.

3. Ibid., 63, 221.

4. Ibid., 64; John L. Sipes Jr. to the author, March 23, 2003.

5. Grinnell, *Cheyenne Indians*, 1:66; E. Adamson Hoebel, *Cheyennes, Indians of the Great Plains* (New York: Holt, Rinehart and Winston, 1978), 68.

6. Grinnell, *Cheyenne Indians*, 1:65, 66.

7. Ibid., 66.

8. Ibid., 129–31, 156; Truman Michelson, "The Narrative of a Southern Cheyenne Woman," Smithsonian *Miscellaneous Collections* 97, no. 5 (1932): 4n; John L. Sipes Jr. to the author, March 23, 2003.

9. John H. Seger, "Cheyenne Marriage Customs," *Journal of American Folk-Lore*, 11, no. 43 (October–December 1898): 298–99; Michelson, "Narrative of a Southern Cheyenne Woman," 6–7; Hoebel, *Cheyennes*, 28; Grinnell, *Cheyenne Indians*, 1:131–45; John L. Sipes Jr. to the author, March 23, 2003.

10. Ibid., 127–29; Hoebel, *Cheyennes*, 95; Grinnell, *Fighting Cheyennes* (New York: Charles Scribner's Sons, 1915), 9.

11. Grinnell, *Cheyenne Indians*, 1:159–60.

12. Ibid., 65–69; Hoebel, *Cheyennes*, 64.

13. Grinnell, *Cheyenne Indians*, 1:67.

14. Ibid., 69–70; John L. Sipes Jr. to the author, March 23, 2003.

15. Dan L. Thrapp, *Encyclopedia of Frontier Biography*, 3 vols. (Glendale, Calif.: Arthur H. Clark, 1988), 1:122–23, cites "c. 1803"; Harvey Markowitz, ed., *American Indians* (Pasadena, Calif.: Salem Press, 1995), 110, cites "1803?"; CISCO, ed., *Biographical Dictionary of the Americas* (Newport Beach, Calif.: American Indian Publishers, 1991), 72, cites "ca. 1803"; Charles Phillips and Alan Axelrod, eds., *Encyclopedia of the American West* (New York: Simon & Schuster Macmillan, 1996), 157, cites "1804?"; John A. Garraty, ed., *American National Biography* (New York: Oxford University Press, 1999), 878, cites "1807?"

16. *New York Times*, December 24, 1868.

17. George E. Hyde, *Life of George Bent: Written from His Letters* (Norman: University of Oklahoma Press, 1968), 322.

18. Ibid., 322–23.

19. Wind Woman to George Bird Grinnell, George Bird Grinnell Papers, Southwest Museum Library, Los Angeles.

20. Wolf Chief to George Bird Grinnell, George Bird Grinnell Papers, Southwest Museum Library, Los Angeles.

21. *Missouri Republican*, October 22, 1867.

22. *New York Times*, December 24, 1868.

23. Berthrong, *Southern Cheyennes*, 71.

24. Ibid., 4–7; Grinnell, *Cheyenne Indians*, 1:4–8, 14–28; Hyde, *Life of George Bent*, 4–9; Tom Weist, *A History of the Cheyenne People* (Billings: Montana Council for Indian Education, 1977), 9–18; Hoebel, *Cheyennes*, 6.

25. Grinnell, *Cheyenne Indians*, 1:2–3; Berthrong, *Southern Cheyennes* (Norman: University of Oklahoma Press, 1963), 27; Hyde, *Life of George Bent*, 9; Peter J. Powell, *Sweet Medicine*, 2 vols. (Norman: University of Oklahoma Press, 1969), 1:24; Weist, *Cheyenne People*, 9.

26. Berthrong, *Southern Cheyennes*, 4–7; Grinnell, *Cheyenne Indians*, 1, 4–8, 14–28; Hyde, *Life of George Bent*, 4–9; Weist, *Cheyenne People*, 9–18.

27. Thom Hatch, *The Custer Companion: A Comprehensive Guide to the Life of George Armstrong Custer and the Plains Indian Wars* (Mechanicsburg, Pa.: Stackpole, 2002), 460–63; Wayne Gard, *The Great Buffalo Hunt* (Lincoln: University of Nebraska Press, 1959), 4–7; John L. Sipes Jr. to the author, March 23, 2003.

28. Ibid., Hyde, *Life of George Bent*, 10.

29. Berthrong, *Southern Cheyennes*, 6, 9; Hyde, *Life of George Bent*, 4–9; Weist, *Cheyenne People*, 9–18.

30. Grinnell, *Cheyenne Indians*, 1:25–27; Grinnell, *Fighting Cheyennes*, 2–3; Hoebel, *Cheyennes*, 8.

31. Grinnell, *Fighting Cheyennes*, 4, 8; Frederick W. Hodge, *Handbook of American Indians North of Mexico* (Bureau of American Ethnology *Bulletin No. 30*, 2 vols., Washington, 1910), 2:660; Berthrong, *Southern Cheyennes*, 10; John L. Sipes Jr. to the author, March 23, 2003.

32. Wind Woman to George Bird Grinnell, August 14, 1913, George Bird Grinnell Papers, Southwest Museum Library, Los Angeles; Hyde, *Life of George Bent*, 322.

33. Powell, *Sweet Medicine*, 1:22–23; Weist, *Cheyenne People*, 18–21; Grinnell, *Cheyenne Indians*, 1:7–13; Grinnell, *Fighting Cheyennes*, 7–11; Hyde, *Life of George Bent*, 322; Hoebel, *Cheyennes*, 20.

34. Grinnell, *Cheyenne Indians*, 1:15; Berthrong, *Southern Cheyennes*, 10–19; Powell, *Sweet Medicine*, 1:23–28; Weist, *Cheyenne People*, 25–29.

35. Meriwether Lewis and William Clark, *Original Journals of the Lewis and Clarke Expedition*, 1804–1806, ed. Reuben Gold Thwaites, 7 vols. (New York: Dodd, Mead & Co., 1904), 1:176, 190; 5:350–57.

36. Grinnell, *Cheyenne Indians*, 1:22–23.

37. Ibid., 107.

38. John L. Sipes Jr. to the author, March 23, 2003.

39. Ibid., Grinnell, *Cheyenne Indians*, 1:104–5, 108.

40. Ibid., 105–6.

41. Hoebel, *Cheyennes*, 98.

42. Grinnell, *Cheyenne Indians*, 1:88–91; Powell, *Sweet Medicine*, 2:433–37; Hoebel, *Cheyennes*, 86.

43. Grinnell, *Cheyenne Indians*, 1:91–94; Powell, *Sweet Medicine*, 2:441; Hoebel, *Cheyennes*, 86; John L. Sipes Jr. to the author, March 23, 2003.

44. Ibid., 86; Powell, *Sweet Medicine*, 2:437–39.

45. Hoebel, *Cheyennes*, 14–18; Berthrong, *Southern Cheyennes*, 57–58; George Bird Grinnell, "Great Mysteries of the Cheyenne," *American Anthropologist* 21, no. 4 (October–December 1910): 545–50; George Bent to George Hyde, February 15, 1905, Western History Department, Denver Public Library; Hyde, *Life of George Bent*, 28; John L. Sipes Jr. to the author, March 23, 2003.

46. Hoebel, *Cheyennes*, 24–25; George Bird Grinnell, "Some Early Cheyenne Tales," loc. cit., N. S., 20, no. 78, 192–94; Robert Anderson, "The Buffalo Men, a Cheyenne Ceremony of Petition Deriving from the Sutaio," *Southwestern Journal of Anthropology* 12, no. 1 (Spring 1956): 92–104; Berthrong, *Southern Cheyennes*, 59–60; Grinnell, *Fighting Cheyennes*, 71–72; John Stands in Timber and Margot Liberty, *Cheyenne Memories* (New Haven: Yale University Press, 1967), 74–78.

47. Grinnell, *Cheyenne Indians*, 2:215–17, 285ff.; Hoebel, *Cheyennes*, 18–23; George A. Dorsey, *The Cheyenne: The Sun Dance*, Field Columbian Museum *Publication No. 103, Anthropological Series* 9, no. 2, Chicago (May 1905); 59–62, 175–77, 181, 186; George Bird Grinnell, "The Cheyenne Medicine Lodge," *American Anthropologist* 16, no. 2 (April–June 1914, 245–48); Leslie Spier, "The Sun Dance of the Plains Indians: Its Development and Diffusion," American Museum of Natural History, *Anthropological Papers* 16, pt. 7, New York (1921): 461–62, 481, 491; Berthrong, *Southern Cheyennes*, 65–67.

48. Grinnell, *Cheyenne Indians*, 2:204–10; Hoebel, *Cheyennes*, 23–24; Berthrong, *Southern Cheyennes*, 61–62.

49. Grinnell, *Cheyenne Indians*, 1:109–26; Berthrong, *Southern Cheyennes*, 40–43; Sister M. Inez Hilger, "Notes on Cheyenne Child Life," *American Anthropologist* 48, no. 1 (January–March 1946): 60–69; George Bird Grinnell, "Coup and Scalp among the Plains Indians, *American Anthropologist* 12, no. 2 (April–June 1910): 296–310.

2. WARRIOR

1. Hoebel, *Cheyennes*, 43–53; James Mooney, *The Cheyenne Indians. Memoirs of the American Anthropological Association*, 1 (Lancaster, Pa., 1905–1907), 371–403; Grinnell, *Cheyenne Indians*, 1:337–46; John L. Sipes Jr. to the author, March 23, 2003; George A. Dorsey, "The Cheyenne, Ceremonial Organization," Field Columbian Museum *Publication 99, Anthropological Series* 9, no. 1, Chicago (1905): 12–15.

2. Ibid., 3–29; Hoebel, *Cheyennes*, 40–42; Robert H. Lowie, "Plains Indians Age-Societies: Historical and Comparative Summary," in Clark Wissler, ed., *Societies of the Plains Indians* (New York: American Museum of Natural History, 1916), 894; Mooney, *Cheyenne Indians*, 413; Grinnell, *Cheyenne Indians*, 2: 48–86; Karen D. Peterson, "Cheyenne Soldier Societies," *Plains Anthropologist* 9, no. 25 (1964): 146–72; John L. Sipes Jr. to the author, March 23, 2003.

3. Father Peter J. Powell, *People of the Sacred Mountain: A History of the Northern Cheyenne Chiefs and Warrior Societies 1830–1879*, 2 vols. (San Francisco: Harper & Row, 1981), 1:188; Hoebel, *Cheyennes*, 40.

4. Ruth Fulton Benedict, "The Vision in Plains Culture," *American Anthropologist* 24, no. 1 (January–March 1922): 5–6; A. L. Kroeber, "Cheyenne Tales,"

Journal of American Folk-Lore 13, no. 50 (July–September 1900); Grinnell, *Cheyenne Indians*, 2:57–62; Powell, *People of the Sacred Mountain*, 1:188.

5. Ibid., 189; Hyde, *Life of George Bent*, 323.

6. For more about early Colorado, see Frank Hall, *History of the State of Colorado* (Chicago: Blakely Printing Company, 1889); Wilbur Fisk Stone, *History of Colorado* (Chicago: S. J. Clarke, 1918); and Carl Abbott, Stephen J. Leonard, and David G. McComb, *Colorado: A History of the Centennial State* (Boulder: Colorado Associated University Press, 1982). For information about the Bent family and Bent's New Fort, see Hyde, *Life of George Bent*; David Lavender, *Bent's Fort* (Lincoln: University of Nebraska Press, 1954); and LeRoy R. Hafen, "When Was Bent's Fort Built?" *Colorado Magazine* 31, no. 2 (April 1954): 105, 114–17.

7. "Journal of a March of a Detachment of Dragoons, under the Command of Colonel Dodge, during the Summer of 1835," *American State Papers, Military Affairs*, 6, Washington, 1861, 138, 144–46, 373–82; Lemuel Ford, "Captain Ford's Journal of an Expedition to the Rocky Mountains," ed. Louis Pelzer, *Mississippi Valley Historical Review* 12, no. 4 (March 1926): 564–65.

8. George Bent to George Hyde, January 23, February 17, 1905, Western History Department, Denver Public Library; Powell, *People of the Sacred Mountain*, 1:38–41; Grinnell, *Fighting Cheyennes*, 47–48; James Mooney, *Calendar History of the Kiowa Indians*, Seventeenth Annual Report, Bureau of American Ethnology (Washington, D.C., 1898), 271–73; Hyde, *Life of George Bent*, 73–74.

9. Powell, *People of the Sacred Mountain*, 1:52–53; Grinnell, *Fighting Cheyennes*, 50–51.

10. The best source for the history of this tribe is Virginia Cole Trenholm's *The Arapahoes, Our People* (Norman: University of Oklahoma Press, 1973).

11. Powell, *People of the Sacred Mountain*, 1; 53–54; Grinnell, *Fighting Cheyennes*, 51–53; Hyde, *Life of George Bent*, 77, 323.

12. Ibid., 77–78; Grinnell, *Fighting Cheyennes*, 53; Powell, *People of the Sacred Mountain*, 1:54; John L. Sipes Jr. to the author, March 23, 2003.

13. Powell, *People of the Sacred Mountain*, 1:158.

14. Francis Densmore, *Cheyenne and Arapaho Music* (Highland Park, Los Angeles, Calif.: Southwest Museum, 1936), 42.

15. Grinnell, *Fighting Cheyennes*, 49, 56–57; Powell, *People of the Sacred Mountain*, 1:45–46; 56–57; Hyde, *Life of George Bent*, 78–79.

16. Ibid., 79–82; Grinnell, *Fighting Cheyennes*, 58–62; Powell, *People of the Sacred Mountain*, 1:57–64; Mooney, *Calendar History of the Kiowa Indians*, 275–76; also contributing to the previous battle was information culled from the following letters: George Bent to George Hyde, January 23, February 17, 1905, Western History Department, Denver Public Library; and George Bent to George Hyde, June 2, 5, July 6, 29, August 3, 7, 1914, Yale Collection of Western Americana, Beinecke Rare Book and Manuscript Library, New Haven, Connecticut.

17. Powell, *People of the Sacred Mountain*, 1:57; Grinnell, *Fighting Cheyennes*, 56–57; Hyde, *Life of George Bent*, 79.

18. Ibid., 42.

19. Powell, *People of the Sacred Mountain*, 1:57–65; Grinnell, *Fighting Cheyennes*, 58–62, 65.

20. Grinnell, *Fighting Cheyennes*, 63; Bent to Hyde, January 23, 1905, and August 3, 1914, Yale Collection.

21. Powell, *People of the Sacred Mountain*, 1:71.

22. Ibid., 72; Grinnell, *Fighting Cheyennes*, 68.

23. Powell, *People of the Sacred Mountain*, 1:75–92; Berthrong, *Southern Cheyennes*, 85–114.

24. Hyde, *Life of George Bent*, 96–97; Powell, *People of the Sacred Mountain*, 1:94–99.

25. Report, *Commissioner of Indian Affairs*, 1851, 288–90; 32nd Cong., 1st sess., House No. 2, 332–37; St. Louis *Missouri Republican*, September 13, 26, October 1, 24, 29, November 2, 9, 30, 1851; LeRoy Hafen and Francis Marion Young, *Fort Laramie and the Pageant of the West, 1834–1890* (Glendale, Calif.: Arthur H. Clark, 1938), 184–96; LeRoy R. Hafen and W. J. Ghent, *Broken Hand: The Life Story of Thomas Fitzpatrick, Mountain Man, Guide and Indian Agent* (Denver: Old West Publishing, 1931), 228–32; Hirum Martin Chittenden and Alfred Talbot Richardson, *Life, Letters and Travels of Father Pierre-Jean De Smet, S. J., 1801–1874* (New York: F. P. Harper, 1905), 4 vols., 2:679–80; Charles J. Kappler, comp. and ed., *Indian Affairs, Laws and Treaties*, 2 vols., Washington, 1904, 1913, 1927, 2:594–96; Powell, *People of the Sacred Mountain*, 1:100–110; Berthrong, *Southern Cheyennes*, 115–23.

26. Grinnell, *Fighting Cheyennes*, 72; Powell, *People of the Sacred Mountain*, 1: 7–10, 112; Berthrong, *Southern Cheyennes*, 58–59; Hyde, *Life of George Bent*, 49–53.

27. Grinnell, *Fighting Cheyennes*, 78–83; Powell, *People of the Sacred Mountain*, 1:111–18.

28. Ibid., 154–57; Grinnell, *Fighting Cheyennes*, 84–85.

29. Ibid., 92; Powell, *People of the Sacred Mountain*, 1:155–57.

30. Ibid., 161–62; Grinnell, *Fighting Cheyennes*, 92–96; Mooney, *Calendar History of the Kiowa Indians*, 249–50.

31. Powell, *People of the Sacred Mountain*, 1:164–69, 175; Mooney, *Cheyenne Indians*, 379; Stands in Timber and Liberty, *Cheyenne Memories*, 163.

32. *Annual Report of the Commissioner of Indian Affairs, 1854*, 93–94; Powell, *People of the Sacred Mountain*, 1:175.

33. Ibid., 177–78.

34. Ibid., 188–89; Bent to Hyde, April 17, 1906, Yale Collection; George Bird Grinnell Papers, Southwest Museum Library; Hyde, *Life of George Bent*, 323. George Bent gives the date of this event as the summer of 1848, but the evidence, especially the timing of the raids into Mexico, indicates that the year would have been 1854.

35. Hyde, *Life of George Bent*, 323; Powell, *People of the Sacred Mountain*, 1:207.

3. THE MIGHT OF THE U.S. ARMY

1. *Engagement between United States Troops and Sioux Indians*, 33rd Cong., 2d sess., House Exec. Doc. No. 63, 1–27; 34th Cong., 1st and 2d sess., Senate Executive Document No. 91, 11–12; Hafen and Young, *Fort Laramie*, 222–29; *Annual*

Report of the Commissioner of Indian Affairs, 1854, 89–94; Eugene Bandel, *Frontier Life in the Army, 1854–61*, ed. R. P. Bieber (Philadelphia: Porcupine Press, 1942), 24–28; George Hyde, *Spotted Tail's Folk* (Norman: University of Oklahoma Press, 1974), 48–53; Grinnell, *Fighting Cheyennes*, 106–8; Robert M. Utley, *Frontiersmen in Blue: The United States Army and the Indian, 1848–1865* (New York: Macmillan, 1967), 112–20; additional details about the Grattan affair and subsequent events can be found in transcripts of interviews with Sioux and white residents of the time, along with letters, newspaper clippings, and comments by Judge Daniel Ricker in the Ricker Tablets, Nebraska State Historical Society.

2. *Report, Commissioner of Indian Affairs, 1854*, 96, and 1855, 400–401.

3. *Report of General Harney, Commander of the Sioux Expedition*, 34th Cong., 1st sess., Sen. Exec. Doc. No. 1, pt. 1, 49–51; St. Louis *Missouri Republican*, September 5, 1855; Grinnell, *Fighting Cheyennes*, 108–10; Berthrong, *Southern Cheyennes*, 130; Doane Robinson, *A History of the Dakota or Sioux Indians* (Minneapolis: Ross and Haines, 1956), 224; Hyde, *Spotted Tail's Folk*, 59–61.

4. J. P. Dunn Jr., *Massacres in the Mountains: A History of the Indian Wars of the Far West, 1815–1875* (New York: Archer House, 1958), 236.

5. Berthrong, *Southern Cheyennes*, 132–33.

6. Grinnell, *Fighting Cheyennes*, 110; Hafen and Young, *Fort Laramie*, 243–45.

7. St. Louis *Missouri Republican*, September 27, 1855; 33rd Cong., 2d sess., House Exec. Doc. No. 36, 3–5; 34th Cong., 3rd sess., Sen. Exec. Doc. No. 59, 4; 34th Cong., 1st sess., House Exec. Doc. No. 130, 1–39.

8. Hoffman to Pleasonton, March 31, 1856, Fort Laramie, Letters Sent, United States Army Commands, Records of the War Department, National Archives.

9. Grinnell, *Fighting Cheyennes*, 111–12; Powell, *People of the Sacred Mountain*, 1:202–3; Hyde, *Life of George Bent*, 100; Hafen and Young, *Fort Laramie*, 227; *Report of the Commissioner of Indian Affairs, 1856*, 87–88, 102.

10. Hoebel, *Cheyennes*, 6–7, 58–64; Berthrong, *Southern Cheyennes*, 62–66; Grinnell, *Fighting Cheyennes*, 226–27.

11. Powell, *People of the Sacred Mountain*, 1:203–4.

12. Grinnell, *Fighting Cheyennes*, 112; *Report of the Commissioner of Indian Affairs, 1856*, 99; Powell, *People of the Sacred Mountain*, 1:204; Hyde, *Life of George Bent*, 101.

13. G. W. Stewart to H. W. Wharton, August 27, 1856, *Kansas Historical Collections* 4, 491–92; H. W. Wharton to S. Cooper, September 8, 1856, *Kansas Historical Collections* 4, 492; Grinnell, *Fighting Cheyennes*, 113; Powell, *People of the Sacred Mountain*, 1:204–5; Hyde, *Life of George Bent*, 100–101; LeRoy R. Hafen and Ann W. Hafen, *Relations with the Indians of the Plains* (Glendale, Calif.: Arthur H. Clark, 1959), 16–17.

14. G. H. Stewart to H. W. Wharton, September 1, 1856, *Kansas Historical Collections* 4, 490–91; H. W. Wharton to S. Cooper, September 8, 1856, *Kansas Historical Collections* 4, 492–94; *Report of the Commissioner*, 1856, 99; Grinnell, *Fighting Cheyennes*, 113; Powell, *People of the Sacred Mountain*, 1:205; Hafen and Young, *Fort Laramie*, 278; Hafen and Hafen, *Relations with the Indians*, 17.

15. Thomas Twiss to A. Cumming, September 25, 1856, and Twiss to Manypenny, October 13, 1856, in Annual Report, Secretary of the Interior, 1856; *Report of the Commissioner of Indian Affairs*, 1856, 102–3; Berthrong, *Southern Cheyennes*,

136; Powell, *People of the Sacred Mountain*, 1:206–7; Hafen and Young, *Fort Laramie*, 279; Hafen and Hafen, *Relations with the Indians*, 18.

16. George Bird Grinnell, *By Cheyenne Campfires* (New Haven, Conn.: Yale University Press, 1926), 59–63.

17. Powell, *People of the Sacred Mountain*, 1:211.

18. Hafen and Young, Fort Laramie, 277; *New York Tribune*, May 21, 1857.

19. Powell, *People of the Sacred Mountain*, 1:210–11.

20. Bent to Hyde, Coe Collection, November 14, 1912.

21. Powell, *People of the Sacred Mountain*, 1:211; Grinnell, *Fighting Cheyennes*, 118–19.

22. General Persifer F. Smith to Cooper, September 10, 1856, and endorsement by Secretary of War Jefferson Davis, October 24, 1856, in *Kansas Historical Collections*, IV, 489–90, 494; Sumner to Adjutant General, September 20, 1857, Office of the Adjutant General, letters received; Sen. Exec. Doc. No. 5, 34th Cong., 3rd sess., 638–45; Alban W. Hoopes, *Indian Affairs and Their Administration with Special Reference to the Far West, 1849–1860* (Philadelphia: University of Pennsylvania Press, 1932), 215; Robert M. Peck, "Recollections of Early Times in Kansas Territory," *Kansas Historical Collections* 8 (1903–1904): 486–94; Hafen and Hafen, *Relations with the Indians*, 49–67, 98–112.

23. Powell, *People of the Sacred Mountain*, 1:212; Hyde, *Life of George Bent*, 102.

24. Berthrong, *Southern Cheyennes*, 138–39.

25. Hyde, *Life of George Bent*, 102; Powell, *People of the Sacred Mountain*, 1:212; Grinnell, *Fighting Cheyennes*, 117–18.

26. Peck, "Recollections," 496–97; S. L. Seabrook, "Expedition of Col. E. V. Sumner against the Cheyenne Indians, 1857," *Kansas Historical Collections* 16 (1923–1925): 311; Powell, *People of the Sacred Mountain*, 1:212; Berthrong, *Southern Cheyennes*, 139.

27. Peck, "Recollections," 497; Powell, *People of the Sacred Mountain*, 1:212–13; Hafen and Hafen, *Relations with the Indians*, 75–80; Berthrong, *Southern Cheyennes*, 212.

28. Powell, *People of the Sacred Mountain*, 1:213; Berthrong, *Southern Cheyennes*, 140; Hyde, *Life of George Bent*, 103; "Report of Colonel E. V. Sumner, August 9, 1857," Annual report, Secretary of War (1857), House Exec. Doc. No. 2, 35th Cong., 1st sess., 2, 96, 99; Peck, "Recollections," 494–98.

29. Grinnell, *Fighting Cheyennes*, 120–21; Powell, *People of the Sacred Mountain*, 1:213; Berthrong, *Southern Cheyennes*, 140; Peck, "Recollections," 494–98; Hyde, *Life of George Bent*, 104; Thom Hatch, *Clashes of Cavalry: The Civil War Careers of George Armstrong Custer and Jeb Stuart* (Mechanicsburg, Pa: Stackpole, 2001), 10–11; the best source for a highly detailed and documented account of this battle, as well as for prior and subsequent events, mainly from the army's point of view, although fair treatment is afforded the circumstances of the Cheyenne, is William Y. Chalfant's *Cheyennes and Horse Soldiers: The 1857 Expedition and the Battle of Solomon's Fork* (Norman: University of Oklahoma Press, 1989).

30. Annual Report, Commissioner of Indian Affairs, 1857, 145–48; Lavender, *Bent's Fort*, 333; Sumner to AAG., August 11, 1857, 35th Cong., 1st sess., House Exec. Doc. No. 2, Vol. 2, 97–98; Hyde, *Life of George Bent*, 121; Berthrong, *Southern Cheyennes*, 141–42.

4. Gold in Colorado Territory

1. Berthrong, *Southern Cheyennes*, 142; Hoopes, *Indian Affairs*, 216; Powell, *People of the Sacred Mountain*, 1:213.

2. Hyde, *Life of George Bent*, 58–62, 83, 94; Lavender, *Bent's Fort*, 20, 186, 188, 323, 347–348.

3. White Antelope, et. al., to Col. Hafferdy (John Haverty), October 28, 1857, Upper Arkansas Agency, Letters Received, National Archives; Berthrong, *Southern Cheyennes*, 142–43; Hoopes, *Indian Affairs*, 216; Powell, *People of the Sacred Mountain*, 1:213–14.

4. William Bent to Hafferday (Haverty), December 11, 1857, Upper Arkansas Agency, Letters Received.

5. Stan Hoig, *The Peace Chiefs of the Cheyennes* (Norman: University of Oklahoma Press, 1980), 106.

6. Powell, *People of the Sacred Mountain*, 1:223–25.

7. Grinnell, *Cheyenne Indians*, 2:380.

8. Robert C. Miller to Charles E. Mix, April 30, 1858, Upper Arkansas Agency, Letters Received; Grinnell, *Fighting Cheyennes*, 124.

9. LeRoy R. Hafen, ed., *Colorado Gold Rush—Contemporary Letters and Reports 1858–59* (Glendale, Calif.: Arthur H. Clark, 1941), 42–44; Stone, *History of Colorado*, vol. 1, 158; Phyllis Flanders Dorset, *The New Eldorado: The Story of Colorado's Gold and Silver Rushes* (New York: Macmillan, 1970), 10–14; Frank M. Cobb, "The Lawrence Party of Gold Seekers," *Colorado Magazine* 10, no. 5 (September 1933): 194–96; James H. Pierce, "With the Green Russell Party," *The Trail* 13, no. 12 (May 1921): 5–14; James H. Pierce, "The First Prospecting in Colorado," *The Trail* 7, no. 5 (October 1914): 5–11.

10. Appendix to the Report of the Commissioner of Indian Affairs (1847), 30th Cong., 1st sess., Sen. Exec. Doc. No. 8, 242.

11. *Report of the Commissioner of Indian Affairs, 1858*, 96–100.

12. Powell, *People of the Sacred Mountain*, 1:224.

13. Ibid., 225.

14. Stone, *History of Colorado*, 134–40; Dorset, *New Eldorado*, 14–18.

15. Sumner to AAG., October 5, 1858, Office of the Adjutant General, Letters Received.

16. *Report of the Commissioner of Indian Affairs, 1858*, 99; Berthrong, *Southern Cheyennes*, 144.

17. Hafen, *Colorado Gold Rush*, 349–57; Stone, *History of Colorado*, 140–43; Dorset, *New Eldorado*, 46–47; Cobb, "Lawrence Party of Gold Seekers," 194–96; Pierce, "With the Green Russell Party," 5–14; Pierce, "First Prospecting in Colorado," 5–11.

18. Curtis to Denver, February 6, 1859, Upper Arkansas Agency, Letters Received; Hyde, *Life of George Bent*, 108.

19. Ibid., 108–9; Grinnell, *Fighting Cheyennes*, 125.

20. Hafen, *Colorado Gold Rush*, intro; Stone, *History of Colorado*, 236–48; Dorset, *New Eldorado*, 25–86; Abbott, et al., *Colorado: A History*, 51–59.

21. Frank A. Root and William E. Connelley, *The Overland Stage to California: Personal Reminiscences and Authentic History of the Great Overland Stage Line*

and Pony Express from the Missouri River to the Pacific Ocean (Topeka: Crane & Co., 1901), 153; Grinnell, *Fighting Cheyennes*, 125.

22. LeRoy R. Hafen, ed., *Overland Routes to the Gold Fields, 1859* (Glendale, Calif.: Arthur H. Clark, 1942), 255–57.

23. Hyde, *Life of George Bent*, 106.

24. Ibid., 107; Lavender, *Bent's Fort*, 364.

25. *Report of the Commissioner of Indian Affairs, 1859*, 137–39; Bent to Robinson, July 23, August 1, 1859, Upper Arkansas Agency, Letters Received; Lavender, *Bent's Fort*, 365–68; Berthrong, *Southern Cheyennes*, 146–47.

26. Hyde, *Life of George Bent*, 113.

27. Ibid., 113; Powell, *People of the Sacred Mountain*, 1:231.

28. Ibid., 232–33; *Report of the Commissioner of Indian Affairs, 1859*, 505.

29. Hyde, *Life of George Bent*, 108; Hatch, *Custer Companion*, 59.

30. Hafen, *Colorado Gold Rush*, 349, 357, 363–64; Albert D. Richardson, *Beyond the Mississippi: From the Great River to the Great Ocean, Life and Adventure on the Prairies, Mountains, and Pacific Coast, 1857–1867* (Hartford: American Publishing Co., 1867), 300.

31. Dorset, *New Eldorado*, 119–20; *Rocky Mountain News*, April 18, 1860.

32. Mooney, *Calendar History of the Kiowa Indians*, 308; George Bent to Hyde, March 6, 1905, Coe Collection; William Bent to Robinson, November 28, 1859, Upper Arkansas Agency, Letters Received; Hafen and Hafen, *Relations with the Indians*, 196–254.

33. *Western Mountaineer*, Golden, Colorado, September 20, 1860; *Annual Report of the Commissioner of Indian Affairs, 1860*, 248, 452.

34. Ibid., 228.

35. *Daily Times*, Leavenworth, Kansas, October 23, 1860.

36. *Western Mountaineer*, October 4, 1860.

37. *Annual Report of the Commissioner of Indian Affairs, 1860*, 228–29.

38. Kappler, *Indian Affairs, Laws and Treaties*, 2:807–11.

39. *Annual Report of the Commissioner of Indian Affairs, 1860*, 230; Berthrong, *Southern Cheyennes*, 149; Hafen and Hafen, *Relations with the Indians*, 284–89; Hyde, *Life of George Bent*, 126; Lavender, *Bent's Fort*, 348, 369.

40. Powell, *People of the Sacred Mountain*, 1:235.

41. Kappler, *Indian Affairs, Laws and Treaties*, 2:810–11.

42. Bent to Hyde, April 17, 1906, May 29, 1906, Coe Collection.

43. Hyde, *Life of George Bent*, 114.

44. Kappler, *Indian Affairs*, 2:810.

5. IN THE WAY OF PROGRESS

1. Stone, *History of Colorado*, 170–71; Abbott, et al., *Colorado: A History*, 64–65.

2. Hall, *History of the State of Colorado*, 265, 275–76; Hubert Howe Bancroft, *History of Nevada, Colorado, and Wyoming* (San Francisco: History Co., 1890), 415; Leroy R. Hafen, *Colorado and Its People* (New York: Lewis Historical, 1948), 1:131–33; Thrapp, *Encyclopedia of Frontier Biography*, 2:557; also see Thomas L.

Kearnes, *William Gilpin: Western Nationalist* (Austin: University of Texas Press, 1970).

3. Gilpin to Fitzpatrick, February 8, 14, 1848, Fitzpatrick to Gilpin, February 10, 1848, Upper Arkansas Agency, Letters Received; Fitzpatrick to Harvey, October 6, 1848, in *Report of the Commissioner of Indian Affairs, 1848*, 470–73; Lavender, *Bent's Fort*, 247–48, 326–30; Berthrong, *Southern Cheyennes*, 111–12.

4. Boone to Robinson, April 25, 1861, Upper Arkansas Agency, Letters Received.

5. Grinnell, *Fighting Cheyennes*, 127.

6. Susan Riley Ashley, "Reminiscences in the Early 'Sixties," *Colorado Magazine* 8 (1936): 222–23.

7. Howard Louis Conrad, *"Uncle Dick" Wootton, the Pioneer Frontiersman of the Rocky Mountain Region: An Account of the Adventures and Thrilling Experiences of the Most Noted American Hunter, Trapper, Guide, Scout, and Indian Fighter Now Living* (Chicago: W. E. Dibble, 1890), 119.

8. Hall, *History of the State of Colorado*, 265, 275–76.

9. Carl Ubbelohde, Maxine Benson, and Duane A. Smith, eds. *A Colorado History* (Boulder, Colo.: Pruett, 1972, 1976, 1982), 104–6; Report, *Commissioner of Indian Affairs*, 1861, 99–101; also see Ovando J. Hollister, *Boldly They Rode: A History of the First Colorado Regiment* (Lakewood, Colo.: Golden Press, 1949).

10. *Report, Commissioner of Indian Affairs, 1861*, 709; *Rocky Mountain News*, September 9, 1861.

11. Boone to Commissioner of Indian Affairs William P. Dole, October 26, November 2, 1861, Upper Arkansas Agency, Letters Received.

12. Boone to Dole, November 16, 1861, Upper Arkansas Agency, Letters Received.

13. Boone to Mix, September 6, 1861, Upper Arkansas Agency, Letters Received; Boone to Dole, November 16, 1861, Upper Arkansas Agency, Letters Received; *Report, Commissioner of Indian Affairs, 1861*, 710.

14. Dorset, *New Eldorado*, 140.

15. Thom Hatch, *The Blue, the Gray, and the Red: Indian Campaigns of the Civil War* (Mechanicsburg, Pa.: Stackpole, 2003), 1–4, 21–22; Hyde, *Life of George Bent*, 115.

16. Ibid., 110, 115–16; Lavender, *Bent's Fort*, 373; *Report, Commissioner of Indian Affairs, 1861*, 99–101, 104–6.

17. The best information about Sibley's invasion of New Mexico and the battle at La Glorieta Pass can be found in Thomas Edington and John Taylor, *The Battle of Glorieta Pass: A Gettysburg in the West, March 26–28, 1862* (Albuquerque: University of New Mexico Press, 1998); Don E. Alberts, *The Battle of Glorieta: Union Victory in the West* (College Station: Texas A & M Press, 1998); William Clarke Whitford, *Colorado Volunteers in the Civil War: The New Mexico Campaign of 1862* (Denver: State Historical and Natural History Society, 1906); and Martin H. Hall, *Sibley's New Mexico Campaign* (Austin: University of Texas Press, 1960).

18. Ubbelohde, et al., *A Colorado History*, 107; also see Kearnes, *William Gilpin*.

19. For biographical information about Evans, see Harry J. Kelsey Jr., *Frontier Capitalist: The Life of John Evans* (Denver: State Historical Society of Colorado, 1969).

20. For details, see Hatch, *The Blue, the Gray, and the Red*, chaps. 3 and 5.

21. Bancroft, *History of Nevada, Colorado, and Wyoming*, 459; Hoig, *Sand Creek Massacre*, 25–26.

22. *Annual Report of the Commissioner of Indian Affairs, 1862*, 229, 373–76.

23. Hoig, *Sand Creek Massacre*, 20; Whitford, *Colorado Volunteers*, 130.

24. Accounts of Chivington's early life can be found in nearly every volume pertaining to Sand Creek. Also see Reyinald S. Craig's sympathetic *The Fighting Parson* (Tucson: Westernlore Press, 1959); and "The First Colorado Regiment," by Colonel J. M. Chivington, Manuscript Collection, Colorado State Historical Society, Denver, Colorado, October 18, 1884.

25. Harry Kelsey, "Background to Sand Creek," *Colorado Magazine* 45, no. 4 (Fall 1968): 279–300; Lavender, *Bent's Fort*, 378; Thrapp, *Encyclopedia of Frontier Biography*, 299–300; Hoig, *Sand Creek Massacre*, 14–16, 24–25; Julia Lambert, "Plain Tales of the Plains," *The Trail* 9 (1916): 17–18.

26. *Leavenworth Times*, March 13, 14, 1863; *New York Tribune*, March 18, April 7, 1863; *Washington Evening Star*, March 27, 1863; *Daily National Intelligencer*, March 28, 1863; *New York Times*, April 8, 11, 13, 1863; Hoig, *Peace Chiefs*, 69–75; Herman J. Viola, *Diplomats in Buckskin: A History of Indian Delegations in Washington City* (Washington, D.C.: Smithsonian Institution Press, 1981), 99–102.

27. Bent to Hyde, July 21, 1915, Coe Collection; Hyde, *Life of George Bent*, 112–13; Powell, *People of the Sacred Mountain*, 1:247–49.

28. Hyde, *Life of George Bent*, 111–13.

29. Grinnell, *Fighting Cheyennes*, 132–33; *The War of the Rebellion: A Compilation of the Official Records of the Union and Confederate Armies*, 128 vols. (Washington, D.C.: U.S. Government Printing Office, 1880–1901) (hereinafter cited as *O. R.*), series 1, vol. 22, pt. 2, 294.

30. *Report of the Commissioner of Indian Affairs, 1863*, 247–48; Grinnell, *Fighting Cheyennes*, 125–28, 132–33; Hoig, *Sand Creek Massacre*, 31–33; Berthrong, *Southern Cheyennes*, 167–68; Powell, *People of the Sacred Mountain*, 1:250–51.

31. *Report of the Commissioner of Indian Affairs, 1863*, 121; Hyde, *Life of George Bent*, 119; Grinnell, *Fighting Cheyennes*, 134.

32. Ibid., 134–35; Berthrong, *Southern Cheyennes*, 172.

33. Ibid., 173; Hyde, *Life of George Bent*, 121; Grinnell, *Fighting Cheyennes*, 135.

34. Berthrong, *Southern Cheyennes*, 173; Alvin M. Josephy Jr., *The Civil War in the American West* (New York: Alfred A. Knopf, 1991), 299.

35. Grinnell, *Fighting Cheyennes*, 135.

36. *Annual Report of the Commissioner of Indian Affairs, 1863*, 393.

37. Trenholm, *Arapahoe*, 78; Grinnell, *Fighting Cheyennes*, 135.

38. *O. R.*, series 1, vol. 34, pt. 2, 742–43; Grinnell, *Fighting Cheyennes*, 131.

6. The Plains Erupt in Flames

1. Hyde, *Life of George Bent*, 121; Grinnell, *Fighting Cheyennes*, 137; Evans to Colley, March 15, 1864, John Evans Collection, Indian Affairs, Colorado Division of State Archives and Public Records.

2. Hyde, *Life of George Bent*, 124.

3. *O. R.*, series 1, vol. 34, pt. 1, 880–82; pt. 3, 85, 98.

4. U.S. Congress, Senate, "Sand Creek Massacre," Report of the Secretary of War, Sen. Exec. Doc. 26, 39th Cong., 2d sess., Washington, G.P.O., 1867 (hereinafter referred to as "Sand Creek Massacre"), 32.

5. Bent to Hyde, March 26, 1906, Yale Collection; *O. R.*, series 1, vol. 34, pt. 1, 883–84, pt. 3, 166; "Condition of Indian Tribes," Report of the Joint Special Committee, appointed under Joint Resolution of March 3, 1865, with appendix. 39th Cong., 2d sess., Sen. Report No. 156, 1867 (hereinafter referred to as "Condition of Indian Tribes"), 68; Grinnell, *Fighting Cheyennes*, 140–41.

6. "Sand Creek Massacre," 32.

7. Bent to Hyde, March 6, 1905, March 26, 1906, March 19, 1912, March 5, 1913, Yale Collection; Grinnell, *Fighting Cheyennes*, 140, n140.

8. *O. R.*, series 1, vol. 34, part 1, pp. 883–85, 887–88.

9. Grinnell, *Fighting Cheyennes*, 141.

10. Bent to Hyde, April 12, 1906, Yale Collection; *O. R.*, series 1, vol. 34, part 1, pp. 881–82, pt. 3, 113, 218–19; "Condition of Indian Tribes," 72; *Rocky Mountain News*, April 27, 1864.

11. *O. R.*, series 1, vol. 34, pt. 3, 167.

12. Ibid., 151.

13. *O. R.*, series 1, vol. 34, pt. 1, 881–82, pt. 3, 113, 218–19.

14. Hyde, *Life of George Bent*, 129; *O. R.*, series 1, vol. 34, pt. 3, 189.

15. Colley to Evans, April 19, 1864, Upper Arkansas Agency, Letters Received.

16. *O. R.*, series 1, vol. 34, pt. 3, 262.

17. Ibid., 304.

18. Hyde, *Life of George Bent*, 129; Grinnell, *Fighting Cheyennes*, 143.

19. *O. R.*, series 1, vol. 34, pt. 1, pp. 907–8; Hyde, *Life of George Bent*, 129–30; Grinnell, *Fighting Cheyennes*, 143–44.

20. Edward W. Wynkoop, *The Tall Chief: The Autobiography of Edward W. Wynkoop*, ed. Christopher B. Gerboth (Denver: Colorado Historical Society, 1994), 1–12; Thomas D. Isern, "The Controversial Career of Edward W. Wynkoop," *Colorado Magazine* 56 (Winter–Spring 1979): 1–18; Louis Kraft, "Edward Wynkoop: A Forgotten Hero," *Research Review: The Journal of the Little Big Horn Associates* 1 (June 1987): 2–11; Edward E. Wynkoop, "Edward Wanshear Wynkoop," *Collections of the Kansas State Historical Society* 13 (1913–1914): 71–79.

21. *O. R.*, series 1, vol. 34, pt. 3, 531–32, 630; Bent to Hyde, March 9, 1905, February 26, 1906, Western History Department, Denver Public Library.

22. Bent to Hyde, March 26, 1906, Yale Collection.

23. *O. R.*, series 1, vol. 34, pt. 4, 101, 403.

24. Bent to Hyde, March 6, 1905, Western History Department, Denver Public Library; Bent to Hyde, March 26, April 12, 1906, Yale Collection.

25. *O. R.*, series 1, vol. 34, pt. 1, p. 934–35, pt. 4, 38–39, 207–8, 402–4; 460–62.

26. U.S. Congress, Senate, "The Chivington Massacre," Reports of the Committee, 39th Cong., 2d sess., Washington, G.P.O., 1867 (hereinafter referred to as "Chivington Massacre"), 72, 75; Bent to Hyde, April 12, 1906, Yale Collection; *O. R.*, series 1, vol. 34, pt. 4, 151.

27. Powell, *People of the Sacred Mountain*, 1:264–65.

28. *O. R.*, series 1, vol. 34, pt. 4, 97–99.

29. Ibid., 353.

30. Hyde, *Life of George Bent*, 127.

31. *Report of the Commissioner of Indian Affairs, 1864*, 228; Berthrong, *Southern Cheyennes*, 191.

32. *O. R.*, series 1, vol. 34, pt. 4, 353–54; Robert Claiborne Pitzer, *Three Frontiers, Memories and a Portrait of Henry Littleton Pitzer as recorded by his son Robert Claiborne Pitzer* (Muscatine, Iowa: Prairie Press, 1938), 162–63.

33. *O. R.*, series 1, vol. 34, pt. 4, 330, 449.

34. Hoig, *Sand Creek Massacre*, 78–79.

35. Original document copied by the author from Special Collections, Tutt Library, Colorado College, Colorado Springs, Colorado; *O. R.*, series 1, vol. 41, pt. 1, 964.

36. Powell, *People of the Sacred Mountain*, 1:270–274.

37. *Annual Report of the Commissioner of Indian Affairs, 1864*, 3; Grinnell, *Fighting Cheyennes*, 145–49; Berthrong, *Southern Cheyennes*, chaps. 8–9; Hoig, *Sand Creek Massacre*, 85–97.

38. U.S. Congress, House of Representatives, "Massacre of Cheyenne Indians," Report of the Conduct of the War, 38th Cong., 2d sess. Washington, G.P.O., 1865 (hereinafter referred to as "Massacre of Cheyenne Indians), 47.

39. Bent to Hyde, February 28, 1906, Yale Collection; Grinnell, *Fighting Cheyennes*, 148–52; *O. R.*, series 1, vol. 41, pt. 2, pp. 276, 368–69, 378–79, 413, 428–29; 445–47, 483–85, 491, 545, 610, 629–30; 722, 752, 765; Berthrong, *Southern Cheyennes*, chaps. 8–9; Hoig, *Sand Creek Massacre*, 85–97.

40. "Sand Creek Massacre," 213.

41. Hyde, *Life of George Bent*, 142.

42. "Sand Creek Massacre," 84.

43. Ibid., 169; original letter to Agent Colley, copied by the author from Special Collections, Tutt Library, Colorado College, Colorado Springs, Colorado.

7. Seeds of Betrayal

1. "Massacre of Cheyenne Indians," 14–15, 30–31, 84–85.

2. "Sand Creek Massacre," 9, 84, 89–90; Edward W. Wynkoop, "Unfinished Colorado History," Wynkoop Papers, Colorado Historical Society, 31; Wynkoop, *Tall Chief*, 17–18.

3. Ibid., 18; "Sand Creek Massacre," 19, 21, 29–34, 54–59, 84–86; Wynkoop, "Unfinished Colorado History," 31; Hyde, *Life of George Bent*, 142–43; *Annual Report of the Commissioner of Indian Affairs, 1864*, 234–35; "Massacre of Cheyenne Indians," 84–87.

4. Wynkoop, "Unfinished Colorado History," 31–32; Wynkoop, *Tall Chief*, 18; "Sand Creek Massacre," 30–31.

5. Wynkoop, "Unfinished Colorado History," 29.

6. Ibid., 32–33; Wynkoop, *Tall Chief*, 92–93; "Sand Creek Massacre," 31–33; Bent to Hyde, March 14, 1905, Western History Department, Denver Public Library; *O. R.*, series 1, vol. 41, pt. 3, 242–43.

7. Wynkoop, *Tall Chief*, 93–94.

8. Ibid., 19–20, 94–96; "Sand Creek Massacre," 44, 213; Bent to Hyde, March 14, 1905, Western History Department, Denver Public Library; *O. R.*, series 1, vol. 41, pt. 3, 242–43; Julia S. Lambert, "Plain Tales of the Plains," *The Trail* 7 (January–September 1916): 7; *Rocky Mountain News*, September, 21, 28, 1864.

9. Bent to Hyde, April 13, 1913, Yale Collection.

10. *O. R.*, series 1, vol. 41, pt. 2, 670–71.

11. Bent to Hyde, September 26, 1905, April 2, 1906, January 29, 1913, Yale Collection; Bent to Hyde, October 15, 1904, Western History Department, Denver Public Library; *O. R.*, series 1, vol. 41, pt. 1, 818.

12. "Sand Creek Massacre," 213.

13. Ibid., 39–43, 60–61, 86–87, 91, 212–18.

14. "Massacre of Cheyenne Indians," 86–87.

15. Ibid., 87.

16. "Sand Creek Massacre," 121.

17. Powell, *People of the Sacred Mountain*, 1:293; *O. R.*, series 1, vol. 41, pt. 3, 798–99, 876.

18. *O. R.*, series 1, vol. 41, pt. 1, 912.

19. *O. R.*, series 1, vol. 41, pt. 4, 62, 63.

20. "Massacre of Cheyenne Indians," 17–18, 20, 87; "Sand Creek Massacre," 128; Bent to Hyde, April 17, 1905, Western History Department, Denver Public Library; Bent to Hyde, April 30, 1906, Yale Collection; Wynkoop, *Tall Chief*, 22.

21. Ibid., 100–101.

22. "Sand Creek Massacre," 106; "Massacre of Cheyenne Indians," 17–18.

23. *O. R.*, series 1, vol. 41, pt. 1, 912–915.

24. Berthrong, *Southern Cheyennes*, 215–16.

25. "Sand Creek Massacre," 93–95.

26. "Massacre of Cheyenne Indians," 5, 8, 29, 31, 87.

27. "Sand Creek Massacre," 87.

8. THE SAND CREEK MASSACRE

1. Bent to Hyde, April 30, 1913, Yale Collection; "Sand Creek Massacre," 134, 138.

2. Ibid., 60, 66, 67, 128, 135–36; "Chivington Massacre," 5, 41, 66, 87–88, 95–96; Hyde, *Life of George Bent*, 152.

3. Bent to Hyde, March 15, 1905, Yale Collection.

4. An excellent source for this march is "Major Hal Sayre's Diary of the Sand Creek Campaign," ed. Lynn I. Perrigo, *Colorado Magazine* 15 (1938): 41–57.

5. *O. R.*, series 1, vol. 41, pt. 4, 771–72.

6. "Sand Creek Massacre," 51, 107.

7. Ibid., 10–11.

8. Ibid., 11, 165.

9. Ibid., 179, 182, 208, 212; "Chivington Massacre," 27.

10. Craig, *Fighting Parson*, 184.

11. "Sand Creek Massacre," 62, 110, 117, 179, 182, 208, 212; "Massacre of Cheyenne Indians," 27–28, 108; "Chivington Massacre," 69–70.

12. "Sand Creek Massacre," 13.

13. Ibid., 46–47.

14. Ibid., 46; "Chivington Massacre," 74.

15. Ibid., 74; "Sand Creek Massacre," 47.

16. Ibid., 129, 147, 153, 156; "Chivington Massacre," 34, 54, 62; "Massacre of Cheyenne Indians," 15.

17. "Sand Creek Massacre," 25, 47, 181–82, 220; "Massacre of Cheyenne Indians," 47.

18. "Sand Creek Massacre," 25, 28, 142; "Chivington Massacre," 96.

19. Irving Howbert, *Memories of a Lifetime in the Pike's Peak Region* (Glorieta, N.M.: Rio Grande Press, 1925), 122–23.

20. Dunn, *Massacres of the Mountains*, 342; Grinnell, *Fighting Cheyennes*, 163.

21. "Sand Creek Massacre," 48–49, 70, 74, 75; "Chivington Massacre," 73; "Condition of Indian Tribes," 66, 73–74.

22. Hyde, *Life of George Bent*, 152.

23. "Sand Creek Massacre," 5, 128; "Chivington Massacre," 51, 95–96; "Massacre of Cheyenne Indians," 5; Hyde, *Life of George Bent*, 152–53; Bent to Hyde, March 15, 1905, Yale Collection.

24. "Condition of Indian Tribes," 41.

25. "Sand Creek Massacre," 6, 70, 74, 75, 137–40.

26. The mystery of Left Hand's disappearance is covered in detail in Margaret Coel's *Chief Left Hand, Southern Arapaho* (Norman: University of Oklahoma Press, 1981), chap. 20.

27. Hyde, *Life of George Bent*, 154; "Sand Creek Massacre," 69; Howbert, *Memories of a Lifetime*, 124–27.

28. "Chivington Massacre," 75.

29. Bent to Hyde, April 25, 1906, Yale Collection.

30. "Sand Creek Massacre," 50–51; Hyde, *Life of George Bent*, 155.

31. Ibid., 171.

32. "Condition of the Indian Tribes," 96.

33. "Sand Creek Massacre," 7, 135–36; "Massacre of Cheyenne Indians," 5–6.

34. "Chivington Massacre," 42; "Massacre of Cheyenne Indians," 9.

35. Ibid., 27.

36. "Chivington Massacre," 53.

37. Ibid., 95–96.

38. "Condition of Indian Tribes," 96.

39. Bent to Hyde, April 14, 1906, Yale Collection.

40. Thomas B. Marquis, *Cheyenne and Sioux: The Reminiscences of Four Indians and a White Soldier*, ed. Ronald H. Limbaugh (Stockton, Calif.: University of the Pacific, 1973), 19.

41. Stands in Timber and Liberty, *Cheyenne Memories*, 169–70.

42. R. R. Perkin, *The First Hundred Years: An Informal History of Denver and the Rocky Mountain News* (Garden City, N.Y.: Doubleday, 1959), 274; "Chivington Massacre," 53.

43. Captain Silas S. Soule to Major Edward W. Wynkoop, December 14, 1864, Colorado State Historical Society.

44. Wynkoop, "Edward Wanshier Wynkoop," 76–77; *O. R.*, series. 1, vol. 16, pt. 1, 948–50.

45. Soule to Wynkoop, December 14, 1864, Colorado State Historical Society.

46. Lieutenant Joseph A. Cramer to Major Edward W. Wynkoop, December 19, 1864, Colorado State Historical Society.

47. "Chivington Massacre," 52.

48. Bent to Hyde, April 30, 1913, Yale Collection.

49. Hyde, *Life of George Bent*, 156–57.

50. Bent to Hyde, April 25, 1906, Yale Collection.

51. *O. R.*, series 1, vol. 41, pt. 1, 948, 949, 954, 961; Bent to Samuel F. Tappan, March 15, 1889, Colorado State Historical Society; Bent to Hyde, April 30, 1913, Yale Collection.

52. Bent to Hyde, April 25, 1906, Yale Collection; Hyde, *Life of George Bent*, 155.

53. Ibid., 157; Bent to Hyde, April 25, 1906, Yale Collection.

54. Hyde, *Life of George Bent*, 158.

55. Grinnell, *Fighting Cheyennes*, 173.

9. REACTION TO THE MASSACRE

1. *O. R.*, series 1, vol. 41, pt. 1, 948; "Chivington Massacre," 91.

2. *O. R.*, series 1, vol. 41, pt. 1, 950–51; "Massacre of Cheyenne Indians," 48.

3. "Sand Creek Massacre," 28, 177; "Massacre of Cheyenne Indians," 22.

4. Ibid., 10.

5. "Chivington Massacre," 92; Hal Sayre, "Early Central City Theatrical and Other Reminiscences," *Colorado Magazine* 6 (1929): 47–53.

6. "Sand Creek Massacre," 71, 136.

7. *O. R.*, series 1, vol. 41, pt. 1, 948–51.

8. Cramer to Wynkoop, December 19, 1864, Colorado State Historical Society.

9. *O. R.*, series 1, vol. 41, pt. 1, 948–50.

10. *Rocky Mountain News*, December 17, 1864.

11. *Rocky Mountain News*, December 22, 1864.

12. Lonnie J. White, *Hostiles and Horse Soldiers* (Boulder, Colo.: Pruett, 1972), 31.

13. *Rocky Mountain News*, December 29, 1864.

14. White, *Hostiles and Horse Soldiers*, 32–34.

15. *Rocky Mountain News*, December 30, 1864.

16. Bent to Hyde, April 30, 1906, Yale Collection; "Condition of Indian Tribes," 94.

17. Bent to Hyde, March 24, 1905, October 3, 1905, December 18, 1905, May 3, 1906, October 18, 1906, October 27, 1914, Yale Collection.

18. Grinnell, *Fighting Cheyennes*, 174–75; Berthrong, *Southern Cheyennes*, 224–25.

19. Hyde, *Life of George Bent*, 169–70.

20. Bent to Hyde, March 24, 1905, October 3, 1905, October 18, 1905, December 18, 1905, May 3, 1906, October 18, 1906, October, 27, 1914, Yale Collection; Grinnell, *Fighting Cheyennes*, 182–88; Hyde, *Life of George Bent*, 170–73; George E. Hyde, *Red Cloud's Folk: A History of the Oglala Sioux Indians* (Norman: University of Oklahoma Press, 1957), 110–11; Hyde, *Spotted Tail's Folk* (Norman: University of Oklahoma Press, 1974), 94–95.

21. Hyde, *Life of George Bent*, 175–76.

22. Bent to Hyde, January 12, 1906, Yale Collection.

23. Hyde, *Life of George Bent*, 244–45.

24. Ibid., 178–196; Grinnell, *Fighting Cheyennes*, 188–203; O. R., series 1, vol. 48, pt. 1, pp. 88–92.

25. "Massacre of Cheyenne Indians," i.

26. O. R., series 1, vol. 41, pt. 1, 959–62, pt. 4, 971.

27. United States Congress, House of Representatives, "Massacre of Cheyenne Indians," *Report on the Conduct of the War*, 38th Cong., 2d sess. Washington, G.P.O., 1865.

28. U.S. Senate. "The Chivington Massacre," *Reports of the Committees*, 39th Cong., 2d sess., Washington, G.P.O., 1867.

29. U.S. Senate. "Sand Creek Massacre," *Report of the Secretary of War*, Sen. Exec. Doc. No. 26, 39th Cong., 2d sess., Washington, G.P.O., 1867.

30. *Rocky Mountain News*, April 14, 24, 27.

31. Wynkoop, *Tall Chief*, 102.

32. "Chivington Massacre," iv–v.

10. Council on the Little Arkansas

1. O. R., series 1, vol. 41, pt. 4, 709.

2. Ibid., 923; vol. 48, pt. 1, 1212, 1295–96; pt. 2, 162–63, 237–38.

3. Carolyn Thomas Foreman, "Col. Jesse H. Leavenworth," *Chronicles of Oklahoma* 13 (1935): 14–29.

4. O. R., series 1, vol. 22, pt. 2, 172–73, 333–34, 400–402.

5. Foreman, "Col. Jesse H. Leavenworth," 14–29.

6. "Massacre of Cheyenne Indians," 4.

7. Ibid.; Hyde, *Life of George Bent*, 247.

8. Leavenworth to Dole, January 9, 19, 1865, Upper Arkansas Agency, Letters Received.

9. O. R., series 1, vol. 48, pt. 1, 862–63.

10. Ibid., 923.

11. Hyde, *Life of George Bent*, 246–47.

12. Berthrong, *Southern Cheyennes*, 233.

13. *Report of the Commissioner of Indian Affairs, 1865*, 391.

14. Ibid., 388–89.

15. Ibid., 389.

16. Ibid., 391.

17. Bent to Hyde, March 24, 1905, May 4, 1906, May 14, 1913, November 5, 1913, Yale Collection.

18. *O. R.*, series 1, vol. 48, pt. 2, 115–16.

19. Berthrong, *Southern Cheyennes*, 235–39.

20. *Report of the Commissioner of Indian Affairs, 1865*, 395.

21. Berthrong, *Southern Cheyennes*, 240–41.

22. Wynkoop, *Tall Chief*, 25.

23. *Report of the Commissioner of Indian Affairs, 1865*, 517.

24. Hyde, *Life of George Bent*, 248.

25. *Report of the Commissioner of Indian Affairs, 1865*, 518.

26. Ibid., 518–19.

27. Ibid., 520.

28. Hyde, *Life of George Bent*, 248.

29. *Report of the Commissioner of Indian Affairs, 1865*, 520–21.

30. Ibid., 522.

31. Ibid., 522–23.

32. Ibid., 524–25.

33. Ibid., 525–26.

34. Kappler, ed., *Laws and Treaties*, 2, 887–89.

35. Hyde, *Life of George Bent*, 250.

36. Berthrong, *Southern Cheyennes*, 256.

37. Ibid., 257.

38. *Report of the Commissioner of Indian Affairs, 1866*, 277–78; Bent to Hyde, May 29, 1906, April 18, 1914, Yale Collection.

39. Berthrong, *Southern Cheyennes*, 259.

40. Hyde, *Life of George Bent*, 253.

41. Berthrong, *Southern Cheyennes*, 38–39.

42. *Report of the Commissioner of Indian Affairs, 1866*, 280.

43. Ibid., 279.

44. Ibid., Berthrong, *Southern Cheyennes*, 262.

45. Hatch, *Custer Companion*, 61.

46. Berthrong, *Southern Cheyennes*, 262–63.

11. Treaty at Medicine Lodge

1. Berthrong, *Southern Cheyennes*, 263.

2. Ibid., 263–64.

3. Ibid., 264.

4. Hyde, *Life of George Bent*, 253–54.

5. "Report of Council at Fort Zarah," Records of the Bureau of Indian Affairs, Washington.

6. Berthrong, *Southern Cheyennes*, 264–65; Wynkoop, *Tall Chief*, 27.

7. Hatch, *Custer Companion*, 35–73.

8. Ibid., 36–37.

9. Bent to Hyde, December 17, 1913, Yale Collection.

10. Grinnell, *Fighting Cheyennes*, 254–58.

11. Hyde, *Life of George Bent*, 278–79.

12. Ibid., 279–80.

13. Ibid., 280–81.

14. Ibid., 281; Grinnell, *Fighting Cheyennes*, 271.

15. Hyde, *Life of George Bent*, 281–82.

16. Ibid., 279–80.

17. Grinnell, *Fighting Cheyennes*, 271.

18. Hyde, *Life of George Bent*, 282.

19. Grinnell, *Fighting Cheyennes*, 272.

20. Berthrong, *Southern Cheyennes*, 290–92.

21. Hyde, *Life of George Bent*, 282.

22. Bent to Hyde, June 5, 1906, Yale Collection.

23. Grinnell, *Fighting Cheyennes*, 272.

24. Ibid.

25. Bent to Hyde, December 17, 1913, Yale Collection; Berthrong, *Southern Cheyennes*, 290.

26. Ibid., 292–93.

27. Hyde, *Life of George Bent*, 283; Grinnell, *Fighting Cheyennes*, 273.

28. Berthrong, *Southern Cheyennes*, 294; *Missouri Republican*, October 28, 1867.

29. Berthrong, *Southern Cheyennes*, 293.

30. "Proceedings of a Council Held at the Arapahoe Village by Supt. Murphy and Col. D. A. Butterfield with Roman Nose, White Beard & Eight Other Cheyenne Warriors, September 27, 1867." Indian Peace Commission, Separated Correspondence, Washington, D.C.; Berthrong, *Southern Cheyennes*, 294.

31. Henry M. Stanley. "A British Journalist Reports the Medicine Lodge Peace Councils of 1867," *Kansas Historical Quarterly* 33, no. 3 (Autumn 1967): 251; Berthrong, *Southern Cheyennes*, 295–96.

32. Stanley, "A British Journalist Reports, 264; Douglas C. Jones, *The Treaty of Medicine Lodge: The Story of the Great Council Treaty as Told by Eyewitnesses* (Norman: University of Oklahoma Press, 1966), 73.

33. Stanley, "A British Journalist Reports," 264–68; *New York Times*, October 23, 1867.

34. Stanley, "A British Journalist Reports," 266.

35. Ibid., 268.

36. Jones, *Treaty of Medicine Lodge*, 82.

37. Ibid., 84–85; Stanley, "A British Journalist Reports," 269; Stan Hoig, *The Battle of the Washita: The Sheridan-Custer Indian Campaign of 1867–69* (Lincoln: University of Nebraska Press, 1976), 27.

38. Jones, *Treaty of Medicine Lodge*, 86–90; Stanley, "A British Journalist Reports," 269–72.

39. Ibid., 269.

40. Ibid., 279–81; Jones, *Treaty of Medicine Lodge*, 110–12.

41. Ibid., 115–27; Stanley, "A British Journalist Reports," 280–87.

42. Kappler, *Indian Affairs, Laws and Treaties*, 2: 977–82; Jones, *Treaty of Medicine Lodge*, 135–37.

43. Ibid., 137–38; Stanley, "A British Journalist Reports," 289.

44. Ibid., 290–91.

45. Ibid., 291.

46. Ibid.

47. Jones, *Treaty of Medicine Lodge*, 159.

48. Stanley, "A British Journalist Reports," 305–6.

49. *New York Tribune*, November 8, 1867.

50. Stanley, "A British Journalist Reports," 307–19; Jones, *Treaty of Medicine Lodge*, 174–76; Kappler, *Indian Affairs, Laws and Treaties*, 2:984–89.

51. Jones, *Treaty of Medicine Lodge*, 176–77.

52. Hoig, *Battle of the Washita*, 37.

53. Stanley, "A British Journalist Reports," 307; Kappler, *Indian Affairs, Laws and Treaties*, 2:989.

54. Hoig, *Battle of the Washita*, 37.

12. BLOOD ALONG THE WASHITA

1. Hyde, *Life of George Bent*, 287.

2. Hatch, *Custer Companion*, 125–27.

3. Hoig, *Battle of the Washita*, 41; Bent to Hyde, June 12, 1906, Yale Collection.

4. Berthrong, *Southern Cheyennes*, 301.

5. Ibid., 302.

6. *Annual Report of the Commissioner of Indian Affairs, 1868*, 66–67; Charles J. Brill, *Conquest of the Southern Plains: Uncensored Narrative of the Battle of the Washita and Custer's Southern Campaign* (Oklahoma City: Golden Saga, 1938), 107.

7. *Annual Report of the Commissioner of Indian Affairs, 1868*, 67–69.

8. *Kansas City Tribune*, August 14, 1868.

9. Bent to Hyde, August 11, 1905, Yale Collection; Berthrong, *Southern Cheyennes*, 305–7; Hoig, *Battle of the Washita*, 46–50.

10. *Annual Report of the Commissioner of Indian Affairs, 1868*, 72.

11. Berthrong, *Southern Cheyennes*, 309–10.

12. Hatch, *Custer Companion*, 49–52, 75, 83–84.

13. Ibid., 98–99.

14. Ibid., 61.

15. Ibid., 75.

16. Hyde, *Life of George Bent*, 316; Brill, *Conquest of the Southern Plains*, 127–33.

17. Hatch, *Custer Companion*, 76.

18. Brill, *Conquest of the Southern Plains*, 135.

19. *Annual Report of the Commissioner of Indian Affairs, 1868*, 76–77; Hoig, *Battle of the Washita*, 86–89.

20. "Record of a Conversation Held between Colonel and Brevet Major General W. B. Hazen, United States Army, on Special Service, and Chiefs of the Cheyenne and Arapaho Tribes of Indians, at Fort Cobb, Indian Territory, November 20, 1868," in 40th Cong., 3rd sess., Sen. Exec. Doc. 18, 22–23.

21. George Armstrong Custer, *My Life on the Plains: or, Personal Experiences with Indians* (Oklahoma City: University of Oklahoma Press, 1962), loc. cit., 390.

22. "Record of a Conversation," 24–25.

23. Hoig, *Battle of the Washita*, 93.

24. House Exec. Doc., 41st Cong., 2d sess., no. 240, 150–51.

25. Paul A. Hutton, *Phil Sheridan and His Army* (Lincoln: University of Nebraska Press, 1985), 63.

26. Grinnell, *Fighting Cheyennes*, 301–2; Brill, *Conquest of the Southern Plains*, 136–38.

27. Ibid., 137.

28. Hoig, *Battle of the Washita*, 93.

29. Ibid., 112–28; Custer, *My Life on the Plains*, 145–64.

30. Brill, *Conquest of the Southern Plains*, 135–36.

31. Theodore A. Ediger and Vinnie Hoffman, "Some Reminiscences of the Battle of the Washita," *Chronicles of Oklahoma* 33 (Summer 1955): 138.

32. Bent to Hyde, August 1, 1913, Yale Collection; Brill, *Conquest of the Southern Plains*, 155–56.

33. Hatch, *Custer Companion* 77.

34. Brill, *Conquest of the Southern Plains*, 155–56; Bent to Hyde, August 1, 1913, Yale Collection.

35. Hatch, *Custer Companion*, 78.

36. Hoig, *Battle of the Washita*, 147.

37. Brill, *Conquest of the Southern Plains*, 159–76; Hatch, *Custer Companion*, 77–78, 84.

38. Ibid., 78; Brill, *Conquest of the Southern Plains*, 177–79.

39. Custer, *My Life on the Plains*, 180; "Report of Lieutenant Colonel G. A. Custer," Philip H. Sheridan Papers, Box 83, Manuscript Division, Library of Congress, Washington, D.C.

40. Ibid.; Sen. Exec. Doc. No. 40, 40th Cong., 3rd sess., 1869, 9.

41. *New York Sun*, May 14, 1899.

42. House Exec. Doc. No. 18, 41st Cong., 2d sess, 1869, 37.

43. Brill, *Conquest of the Southern Plains*, 313.

44. *Annual Report of the Commissioner of Indian Affairs, 1869*, 525.

45. Bent to Hyde, August 28, 1913, Coe Collection.

46 Hoig, *Battle of the Washita*, 140.

47. Ibid., 145.

48. Brill, *Conquest of the Southern Plains*, 25–26.

49. John L. Sipes Jr. to the author, May 19, 2003.

13. LEGACY

1. *Annual Report of the Secretary of War, 1869–70*, 47–48.

2. The best accounts of this debate can be found in Hutton, *Phil Sheridan and His Army*, 95–100; and Hoig, *Battle of the Washita*, chap. 12.

3. Hatch, *Custer Companion*, 88.

4. *New York Times*, December 22, 1868.

5. Ibid.

6. *Report of the Secretary of the Interior* (1868), 834.

7. Wynkoop to Taylor, January 26, 1869, Indian Bureau Records, No. 32, National Archives.

8. Hatch, *Custer Companion,* 72.

9. *Report of the Secretary of the Interior* (1868), 834.

10. Ibid.

11. Hatch, *Custer Companion,* 45, 78–80, 84–85, 101–2.

12. Hoebel, *Cheyennes,* 47, 70.

13. Wynkoop, *Tall Chief,* 93–94.

14. "Sand Creek Massacre," 213.

15. Mari Sandoz, *Cheyenne Autumn* (New York: McGraw-Hill, 1953), 215.

16. *New York Times,* December 24, 1868.

BIBLIOGRAPHY

NEWSPAPERS

Commonwealth Weekly, Denver
The Cincinnati Commercial
Daily National Intelligencer, Washington, D.C.
The Daily Oklahoman
Daily Times, Leavenworth, Kansas
Denver Republican
Kansas City Star
Kansas City Tribune, Lawrence
Leavenworth Times
Missouri Democrat, St. Louis
National Republican, Washington, D.C.
New York Herald
New York Sun
New York Times
New York Tribune
Rocky Mountain Herald, Denver
Rocky Mountain News, Denver (daily and weekly)
St. Louis *Missouri Republican*
Washington *Daily National Intelligencer*
Washington Evening Star
Washington Daily Morning Chronicle
Western Mountaineer, Golden, Colorado

COLLECTIONS

Bent, George. "Letters to George Hyde," MS 21, Denver, Colorado State Historical Society.
Bent, George. "Letters." Yale Collection of Western Americana, Beinecke Rare Book and Manuscript Library, Yale University, New Haven, Connecticut.
Chivington, Colonel J. M. "The First Colorado Regiment," Colorado State Historical Society, Denver.
Evans, John. Collection, Indian Affairs, Colorado Division of State Archives and Public Records.
Grinnell, George Bird. "George Bird Grinnell Papers," Southwest Museum Library, Los Angeles, California.
Nebraska State Historical Society, Lincoln.
Sheridan, Philip H. Papers. Manuscript Division, Library of Congress, Washington, D.C.

Tappan, Samuel F. "Unpublished Autobiography," Kansas State Historical Society, Topeka, Kansas.
Tutt Library. Special Collections. Colorado College, Colorado Springs, Colorado.
Wynkoop, Edward W. "Unfinished Colorado History," Wynkoop Papers. Colorado Historical Society, Denver.
Western History Department, Denver Public Library.

CORRESPONDENCE

John L. Sipes Jr. to the author, February–May 2003.

GOVERNMENT DOCUMENTS

American State Papers, Military Affairs, vol. 6, Washington, 1861.
Annual Report of the Commissioner of Indian Affairs (1851–1869), Washington, D.C.
Annual Report of the Secretary of the Interior (1856–1868), Washington, D.C.
Annual Report of the Secretary of War (1861–1870), Washington, D.C.

CONGRESSIONAL DOCUMENTS

Senate Documents

U.S. Senate. Executive Document No. 8, 30th Cong., 1st sess., 1847.
———. Executive Document No. 5, 34th Cong., 1st sess., 1855.
———. Executive Document No. 91, 34th Cong., 1st and 2d sess., 1855.
———. Executive Document No. 1, 34th Cong., 3rd sess., 1856.
———. Executive Document No. 59, 34th Cong., 3rd sess., 1856.
———. Executive Document No. 26, 39th Cong., 2d Sess., 1867.
———. Executive Document No. 40, 40th Cong., 3rd sess., 1869.
———. Executive Document No. 18, 40th Cong., 3rd sess., 1869.
———. Report No. 156, 39th Cong., 2d sess., 1867.

House of Representatives Documents

U.S. House of Representatives. Executive Document No. 2, 32nd Cong., 1st sess., 1853.
———. Executive Document No. 36, 33rd Cong., 2d sess., 1854.
———. Executive Document No. 63, 33rd Cong., 2d sess., 1854.
———. Executive Document No. 130, 34th Cong. 1st sess., 1855.
———. Executive Document No. 2, 35th Cong., 1st sess., 1857.
———. Executive Document No. 18, 41st Cong., 2d sess, 1869.
———. Executive Document No. 240, 41st Cong., 2d sess., 1869.
Indian Peace Commission. Separated Correspondence, National Archives, Washington, D.C., 1867.
Kappler, Charles J., comp. and ed. *Indian Affairs, Laws and Treaties.* 2 vols. Government Printing Office, Washington, D.C., 1904, 1913, 1927.

"Report of the Conduct of the War," 38th Cong., 2d sess., 1865.

United States Army Commands. Records of the War Department, National Archives, Washington, D.C.

Upper Arkansas Agency. Letters Received. Department of the Missouri, National Archives, Washington, D.C.

The War of the Rebellion: A Compilation of the Official Records of the Union and Confederate Armies. 128 vols. Washington, D.C.: U.S. Government Printing Office, 1880–1901.

JOURNAL ARTICLES

Adams, Blanche V. "The Second Colorado Cavalry in the Civil War." *Colorado Magazine* 8 (May 1931).

Anderson, Robert. "The Buffalo Men, A Cheyenne Ceremony of Petition Deriving from the Sutaio." *Southwestern Journal of Anthropology* 12, no. 1 (spring 1956).

Ashley, Susan Riley. "Reminiscences in the Early 'Sixties." *Colorado Magazine* 8 (1936).

Benedict, Ruth Fulton. "The Vision in Plains Culture." *American Anthropologist* 24, no. 1 (January–March 1922).

Bent, Charles. "The Charles Bent Papers." *New Mexico Historical Review* 30, no. 2 (April 1955).

Bent, George. "Forty Years with the Cheyennes," ed. George E. Hyde. *The Frontier* (October 1905–February 1906).

Burkey, Elmer R. "The Site of the Murder of the Hungate Family by Indians in 1864." *Colorado Magazine* 12, no. 4 (July 1935).

Campbell, W. S. "The Cheyenne Dog Soldier." *Chronicles of Oklahoma,* 11 (January 1921).

Carey, R. G. "The Puzzle of Sand Creek." *Colorado Magazine* 41, no. 4 (1964).

Chivington, J. M. "The Pet Lambs." *Denver Republican,* April 20–May 18, 1890.

Cobb, Frank M. "The Lawrence Party of Gold Seekers." *Colorado Magazine* 10, no. 5 (September 1933).

Connelley, William E. "The Treaty Held at Medicine Lodge." *Kansas Historical Collections* 17 (Winter 1926–1927).

Davis, Theodore. "Henry M. Stanley's Indian Campaign in 1867." *The Westerner's Brand Book.* Chicago: Chicago Westerners Posse, 1947.

———. "A Summer on the Plains." *Harper's New Monthly Magazine* 36 (February 1868).

Dawson, Thomas F. "Colonel Boone's Treaty with the Plains Indians." *The Trail* 14 (July 1921).

D'Elia, J. "The Argument over Civilian or Military Indian Control, 1865–1880," *The Historian* 24 (February 1962).

Dormis, John T., ed. "The Chivingtons." *Masonic News-Digest* 36 (June 28, 1957).

Dorsey, George A. "The Cheyenne: The Sun Dance." Field Columbian Museum *Publication No. 103, Anthropological Series* 9, no. 2, Chicago (1905).

———. "The Cheyenne, Ceremonial Oganization." Field Columbian Museum *Publication 99, Anthropological Series,* 9, no. 1, Chicago (1905).

————. "How the Pawnees Captured the Cheyenne Medicine Arrows." *American Anthropologist* 5, no. 4 (October–December 1903).

Ediger, Theodore A., and Vinnie Hoffman. "Some Reminiscences of the Battle of the Washita." *Chronicles of Oklahoma* 33 (Summer 1955).

Flores, Dan L. "Bison Ecology and Bison Diplomacy: The Southern Plains from 1800 to 1850." *Journal of American History* 78 (September 1991).

Ford, Lemuel. "Captain Ford's Journal of an Expedition to the Rocky Mountains," ed. Louis Pelzer, *Mississippi Valley Historical Review* 12, no. 4 (March 1926).

Foreman, Carolyn Thomas. "Col. Jesse H. Leavenworth." *Chronicles of Oklahoma* 13 (1935).

Garfield, Marvin H. "Defense of the Kansas Frontier, 1866–1869," *Kansas Historical Quarterly* 1, nos. 4 and 5 (August, November 1932).

————. "The Military Fort as a Factor in the Frontier Defense of Kansas, 1865–69." *Kansas Historical Quarterly* 1 (November 1931).

Godfrey, General Edward S. "Medicine Lodge Treaty 60 Years Ago." *Winners of the West* 6, no. 4 (March 30, 1929).

Green, James. "Incidents of the Indian Outbreak of 1864." *Publications of the Nebraska State Historical Society* 19 (1919).

Grinnell, George Bird. "The Cheyenne Medicine Lodge." *American Anthropologist* 16, no. 2 (April–June 1914).

————. "Coup and Scalp among the Plains Indians." *American Anthropologist* 12, no. 2 (April–June 1910).

————. "Early Cheyenne Villages," *American Anthropologist* 20, no. 4 (October–December 1918).

————. "Great Mysteries of the Cheyenne." *American Anthropologist* 21, no. 4 (October–December 1910).

————. "Social Organization of the Cheyennes." *International Congress of Americanists*, 13th sess. New York, 1902, Easton, Pa. (1905).

————. "Some Early Cheyenne Tales." *Journal of American Folk-Lore* 10–21, nos. 78 and 82 (July–September 1907, October–December 1908).

Hafen, LeRoy R. "When Was Bent's Fort Built?" *Colorado Magazine* 31, no. 2 (April 1954).

Hagerty, Leroy W., "Indian Raids along the Platte and Little Blue Rivers, 1864–1865." *Nebraska History* 28, no. 4 (October–December 1947).

Hilger, Sister M. Inez. "Notes on Cheyenne Child Life." *American Anthropologist*, vol. 48, no. 1 (January–March 1946).

Hornbeck, Lewis N. "The Battle of the Washita." *Sturm's Oklahoma Magazine* 5, no. 5 (January 1908).

Isern, Thomas D. "The Controversial Career of Edward W. Wynkoop." *Colorado Magazine* 56 (Winter–Spring 1979).

Kelsey, Harry. "Background to Sand Creek." *Colorado Magazine* 45, no. 4 (Fall 1968).

Kraft, Louis. "Edward Wynkoop: A Forgotten Hero." *Research Review: The Journal of the Little Big Horn Associates* 1 (June 1987).

Kroeber, A. L. "Cheyenne Tales." *Journal of American Folk-Lore* 13, no. 50 (July–September 1900).

Lambert, Julia S. "Plain Tales of the Plains." *The Trail* 7 (January–September 1916).

Lowie, Robert H. "Plains Indians Age-Societies: Historical and Comparative Summary." In Clark Wissler, ed., *Societies of the Plains Indians.* New York: American Museum of Natural History, 1916.

Lubers, H. L. "William Bent's Family and the Indians of the Plains." *Colorado Magazine* 13 (January 1936).

Mardock, Robert. "The Plains Frontier and the Indian Peace Policy, 1865–1880." *Nebraska History* 49 (Summer 1968).

Mellor, William J. "The Military Investigation of Col. John M. Chivington Following the Sand Creek Massacre." *Chronicles of Oklahoma* 16, no. 4 (1938).

Michelson, Truman. "The Narrative of a Southern Cheyenne Woman." Smithsonian *Miscellaneous Collections* 97, no. 5 (1932).

Mumey, Nolie. "John Milton Chivington, the Misunderstood Man." *1956 Brand Book of the Denver Westerners.* Boulder, Colo.: Johnson, 1957.

Peck, Robert M. "Recollections of Early Times in Kansas Territory." *Kansas Historical Collections* 8 (1903–1904).

Perrigo, Lynn I., ed. "Major Hal Sayre's Diary of the Sand Creek Campaign." *Colorado Magazine* 15 (1938).

Peterson, Karen D. "Cheyenne Soldier Societies." *Plains Anthropologist* 9, no. 25 (1964).

Pierce, James H. "The First Prospecting in Colorado." *The Trail* 7, no. 5 (October 1914).

————. "With the Green Russell Party." *The Trail* 13, no. 12 (May 1921).

Prentice, C. A. "Captain Silas S. Soule, a Pioneer Martyr." *Colorado Magazine* 4 (May 1927).

Rister, Carl C. "Indians as Buffalo Hunters." *Frontier Times* 5 (September 1928).

Sanford, Albert B. "Life at Camp Weld and Fort Lyon in 1861–62." *Colorado Magazine* 7 (May 1930).

Sayre, Hal. "Early Central City Theatrical and Other Reminiscences." *Colorado Magazine* 6 (1929).

Seabrook, S. L. "Expedition of Col. E. V. Sumner against the Cheyenne Indians, 1857." *Kansas Historical Collections* 16 (1923–1925).

Seger, John H. "Cheyenne Marriage Customs." *Journal of American Folk-Lore* 11, no. 43 (October–December 1898).

Spier, Leslie. "The Sun Dance of the Plains Indians: Its Development and Diffusion." American Museum of Natural History, *Anthropological Papers* 16, pt. 7, New York (1921).

Stanley, Henry M. "A British Journalist Reports the Medicine Lodge Peace Councils of 1867." *Kansas Historical Quarterly* 33, no. 3 (Autumn 1967).

Taylor, Alfred A. "The Medicine Lodge Peace Council." *Chronicles of Oklahoma* 2, no. 2 (June 1924).

Unrau, William E. "The Story of Fort Larned." *Kansas Historical Quarterly* 23, no. 3 (August 1957).

Wynkoop, Edward E. "Edward Wanshear Wynkoop." *Collections of the Kansas State Historical Society* 13 (1913–1914).

BOOKS

Abbott, Carl, Stephen J. Leonard, and David G. McComb. *Colorado: A History of the Centennial State*. Boulder: Colorado Associated University Press, 1982.

Alberts, Don E. *The Battle of Glorieta: Union Victory in the West*. College Station: Texas A & M Press, 1998.

Bancroft, Hubert Howe. *History of Nevada, Colorado, and Wyoming*. San Francisco: History Co., 1890.

Bandel, Eugene. *Frontier Life in the Army, 1854–61*. Edited by R. P. Bieber. Philadelphia: Porcupine Press, 1942.

Berthrong, Donald J. *The Southern Cheyennes*. Norman: University of Oklahoma Press, 1963.

Brady, Cyrus T. *Indian Fights and Fighters*. Lincoln: University of Nebraska Press, 1971.

Brill, Charles J. *Conquest of the Southern Plains: Uncensored Narrative of the Battle of the Washita and Custer's Southern Campaign*. Oklahoma City: Golden Saga, 1938.

Carroll, John, ed. *General Custer and the Battle of the Washita: The Federal View*. Bryan, Tex.: Guidon Press, 1978.

Chalfant, William Y. *Cheyennes and Horse Soldiers: The 1857 Expedition and the Battle of Solomon's Fork*. Norman: University of Oklahoma Press, 1989.

Chittenden, Hirum Martin, and Alfred Talbot Richardson. *Life, Letters and Travels of Father Pierre-Jean De Smet, S. J., 1801–1874*. 4 vols. New York: F. P. Harper, 1905.

CISCO, ed. *Biographical Dictionary of the Americas*. Newport Beach, Calif.: American Indian Publishers, 1991.

Coel, Margaret. *Chief Left Hand, Southern Arapaho*. Norman: University of Oklahoma Press, 1981.

Conrad, Howard Louis. *"Uncle Dick" Wootton, the Pioneer Frontiersman of the Rocky Mountain Region: An Account of the Adventures and Thrilling Experiences of the Most Noted American Hunter, Trapper, Guide, Scout, and Indian Fighter Now Living*. Chicago: W. E. Dibble, 1890.

Craig, Reyinald S. *The Fighting Parson*. Tucson, Ariz.: Westernlore Press, 1959.

Custer, George Armstrong. *My Life on the Plains: Or, Personal Experiences with Indians*. Oklahoma City: University of Oklahoma Press, 1962.

Densmore, Francis. *Cheyenne and Arapaho Music*. Highland Park, Los Angeles, Calif.: Southwest Museum, 1936.

Dorsett, Phyllis Flanders. *The New Eldorado: The Story of Colorado's Gold and Silver Rushes*. New York: Macmillan, 1970.

Dunn, J. P., Jr. *Massacres in the Mountains: A History of the Indian Wars of the Far West, 1815–1875*. New York: Archer House, 1958.

Edington, Thomas, and John Taylor. *The Battle of Glorieta Pass: A Gettysburg in the West, March 26–28, 1862*. Albuquerque: University of New Mexico Press, 1998.

Epple, Jess C. *Custer's Battle of the Washita and a History of the Plains Indian Tribes*. New York: Exposition Press, 1970.

Fritz, Henry E. *The Movement for Indian Assimiliation, 1860–1890*. Philadelphia: University of Pennsylvania Press, 1963.

Frost, Lawrence A. *The Court-Martial of George Armstrong Custer.* Norman: University of Oklahoma Press, 1968.

Gard, Wayne. *The Great Buffalo Hunt.* Lincoln: University of Nebraska Press, 1959.

Garraty, John A., ed. *American National Biography.* New York: Oxford University Press, 1999.

Grinnell, George Bird. *By Cheyenne Campfires.* New Haven, Conn.: Yale University Press, 1926.

————. *The Cheyenne Indians: Their History and Ways of Life.* 2 vols. New Haven: Yale University Press, 1923.

————. *The Fighting Cheyennes.* New York: Charles Scribner's Sons, 1915.

Hafen, LeRoy R., *Colorado and Its People.* New York: Lewis Historical Publishing Co., 1948.

Hafen, LeRoy R., ed. *Colorado Gold Rush—Contemporary Letters and Reports 1858–59.* Glendale, Calif.: Arthur H. Clark, 1941.

Hafen, LeRoy R., ed. *Overland Routes to the Gold Fields, 1859.* Glendale, Calif.: Arthur H. Clark Company, 1942.

Hafen, LeRoy R., and W. J. Ghent. *Broken Hand: The Life Story of Thomas Fitzpatrick, Mountain Man, Guide and Indian Agent.* Denver: Old West Publishing, 1931.

Hafen, LeRoy R., and Ann W. Hafen. *Relations with the Indians of the Plains.* Glendale, Calif.: Arthur H. Clark, 1959.

Hafen, LeRoy R., and Francis Marion Young. *Fort Laramie and the Pageant of the West, 1834–1890.* Glendale, Calif.: Arthur H. Clark, 1938.

Haines, Francis. *The Buffalo: The Story of American Bison and Their Hunters from Prehistoric Times to the Present.* New York: Thomas Y. Crowell, 1976.

Hall, Frank. *History of the State of Colorado.* Chicago: Blakely Printing, 1889.

Hall, Martin H. *Sibley's New Mexico Campaign.* Austin: University of Texas Press, 1960.

Hatch, Thom. *The Blue, the Gray, and the Red: Indian Campaigns of the Civil War.* Mechanicsburg, Pa.: Stackpole, 2003.

————. *Clashes of Cavalry: The Civil War Careers of George Armstrong Custer and Jeb Stuart.* Mechanicsburg, Pa.: Stackpole, 2001.

————. *The Custer Companion: A Comprehensive Guide to the Life of George Armstrong Custer and the Plains Indian Wars.* Mechanicsburg, Pa.: Stackpole, 2002.

Hill, Alice Polk. *Tales of the Colorado Pioneers.* Denver: Pierson and Gardiner, 1884.

Hodge, Frederick W. *Handbook of American Indians North of Mexico.* Bureau of American Ethnology *Bulletin No. 30.* 2 vols. Washington, 1910.

Hoebel, E. Adamson. *The Cheyennes: Indians of the Great Plains.* New York: Holt, Rinehart and Winston, 1978.

Hoig, Stan. *The Battle of the Washita: The Sheridan-Custer Indian Campaign of 1867–69.* Lincoln: University of Nebraska Press, 1976.

————. *The Peace Chiefs of the Cheyennes.* Norman: University of Oklahoma Press, 1980.

————. *The Sand Creek Massacre.* Norman: University of Oklahoma Press, 1961.

Hollister, Ovando J. *Boldly They Rode: A History of the First Colorado Regiment.* Lakewood, Colo.: Golden Press, 1949.

Hoopes, Alban W. *Indian Affairs and Their Administration with Special Reference to the Far West, 1849–1860.* Philadelphia: University of Pennsylvania Press, 1932.

Howbert, Irving. *The Indians of the Pike's Peak Region.* New York: Knickerbocker Press, 1914.

————. *Memories of a Lifetime in the Pike's Peak Region.* Glorieta, N. Mex.: Rio Grande Press, 1925.

Hutton, Paul A. *Phil Sheridan and His Army.* Lincoln: University of Nebraska Press, 1985.

Hyde, George E. *Life of George Bent: Written from His Letters.* Norman: University of Oklahoma Press, 1968.

————. *Red Cloud's Folk: A History of the Oglala Sioux Indians.* Norman: University of Oklahoma Press, 1957.

————. *Spotted Tail's Folk.* Norman: University of Oklahoma Press, 1974.

Jablow, Joseph. *The Cheyenne in Plains Trade Relations, 1795–1840.* New York: J. J. Augustin, 1951.

Jackson, Helen Hunt. *A Century of Dishonor.* Boston: Roberts Brothers, 1887.

Jones, Douglas C. *The Treaty of Medicine Lodge: The Story of the Great Council Treaty as Told by Eyewitnesses.* Norman: University of Oklahoma Press, 1966.

Josephy, Alvin M., Jr. *The Civil War in the American West.* New York: Alfred A. Knopf, 1991.

Kearnes, Thomas L. *William Gilpin: Western Nationalist.* Austin: University of Texas Press, 1970.

Kelsey, Harry J., Jr. *Frontier Capitalist: The Life of John Evans.* Denver: State Historical Society of Colorado, 1969.

Keim, B. Randolph De. *Sheridan's Troopers on the Borders: A Winter Campaign on the Plains.* Philadelphia: David McKay, 1885.

Lavender, David. *Bent's Fort.* Lincoln: University of Nebraska Press, 1954.

Leckie, William H. *The Military Conquest of the Southern Plains.* Norman: University of Oklahoma Press, 1963.

Lewis, Meriwether, and William Clark. *Original Journals of the Lewis and Clarke Expedition, 1804–1806.* 7 vols. New York: Dodd, Mead & Co., 1904.

McMechen, Edgar Carlisle. *Life of Governor Evans.* Denver: Walgren, 1924.

Manypenny, George W. *Our Indian Wards.* Cincinnati: Robert Clarke, 1880.

Mardock, Robert Winston. *The Reformers and the American Indian.* Columbia: University of Missouri Press, 1971.

Markowitz, Harvey, ed. *American Indians.* Pasadena, Calif.: Salem Press, 1995.

Marquis, Thomas B. *Cheyenne and Sioux: The Reminiscences of Four Indians and a White Soldier.* Edited by Ronald H. Limbaugh. Stockton, Calif.: Pacific Center for Western Historical Studies, University of the Pacific, 1973.

Mendoza, Patrick. *Song of Sorrow: Massacre at Sand Creek.* Denver: Willow Word, 1993.

Mooney, James. *Calendar History of the Kiowa Indians,* Seventeenth Annual Report, Bureau of American Ethnology. Washington, D.C., 1898.

————. *The Cheyenne Indians.* Memoirs of the American Anthropological Association. Lancaster, Pa., 1905–1907.

Mumey, Nolie. *History of Early Settlements of Denver (1859–1860)*. Glendale, Calif.: Arthur H. Clark, 1942.

Perkin, R. R. *The First Hundred Years: An Informal History of Denver and the Rocky Mountain News*. Garden City, N.Y.: Doubleday, 1959.

Phillips, Charles, and Alan Axelrod, eds. *Encyclopedia of the American West*. New York: Simon & Schuster Macmillan, 1996.

Pitzer, Robert Claiborne. *Three Frontiers, Memories and a Portrait of Henry Littleton Pitzer as Recorded by His Son Robert Claiborne Pitzer*. Muscatine, Iowa: Prairie Press, 1938.

Powell, Father Peter J. *People of the Sacred Mountain: A History of the Northern Cheyenne Chiefs and Warrior Societies 1830–1879*. 2 vols. San Francisco: Harper & Row, 1981.

————. *Sweet Medicine*. 2 vols. Norman: University of Oklahoma Press, 1969.

Priest, Loring B. *Uncle Sam's Stepchildren: The Reformation of the United States Indian Policy, 1865–1887*. New York: Octagon, 1969.

Prucha, Francis P. *American Indian Policy in Crisis: Christian Reformers and the Indian, 1865–1900*. Chicago: University of Chicago Press, 1977.

Reiger, John F., ed. *The Passing of the Great West: Selected Papers of George Bird Grinnell*. New York: Charles Scribner's Sons, 1972.

Richardson, Albert D. *Beyond the Mississippi: From the Great River to the Great Ocean, Life and Adventure on the Prairies, Mountains, and Pacific Coast, 1857–1867*. Hartford, Conn.: American Publishing Co., 1867.

Robinson, Doane. *A History of the Dakota or Sioux Indians*. Minneapolis: Ross and Haines, 1956.

Root, Frank A., and William E. Connelley. *The Overland Stage to California: Personal Reminiscences and Authentic History of the Great Overland Stage Line and Pony Express from the Missouri River to the Pacific Ocean*. Topeka, Kans.: Crane & Co., 1901.

Sandoz, Mari. *The Buffalo Hunters: The Story of the Hide Men*. New York: McGraw-Hill, 1954.

————. *Cheyenne Autumn*. New York: McGraw-Hill, 1953.

Sheridan, Philip H. *Record of Engagements with Hostile Indians within the Military Division of the Missouri, from 1868 to 1882, Lieutenant-General P. H. Sheridan, Commanding*. Facsimile edition. Fort Collins, Colo.: Old Army Press, 1972.

Schultz, Duane. *Month of the Freezing Moon: The Sand Creek Massacre*. New York: St. Martin's, 1990.

Stands in Timber, John, and Margot Liberty. *Cheyenne Memories*. New Haven: Yale University Press, 1967.

Stone, Wilbur Fisk, ed. *History of Colorado*. 3 vols. Chicago: S. J. Clarke, 1918.

Thrapp, Dan L. *Encyclopedia of Frontier Biography*. 3 vols. Glendale, Calif.: Arthur H. Clark, 1988.

Trenholm, Virginia Cole. *The Arapahoes, Our People*. Norman: University of Oklahoma Press, 1973.

Turner, Don. *Custer's First Massacre: The Battle of the Washita*. Amarillo, Tex.: Humbug Gulch Press, 1968.

Ubbelohde, Carl, Maxine Benson, and Duane A. Smith, eds. *A Colorado History*. Boulder, Colo.: Pruett, 1972, 1976, 1982.

Utley, Robert. *Frontier Regulars: The United States Army and the Indian, 1866–1891*. New York: Macmillian, 1973.

————. *Frontiersmen in Blue: The United States Army and the Indian, 1848–1865*. New York: Macmillan, 1967.

————. *The Indian Frontier of the American West, 1846–1890*. Albuquerque: University of New Mexico Press, 1984.

Viola, Herman J. *Diplomats in Buckskin: A History of Indian Delegations in Washington City*. Washington, D.C.: Smithsonian Institution Press, 1981.

Ware, Captain Eugene F. *The Indian War of 1864*. New York: St. Martin's, 1960.

Webb, Walter P. *The Great Plains*. Boston: Gin and Company, 1931.

Weist, Tom. *A History of the Cheyenne People*. Billings: Montana Council for Indian Education, 1977.

White, Lonnie J. *Hostiles and Horse Soldiers*. Boulder, Colo.: Pruett, 1972.

Whitford, William Clarke. *Colorado Volunteers in the Civil War: The New Mexico Campaign of 1862*. Denver: State Historical and Natural History Society, 1906.

Williams, Mrs. Ellen. *Three Years and a Half in the Army: or History of the Second Colorados*. New York: Fowler and Wells, 1885.

Willison, George F. *Here They Dug the Gold*. New York: Brentano's, 1931.

Wooster, Robert. *The Military and United States Indian Policy, 1865–1903*. New Haven, Conn.: Yale University Press, 1988.

Wynkoop, Edward W. *The Tall Chief: The Autobiography of Edward W. Wynkoop*. Edited by Christopher B. Gerboth. Denver: Colorado Historical Society, 1994.

INDEX

CPSIA information can be obtained
at www.ICGtesting.com
Printed in the USA
BVHW01*1144180218
507681BV00021B/43/P

9 780471 445920